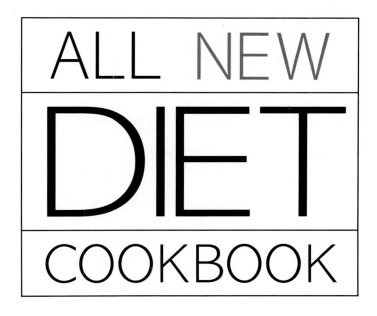

ALL NEW
DIET
COOKBOOK

Publications International, Ltd.

ISBN 1-56173-549-3

Library of Congress Catalog Card Number: 91-68328

Pictured on the front cover, clockwise from top right: Cappuccino Bon Bons (page 209), Pasta Delight (page 153), Marinated Vegetable Spinach Salad (page 151) and Chicken with Pineapple Salsa (page 107).

Pictured on the back cover, top to bottom: Rice Crêpes (page 56), Turkey and Rice Quiche (page 105) and Lovely Lemon Cheesecake (page 182).

CONTENTS

INTRODUCTION

The All New Way to Diet

There definitely is a *new* way to diet that is revolutionizing the way we think about food. Remember the once-popular high-protein diet, grapefruit diet and all-liquid diet? These dieting fads have been replaced by a healthier, more balanced approach toward eating. The best way to lose weight, indicated in study after study, is to follow a low-fat, high-carbohydrate diet. Besides keeping hunger pangs at bay, following this approach toward eating can also help lower your blood cholesterol levels and reduce your risk of heart disease. So whether you are looking to lose a few pounds or would just like to shape up your eating habits, this marvelous recipe collection can help you achieve your goal with hundreds of recipes "fit" for any meal or occasion.

Everyone is concerned with calories, fat, cholesterol and sodium. Because of this concern, there seems to be an abundance of advice, often conflicting, pertaining to food and diets. There is no question, though, that when it comes to fat, health professionals agree—we need to decrease our fat intake. More specifically, we need to limit our total fat intake to no more than 30 percent of our daily calories, instead of our typical 40 percent. This recommendation applies to healthy adults and children over the age of two, whether or not they have a high blood cholesterol level.

Why has fat become such a villain in our diet? Why is this usually flavorless substance, which adds such richness and creaminess to so many of our favorite foods, something we should cut back on? The reason is that consuming excess saturated fat, the type found in meat and whole-milk dairy products, suppresses the body's natural mechanism for pulling cholesterol out of the bloodstream. Instead, cholesterol may be deposited on the inner walls of arteries. Over time, this buildup can constrict the blood flow to the heart. The latest research also links a high-fat diet with an increased

risk for certain types of cancers. A high-fat diet also contributes to weight gain, further increasing health risks. For these reasons, experts recommend decreasing our daily fat intake.

The good news is that substituting complex carbohydrates, such as grains, beans, fruits and vegetables, for high-fat foods, allows you to lose weight without feeling hungry or deprived. One reason consuming fat can make you gain weight is that a gram of fat has nine calories while a gram of carbohydrate or protein has only four. In other words, a teaspoon of fat has 45 calories, versus 20 calories for the same amount of carbohydrate or protein. Of course, to lose weight you still have to take in fewer calories than you expend in energy. But consider that for the same number of calories, you can substitute a plain 12-ounce baked potato for a 1.5-ounce bag of potato chips and feel full and satisfied. Substituting complex carbohydrates for fats allows you to eat larger quantities of food without gaining weight. Substituting skim milk for whole and low-fat or nonfat frozen yogurt for ice cream and choosing lean meats are other ways to reduce your fat consumption.

Making Smart Choices

The recipes in this cookbook can help you make smart choices about the foods you prepare. From breakfast to dinner, simple family suppers to elegant entertaining, there are hundreds of wonderful, low-calorie, low-fat recipes to choose from. Every recipe is followed by a nutritional chart that tells you the number of calories, the grams (g) of fat, the milligrams (mg) of cholesterol and the milligrams (mg) of sodium for each serving of that recipe.

Each recipe in this book contains no more than 300 calories and no more than 10 grams of fat per serving. If you do choose higher fat items for a meal, try to choose other foods that day that are low in fat. By mixing and matching your selection of recipes and foods, your weekly diet will follow the guidelines for healthy eating. Many of the recipes are low-cholesterol and low-sodium as well. These recipes contain less than 50 mg of cholesterol and less than 300 mg of sodium. These values were chosen after careful consideration of a number of factors. The Food and Nutrition Board of the National Academy of Sciences proposes the Recommended Dietary Allowances (RDA) for essential nutrients including calories, carbohydrates, fat, protein, amino acids, vitamins and minerals.

The RDA were most recently revised in 1989. The RDA for calories are broken down according to age groups and sex. For healthy men between the ages of 19 and 50, for example, the RDA for total calorie intake are 2,900 calories per day. For healthy women between the ages of 19 and 50 (who are neither pregnant nor lactating), they are 2,200 calories per day. Thus, the 300 calories or less per serving for the recipes in this book represents only about 10 percent of the RDA for most men and about 14 percent of the RDA for most women.

The American Heart Association recommends that total fat intake be no more than 30 percent of calories. For most women, that amounts to about 660 calories from fat (or about 73 grams of fat) per day; for most men, that amounts to about 870 calories from fat (or about 97 grams of fat) per day. Thus, the 10 grams of fat or less per serving for each recipe in this book is well within recommended guidelines. The American Heart Association also recommends that cholesterol intake be less than 300 mg a day and sodium intake not exceed 3,000 mg a day.

About the Nutritional Information

The analysis of each recipe includes all the ingredients that are listed in that recipe, except ingredients labeled as "optional" or "for garnish." If a range is given in the yield of a recipe ("Makes 6 to 8 servings," for example), the *higher* yield was used to calculate the per serving information. If a range is offered for an ingredient (¼ to ⅛

teaspoon, for example) the *first* amount given was used to calculate the nutrition information. If an ingredient is presented with an option ("2 tablespoons margarine or butter") the *first* item listed was used to calculate the nutrition information. Foods shown in photographs on the same serving plate and offered as "serve with" suggestions at the end of a recipe are also *not* included in the recipe analysis unless it is stated in the per serving line.

The nutrition information that appears with each recipe was submitted in part by the participating companies and associations. **Every effort has been made to check the accuracy of these numbers. However, because numerous variables account for a wide range of values for certain foods, nutritive analyses in this book should be considered approximate.**

This cookbook offers you a wide variety of recipes that are, on a per serving basis, low in calories, fat and cholesterol. **The recipes in this book are NOT intended as a medically therapeutic program, nor as a substitute for medically approved diet plans for people on fat-, cholesterol- or sodium-restricted diets. You should consult your physician before beginning any diet plan.** The recipes offered here can be part of a healthy lifestyle that meets recognized dietary guidelines. A healthy lifestyle includes not only eating a balanced diet, but engaging in proper exercise as well.

Microwave cooking times in this book are approximate. Numerous variables, such as the microwave oven's rated wattage and the starting temperature, shape, amount and depth of the food, can affect cooking time. Use the cooking times as a guideline and check doneness before adding more time. Lower wattage ovens may consistently require longer cooking times.

Tempting, satisfying recipes for any meal or occasion, combined with easy-to-follow instructions and beautiful color photographs, can get you started on the road to better living as you learn this healthy new approach to eating.

Appetizers and Beverages

Left: Indonesian Satay
Right: Lemony Light Cooler (page 8)

INDONESIAN SATAY

- ¼ cup lime juice
- 2 cloves garlic, minced
- 1 teaspoon grated lime peel
- ½ teaspoon ground ginger
- ½ teaspoon ground red pepper
- 4 boneless skinless chicken breasts (about 2 pounds), cut into strips
  Spicy Peanut Sauce (recipe follows)

Mix together lime juice, garlic, peel, ginger and pepper; pour over chicken. Cover. Refrigerate 1 hour. Drain.

Prepare coals for grilling.

Thread chicken on individual skewers; place on greased grill over hot coals (coals will be glowing).

Grill, uncovered, 3 to 5 minutes on each side or until tender. Serve with Spicy Peanut Sauce.   *Makes 15 servings*

SPICY PEANUT SAUCE

- 1 package (8 ounces) PHILADELPHIA BRAND® Cream Cheese, cubed
- ½ cup milk
- 3 tablespoons peanut butter
- 2 tablespoons firmly packed brown sugar
- ½ teaspoon ground cardamom
- ⅛ teaspoon ground red pepper

Stir ingredients in small saucepan over low heat until smooth.

Prep time: 20 minutes plus marinating
Cook time: 10 minutes

Nutrients per serving:

Calories	130	Cholesterol	35 mg
Fat	8 mg	Sodium	85 mg

BLACK BEAN DIP

1 can (15 ounces) black beans,
    rinsed, drained
½ cup **MIRACLE WHIP® FREE®**
    Nonfat Dressing
½ cup reduced-calorie sour
    cream
1 can (4 ounces) chopped green
    chilies, drained
2 tablespoons chopped cilantro
1 teaspoon chili powder
½ teaspoon garlic powder
    Few drops hot pepper sauce

Mash beans with fork. Stir in remaining
ingredients until well blended; refrigerate.
Serve with tortilla chips.

Makes 2¼ cups

Prep time: 10 minutes plus
refrigerating

Nutrients per serving (2 tablespoons):			
Calories	70	Cholesterol	0 mg
Fat	1 g	Sodium	119 mg

Black Bean Dip

LEMONY LIGHT COOLER

3 cups white grape juice *or*
    1 bottle (750 ml) dry white
    wine, chilled
½ to ¾ cup sugar
½ cup **REALEMON®** Lemon
    Juice from Concentrate
1 (32-ounce) bottle club soda,
    chilled
    Strawberries, plum, peach or
    orange slices or other fresh
    fruit
    Ice

In pitcher, combine grape juice, sugar
and ReaLemon® brand; stir until sugar
dissolves. Cover; chill. Just before
serving, add club soda and fruit. Serve
over ice.

Makes about 7 cups, 7 servings

Tip: Recipe can be doubled.

Nutrients per serving (without fruit):			
Calories	110	Cholesterol	0 mg
Fat	trace	Sodium	31 mg

BRUSCHETTA

2 Italian rolls (each 5 inches
    long)
1¾ cups (14½ ounce can)
    CONTADINA® Italian-Style
    Tomatoes
2 tablespoons chopped fresh
    basil
1 tablespoon finely chopped
    onion
1 tablespoon olive oil
1 small clove garlic, crushed
¼ teaspoon dried oregano leaves
¼ teaspoon salt
⅛ teaspoon black pepper

Cut rolls lengthwise in half. Cut each half crosswise into 2 pieces. Toast cut sides. Drain tomatoes thoroughly; chop tomatoes. Combine tomatoes with remaining ingredients. Spoon tomato mixture on toasted rolls. Broil 5 inches from heat source until tomato mixture is hot, about 2 minutes.

Makes 8 servings

Nutrients per serving:

Calories	100	Cholesterol	17 mg
Fat	3 g	Sodium	280 mg

SWEET & SPICY SALSA

- ¾ cup fresh pineapple, peeled, cored and cut into ¼-inch cubes
- ½ cup red bell pepper, cut into ¼-inch pieces
- ½ cup yellow bell pepper, cut into ¼-inch pieces
- ½ cup red onion, finely chopped
- ½ cup cilantro, finely chopped
- 1 jalapeño, seeded and minced
- 2 tablespoons fresh lime juice
- 1½ teaspoons firmly packed brown sugar
  Dash salt
  Dash black pepper

In medium bowl, combine pineapple, red and yellow peppers, onion, cilantro, jalapeño, lime juice, brown sugar, salt and black pepper. Cover and refrigerate 30 minutes before serving.

Makes 8 servings

Nutrients per serving:

Calories	19	Cholesterol	0 mg
Fat	0 g	Sodium	18 mg

Favorite recipe from **National Turkey Federation**

Hawaiian Tea

HAWAIIAN TEA

- 3 cups DOLE® Pineapple Orange Juice
- 1 cinnamon stick
- 2 tablespoons chopped crystallized ginger
- ¼ teaspoon anise seeds
- ¼ teaspoon whole cloves
- 1 orange tea bag
- 1 peppermint tea bag
  Brown sugar (optional)
  Additional cinnamon sticks for garnish (optional)

Combine juice and spices in saucepan. Bring to a boil. Reduce heat; simmer 1 minute. Add tea bags. Cover and steep 5 to 7 minutes. Remove tea bags and spices. Sweeten with brown sugar, if desired. Garnish with cinnamon sticks, if desired.

Makes 3 servings

Nutrients per serving:

Calories	170	Cholesterol	0 mg
Fat	trace	Sodium	17 mg

Birthday Punch

BIRTHDAY PUNCH

2 quarts DOLE® Pineapple Juice, chilled
1 bottle (32 ounces) lemon-lime soda, chilled
1 can (12 ounces) frozen DOLE® Pine-Orange Banana Juice concentrate, thawed
DOLE® citrus slices for garnish
DOLE® Fresh or frozen Strawberries, halved (optional)

Combine all ingredients in large punch bowl.   *Makes 18 servings*

Nutrients per serving (6 ounces):			
Calories	89	Cholesterol	0 mg
Fat	trace	Sodium	7 mg

GINGER SHRIMP

1 cup (8 ounces) Lite WISH-BONE® Italian Dressing
½ cup sherry
4 medium shallots, peeled and halved*
3 medium green onions, cut into pieces
1 (2-inch) piece fresh ginger, peeled and cut into pieces**
1 teaspoon soy sauce
1 teaspoon lemon juice
1 pound uncooked large shrimp, cleaned (keep tails on)

In food processor or blender, purée all ingredients except shrimp. In large shallow baking dish, combine dressing mixture with shrimp. Cover and marinate in refrigerator, stirring occasionally, at least 3 hours.

Remove shrimp and marinade to large shallow baking pan or aluminum-foil-lined broiler rack. Broil shrimp with marinade, turning once, 10 minutes or until done. Serve remaining marinade with shrimp. Garnish as desired.

Makes about 2 dozen

*Substitution: Use ⅓ medium onion, cut into pieces.
**Substitution: Use 1 teaspoon ground ginger.

Nutrients per serving (1 appetizer):			
Calories	24	Cholesterol	23 mg
Fat	0 g	Sodium	178 mg

TWO–TONE RICOTTA LOAF

2 envelopes unflavored gelatin
1 cup cold skim milk

Pepper Layer
1 container (15 ounces)
      POLLY-O FREE® Natural
      Nonfat Ricotta Cheese or
      POLLY-O LITE®
      Reduced-Fat Ricotta Cheese
1 jar (7 ounces) roasted red
      peppers, undrained
¼ teaspoon salt
      Pinch ground black pepper

Basil Layer
1 container (15 ounces)
      POLLY-O FREE® Natural
      Nonfat Ricotta Cheese or
      POLLY-O LITE®
      Reduced-Fat Ricotta Cheese
1 cup fresh basil leaves
⅓ cup fresh parsley leaves
¾ teaspoon salt
1 small garlic clove, crushed
      Pinch ground black pepper
½ cup skim milk
      Additional basil leaves
      (optional garnish)

In small saucepan, sprinkle gelatin over 1 cup cold milk; let stand 5 minutes. Stir over low heat until gelatin is completely dissolved.

Pepper Layer: In food processor, purée ricotta with roasted red peppers and their juice, salt and black pepper. Add ½ cup dissolved gelatin mixture and process until combined. Pour into an 8×4-inch loaf pan; refrigerate until partially set, about 20 minutes.

Basil Layer: In food processor, combine ricotta, basil, parsley, salt, garlic and black pepper. Process until herbs are finely chopped. Add remaining gelatin mixture and ½ cup skim milk. Pour into a bowl and chill, stirring occasionally, until mixture is consistency of unbeaten egg whites. Spoon over partially set pepper layer; smooth top. Cover and refrigerate until set, at least 4 hours or overnight. To serve, unmold onto a serving dish. If desired, garnish with fresh basil leaves.   *Makes 8 servings*

Nutrients per serving:

Calories	167	Cholesterol	20 mg
Fat	4 g	Sodium	382 mg

Two-Tone Ricotta Loaf

Tuna-Stuffed Artichokes

TUNA–STUFFED ARTICHOKES

4 medium artichokes
Lemon juice
1½ cups chopped fresh mushrooms
1 cup diced yellow squash or
    zucchini
⅓ cup chopped green onions
1 clove garlic, minced
2 tablespoons vegetable oil
1 can (12½ ounces) STARKIST®
    Tuna, drained and flaked
½ cup (2 ounces) shredded
    low-fat Cheddar, mozzarella
    or Monterey Jack cheese
¼ cup seasoned bread crumbs
2 tablespoons diced drained
    pimento

With kitchen shears trim sharp points from artichoke leaves. Trim stems; remove loose outer leaves. Cut 1 inch from the tops. Brush cut edges with lemon juice. In a large covered saucepan or Dutch oven bring artichokes and salted water to a boil; reduce heat. Simmer until a leaf pulls out easily, 20 to 30 minutes. Drain upside down.

Preheat oven to 450°F. Cut cooled artichokes lengthwise into halves. Remove fuzzy chokes and hearts. Finely chop hearts; discard chokes. In a medium skillet sauté mushrooms, artichoke hearts, squash, onions and garlic in oil for 3 minutes, stirring frequently. Stir in tuna. Place artichoke halves, cut-side-up, in a lightly oiled baking dish. Mound tuna mixture in centers of artichokes. In a small bowl stir together remaining ingredients; sprinkle over filling. Bake 5 to 8 minutes, or until cheese is melted and topping is golden.

Makes 8 appetizer servings

Nutrients per serving:

Calories	136	Cholesterol	47 mg
Fat	10 g	Sodium	522 mg

GREEK ISLES APPETIZERS

1 pound ground beef
1 pound ground lamb
2 eggs
½ cup finely chopped onion
2 garlic cloves, minced
2 teaspoons dry mustard
1 teaspoon dried thyme leaves,
    crushed
1 teaspoon ground coriander
½ teaspoon salt
½ teaspoon pepper
    Cucumber Sauce (recipe
    follows)

Heat oven to 350°F. Mix meat, eggs, onions, garlic and seasonings in large bowl until well blended. Shape into 1-inch balls. Place meatballs on rack in 15×10×1-inch jelly-roll pan. Bake 15 to 20 minutes or until lightly browned. Serve with Cucumber Sauce.

Makes 70 meatballs

CUCUMBER SAUCE

1 container (8 ounces)
    PHILADELPHIA BRAND®
    Soft Cream Cheese with
    Herb & Garlic
½ cup plain yogurt
1 tablespoon lemon juice
½ cup shredded cucumber, well
    drained

Stir together cream cheese, yogurt and lemon juice in small bowl until well blended. Stir in cucumber.

Prep time: 35 minutes
Cook time: 20 minutes

Nutrients per serving (3 meatballs plus 2 tablespoons sauce):

Calories	128	Cholesterol	55 mg
Fat	9 g	Sodium	161 mg

GROUND TURKEY CHINESE SPRING ROLLS

1 pound Ground Turkey
1 large clove garlic, minced
1½ teaspoons minced fresh ginger root
2 cups thinly sliced bok choy
½ cup thinly sliced green onions
2 tablespoons reduced-sodium soy sauce
1 teaspoon dry sherry or rice wine
1 teaspoon sesame oil
8 sheets phyllo pastry
Nonstick cooking spray

Preheat oven to 400°F.

In medium nonstick skillet, over medium-high heat, sauté turkey, garlic and ginger 4 to 5 minutes or until turkey is no longer pink. Drain thoroughly.

In medium bowl combine turkey mixture, bok choy, onions, soy sauce, sherry and oil.

On clean, dry counter, layer phyllo sheets into a stack and cut into 2 (18×7-inch) rectangles. Work with one rectangle of phyllo at a time. (Keep remaining phyllo covered with a damp cloth following package instructions.)

Coat rectangle of phyllo with nonstick cooking spray. On counter, arrange phyllo sheet so 7-inch side is parallel to counter edge. Place ¼ cup of turkey mixture in 5-inch strip, 1 inch away from bottom and side edges of phyllo. Fold 1-inch bottom edge of phyllo over filling and fold longer edges of phyllo toward center; roll up, jelly-roll style. Phyllo may break during rolling, but will hold filling once the roll is completed.

Ground Turkey Chinese Spring Rolls

Repeat process with remaining rectangles of phyllo to make remaining spring rolls. Place rolls, seam-side-down, on 2 (10×15-inch) cookie sheets coated with nonstick cooking spray. Coat tops of rolls with nonstick cooking spray. Bake 14 to 16 minutes or until all surfaces of rolls are golden brown.

Serve immediately with Chinese mustard, hoisin sauce and additional soy sauce, if desired.

Makes 16 spring rolls

Nutrients per serving (1 spring roll):

Calories	86	Cholesterol	14 mg
Fat	3 g	Sodium	140 mg

Favorite recipe from **National Turkey Federation**

Hot Orchard Peach Cup

SKIM MILK HOT COCOA

3 tablespoons sugar
2 tablespoons HERSHEY'S® Cocoa
¼ cup hot water
1½ cups skim milk
⅛ teaspoon vanilla extract

Blend sugar and cocoa in small saucepan; gradually add hot water. Cook over medium heat, stirring constantly, until mixture boils; boil and stir for 2 minutes. Add milk; heat thoroughly. Stir occasionally; *do not boil.* Remove from heat; add vanilla. Serve hot.

Makes two (7-ounce) servings

Nutrients per serving:

Calories	160	Cholesterol	5 mg
Fat	1 g	Sodium	100 mg

HOT ORCHARD PEACH CUP

1 bottle (40 ounces) DOLE® Pure & Light Orchard Peach Juice
¼ cup packed brown sugar
2 cinnamon sticks
2 tablespoons margarine
½ cup peach schnapps (optional) Additional cinnamon sticks for garnish (optional)

Combine juice, brown sugar, cinnamon and margarine in Dutch oven. Heat to a boil. Remove from heat; discard cinnamon sticks. Add schnapps, if desired. Garnish with cinnamon sticks, if desired.

Makes 6 servings

Nutrients per serving (7 ounces):

Calories	181	Cholesterol	0 mg
Fat	4 g	Sodium	70 mg

15

TANGY OLIVE SALSA

    1 cup tomatoes, peeled, seeded
        and diced
   ⅓ cup fresh parsley, chopped
   ¼ cup yellow bell pepper,
        chopped
    2 tablespoons Greek olives,
        pitted
    2 tablespoons fresh lime juice
  1½ tablespoons capers, drained
  1½ tablespoons olive oil
  1½ teaspoons fresh basil, chopped
    1 teaspoon balsamic vinegar
      Dash ground red pepper
      Dash black pepper

In medium bowl, combine tomatoes,
parsley, yellow pepper, olives, lime juice,
capers, oil, basil, vinegar, ground red
pepper and black pepper. Cover and
refrigerate for at least 1 hour to allow
flavors to blend.   *Makes 8 servings*

Nutrients per serving:

Calories	37	Cholesterol	0 mg
Fat	3 g	Sodium	119 mg

Favorite recipe from **National Turkey
Federation**

GRILLED MUSHROOMS WITH LAMB AND HERBS

   ¼ cup olive oil
   ¼ cup fresh lime juice
    1 small green onion, minced
   ½ teaspoon grated fresh ginger
   ¼ teaspoon salt
   ¼ teaspoon black pepper
    1 bunch parsley
   36 medium mushroom caps
    6 ounces cooked American
        lamb,* cut in ½-inch cubes
        or to fit mushroom caps

Combine all ingredients except
mushrooms and lamb in blender and
process until finely minced. Brush each
mushroom generously with mixture and
arrange on baking sheet. Top each
mushroom with a lamb cube. Broil about
4 inches from heat source until hot.
Garnish with parsley, if desired.
                    Makes 6 servings

*Leftover leg of lamb may be used.

Nutrients per serving:

Calories	62	Cholesterol	20 mg
Fat	4 g	Sodium	14 mg

Favorite recipe from **American Lamb
Council**

MULLED CIDER

    2 quarts apple cider
   ¾ to 1 cup REALEMON® Lemon
        Juice from Concentrate
    1 cup firmly packed light brown
        sugar
    8 whole cloves
    2 cinnamon sticks
   ¾ cup rum (optional)
      Additional cinnamon sticks for
        garnish (optional)

In large saucepan, combine all
ingredients except rum and garnish;
bring to a boil. Reduce heat; simmer,
uncovered, 10 minutes to blend flavors.
Remove spices; add rum just before
serving, if desired. Serve hot with
additional cinnamon sticks, if desired.
                    Makes about 2 quarts

Tip: Can be served cold.

Nutrients per serving (¾ cup):

Calories	135	Cholesterol	0 mg
Fat	trace	Sodium	7 mg

TUNA–STUFFED ENDIVE

4 ounces soft-spread herb cheese
4 ounces reduced-calorie cream cheese, softened
1 teaspoon lemon or lime juice
2 heads Belgian endive or small lettuce leaves _or_ crackers
1 can (3¼ ounces) STARKIST® Tuna, drained and finely flaked
Watercress sprigs or pimento strips for garnish

In blender container or food processor bowl, place cheeses and lemon juice. Cover and process until mixture is well blended. Trim ½ inch from bottom stems of endive; separate heads into leaves. Sprinkle 1 to 2 teaspoons tuna into each endive leaf; spoon or pipe 2 teaspoons of the cheese filling into each endive leaf. Garnish each with a sprig of watercress.

Makes about 24 appetizers

Nutrients per serving (1 appetizer):

Calories	29	Cholesterol	7 mg
Fat	2 g	Sodium	65 mg

PINEAPPLE SHRIMP APPETIZERS

1 can (8 ounces) DOLE® Crushed Pineapple, drained
1 can (4¼ ounces) Pacific shrimp, drained
¼ cup reduced-calorie mayonnaise
1 tablespoon minced DOLE® Green Onion
2 teaspoons Dijon-style mustard
½ teaspoon dill weed
2 cucumbers

Combine all ingredients except cucumbers. Cut cucumbers in ⅛- to ¼-inch-thick slices. Spoon heaping teaspoon of pineapple mixture on top of each slice. Garnish with dill or minced green onion if desired.

Makes 30 appetizers

Nutrients per serving (1 appetizer):

Calories	15	Cholesterol	6 mg
Fat	trace	Sodium	15 mg

SPINACH RICE BALLS

2 cups cooked rice
1 package (10 ounces) frozen chopped spinach, thawed and squeezed dry*
⅔ cup dry Italian-style bread crumbs, divided
½ cup grated Parmesan cheese
⅓ cup minced onion
3 egg whites, beaten
¼ cup skim milk
1 tablespoon Dijon mustard
Nonstick cooking spray

Combine rice, spinach, ⅓ cup bread crumbs, cheese, onion, egg whites, milk, and mustard in large bowl. Shape into 1-inch balls. Roll each ball in remaining ⅓ cup bread crumbs. Place on baking sheet coated with nonstick cooking spray. Bake at 375°F for 10 to 15 minutes. Serve warm.

Makes about 3 dozen rice balls

*Substitute 1 package (10 ounces) frozen chopped broccoli, thawed and well drained, for the spinach, if desired.

Nutrients per serving:

Calories	32	Cholesterol	1 mg
Fat	1 g	Sodium	102 mg

Favorite recipe from **USA Rice Council**

17

WHITE SANGRIA

2 quarts DOLE®
    Pine-Orange-Guava Juice
2 cups fruity white wine
¼ cup orange-flavored liqueur
¼ cup sugar
1 DOLE® Orange, thinly sliced
1 lime, thinly sliced
2 cups sliced DOLE® Fresh or
    frozen Strawberries
    Ice cubes
    Mint sprigs for garnish

Combine all ingredients except ice and
mint in 2 large pitchers; cover and
refrigerate for 2 hours to blend flavors.
Serve over ice. Garnish with mint sprig.

Makes 20 servings

Nutrients per serving (4 ounces):

Calories	93	Cholesterol	0 mg
Fat	trace	Sodium	7 mg

White Sangria

TWELVE CARAT BLACK–EYED PEA RELISH

1 cup vinegar
¼ cup vegetable oil
2 cans (15 ounces each)
    black-eyed peas, drained
12 small carrots, steamed until
    crisp-tender, coarsely
    chopped
1 sweet onion, finely chopped
1 green bell pepper, finely
    chopped
1 cup sugar
¼ cup Worcestershire sauce
2 teaspoons black pepper
2 teaspoons salt (optional)
2 dashes ground red pepper

Combine vinegar and oil in small
saucepan. Bring to a boil over high heat.
Meanwhile, combine black-eyed peas,
carrots, onion, green pepper, sugar,
Worcestershire sauce, black pepper, salt
and ground red pepper in large bowl.
Pour oil mixture over vegetable mixture.
Cover and refrigerate at least 24 hours to
allow flavors to blend. Store, covered, in
glass containers in refrigerator. Serve
cold; garnish as desired.

Makes 2 to 3 pints

Nutrients per serving (⅓ cup):

Calories	112	Cholesterol	0 mg
Fat	3 g	Sodium	45 mg

Favorite recipe from the **Black-Eyed Pea
Jamboree—Athens, Texas**

GUACAMOLE WITH TORTILLA CHIPS

1 package (4-serving size)
    JELL-O® Brand Lemon
    Flavor Sugar Free Gelatin
1 cup boiling water
1 container (16 ounces)
    1% low-fat cottage cheese
1 cup chopped ripe avocado
¾ cup chopped scallions, divided
¼ cup drained pickled jalapeño
    slices
¼ cup lemon juice
2 cloves garlic
1 to 2 teaspoons chili powder
¼ cup diced tomato
4 sliced ripe olives
    Chili Tortilla Chips (recipe
    follows)

Completely dissolve gelatin in boiling water in small bowl. Pour into blender container. Add cottage cheese, avocado, ½ cup of scallions, jalapeños, lemon juice, garlic and chili powder. Blend on low speed, scraping down sides occasionally, about 2 minutes or until mixture is completely smooth. Pour into shallow 5-cup serving dish; smooth top. Chill until set, about 4 hours.

Just before serving, garnish with remaining ¼ cup chopped scallions, tomato and ripe olives. Serve as a dip with fresh vegetables or Chili Tortilla Chips. *Makes 12 servings*

Nutrients per serving:			
Calories	60	Cholesterol	0 mg
Fat	3 g	Sodium	230 mg

Guacamole with Tortilla Chips

CHILI TORTILLA CHIPS

6 flour tortillas (7 inches in
    diameter)
    Nonstick cooking spray
    Chili powder

Heat oven to 350°F. Lightly spray tortillas with nonstick cooking spray; sprinkle with chili powder. Turn tortillas over; repeat process. Cut into 8 pie-shaped wedges. Place on cookie sheet; bake 8 to 10 minutes until crisp and lightly browned. *Makes 12 servings*

Nutrients per serving (4 chips):			
Calories	60	Cholesterol	0 mg
Fat	1 g	Sodium	90 mg

CRAB CURRY DIP

½ cup *undiluted* CARNATION®
    Lite Evaporated Skimmed
    Milk
1 package (8 ounces) light
    Neufchâtel cream cheese,
    softened
4 ounces (¾ cup) imitation crab
    meat, shredded
2 tablespoons finely sliced green
    onion
2 tablespoons finely chopped red
    pepper
½ teaspoon curry powder
¼ teaspoon garlic salt

In small mixer bowl, beat evaporated
skimmed milk and cream cheese. Stir in
crab, onion, red pepper, curry powder
and garlic salt. Cover and chill. Serve
with assorted raw vegetables.

Makes 2 cups

Variation: For Crab Horseradish Dip,
substitute 1 to 2 teaspoons prepared
horseradish for curry powder.

Nutrients per serving (¼ cup):

Calories	108	Cholesterol	28 mg
Fat	7 g	Sodium	320 mg

CHERRY PUNCH

1 can (6 ounces) frozen
    lemonade concentrate,
    thawed
5 cups DOLE® Pure & Light
    Mountain Cherry Juice,
    chilled
1 bottle (28 ounces) mineral
    water, chilled
    DOLE® Lemon slices for
    garnish
    Mint sprigs for garnish

Reconstitute lemonade according to
label directions in large punch bowl. Add
remaining ingredients.

Makes 16 servings

Nutrients per serving:

Calories	61	Cholesterol	0 mg
Fat	trace	Sodium	4 mg

SCANDINAVIAN SMÖRGÅSBORD

36 slices party bread, crackers or
    flat bread
    Reduced-calorie mayonnaise
    or salad dressing
    Mustard
36 small lettuce leaves or Belgian
    endive leaves
1 can (6½ ounces) STARKIST®
    Tuna, drained and flaked or
    broken into chunks
2 hard-cooked eggs, sliced
¼ pound frozen cooked bay
    shrimp, thawed
½ medium cucumber, thinly
    sliced
36 pieces steamed asparagus tips
    or pea pods
    Capers, plain yogurt, dill
    sprigs, pimento strips, red
    or black caviar, sliced green
    onion for garnish (optional)

Arrange party bread on a tray; spread
each with 1 teaspoon mayonnaise and/or
mustard. Top with a small lettuce leaf.
Top with tuna, egg slices, shrimp,
cucumber or steamed vegetables.
Garnish as desired.

Makes 36 appetizers

Nutrients per serving (1 appetizer):

Calories	47	Cholesterol	24 mg
Fat	1 g	Sodium	103 mg

Scandinavian Smörgåsbord

Clockwise from top right: Minted ReaLemonade, Sparkling ReaLemonade, Slushy ReaLemonade, Pink ReaLemonade

REALEMONADE

½ cup sugar
½ cup REALEMON® Lemon
    Juice from Concentrate
3¼ cups cold water
    Ice

In pitcher, dissolve sugar in ReaLemon® brand; add water. Cover; chill. Serve over ice.   *Makes about 1 quart*

Variations:
Sparkling: Substitute club soda for cold water.

Slushy: Reduce water to ½ cup. In blender container, combine sugar, ReaLemon® brand and ½ cup water. Gradually add 4 cups ice cubes, blending until smooth. Serve immediately.

Pink: Stir in 1 to 2 teaspoons grenadine syrup or 1 to 2 drops red food coloring.

Minted: Stir in 2 to 3 drops peppermint extract.

Low Calorie: Omit sugar. Add 4 to 8 envelopes sugar substitute or 1½ teaspoons liquid sugar substitute.

Strawberry: Increase sugar to ¾ cup. In blender or food processor, purée 1 quart fresh strawberries, cleaned and hulled (about 1½ pounds); add to lemonade.

Grape: Stir in 1 (6-ounce) can frozen grape juice concentrate, thawed.

Nutrients per serving (1 cup):			
Calories	97	Cholesterol	0 mg
Fat	trace	Sodium	6 mg

SHRIMP CUCUMBER SPREAD

¼ cup MIRACLE WHIP® FREE®
    Nonfat Dressing
2 ounces Light PHILADELPHIA
    BRAND® Neufchatel Cheese,
    softened
¼ cup chopped cooked shrimp or
    flaked canned tuna
3 tablespoons seeded chopped
    cucumber
1 tablespoon green onion slices
1 tablespoon chili sauce

Mix together ingredients until well blended; refrigerate. Serve with assorted crackers.   *Makes 1 cup*

Prep time: 10 minutes plus refrigerating

Nutrients per serving (3 tablespoons):			
Calories	60	Cholesterol	20 mg
Fat	3 g	Sodium	249 mg

ORANGE TEA PUNCH

4 cups brewed tea
2 cups orange juice, chilled
1 cup REALEMON® Lemon
    Juice from Concentrate
1 cup sugar
1 (32-ounce) bottle ginger ale,
    chilled
1 quart BORDEN® or
    MEADOW GOLD® Orange
    Sherbet

In pitcher, combine tea, orange juice,
ReaLemon® brand and sugar; stir until
sugar dissolves. Chill. Just before
serving, pour tea mixture into large
punch bowl; add ginger ale and scoops
of sherbet.

Makes about 4 quarts, 16 servings

Nutrients per serving:

Calories	82	Cholesterol	0 mg
Fat	trace	Sodium	9 mg

Garden Vegetable Platter

GARDEN VEGETABLE PLATTER

1 cup torn spinach
½ cup fresh parsley, stemmed
¼ cup cold water
3 tablespoons sliced green onions
½ teaspoon dried tarragon
    leaves, crushed
1 package (8 ounces) Light
    PHILADELPHIA BRAND®
    Neufchatel Cheese, softened
¾ cup chopped cucumber
½ teaspoon lemon juice
3 drops hot pepper sauce
¼ teaspoon salt

Bring to boil spinach, parsley, water,
onions and tarragon in small saucepan.
Reduce heat. Cover; simmer 1 minute.
Drain.

Place spinach mixture and all remaining
ingredients in blender or food processor
container; cover. Blend until smooth.
Cover. Refrigerate. Serve with assorted
vegetable dippers.   *Makes 1½ cups*

Prep time: 30 minutes plus
refrigerating

**Nutrients per serving (about 1
tablespoon):**

Calories	25	Cholesterol	5 mg
Fat	2 g	Sodium	60 mg

Clockwise from top: Sparkling Raspberry Mint Cooler, Kokomo Quencher, Sunlight Sipper

KOKOMO QUENCHER

1 carton (64 ounces) DOLE®
   Pine-Orange-Guava Juice
2 bottles (32 ounces each)
   lemon-lime soda, chilled
1 can (46 ounces) DOLE®
   Pineapple Juice, chilled
1 package (16 ounces) frozen
   blackberries
1 can (15 ounces) real cream of
   coconut
1 lime, thinly sliced

Combine all ingredients in large punch bowl. *Makes 47 servings*

Nutrients per serving (4 ounces):			
Calories	82	Cholesterol	0 mg
Fat	2 g	Sodium	13 mg

SPARKLING RASPBERRY MINT COOLER

1 to 2 cups fresh mint leaves
1 can (46 ounces) DOLE®
   Pineapple Juice, chilled
1 bottle (40 ounces) DOLE®
   Pure & Light Country
   Raspberry Juice
1 bottle (32 ounces) lemon-lime
   soda, chilled
1 package (12 ounces) frozen
   raspberries
1 DOLE® Lemon, thinly sliced

Rub mint leaves around sides of punch bowl, then drop the bruised leaves in bottom of bowl. Combine remaining ingredients in punch bowl.

Makes 32 servings

Nutrients per serving (4 ounces):			
Calories	66	Cholesterol	0 mg
Fat	trace	Sodium	7 mg

SUNLIGHT SIPPER

¾ cup DOLE® Pine-Passion-
   Banana Juice, chilled
1 tablespoon puréed peaches
1 tablespoon orange-flavored
   liqueur (optional)
1 teaspoon rum extract
   Cracked ice

Combine all ingredients in glass.

Makes 1 serving

Nutrients per serving:			
Calories	106	Cholesterol	0 mg
Fat	trace	Sodium	9 mg

SHANGHAI PARTY PLEASERS

1 can (20 ounces) crushed
     pineapple in juice, undrained
¼ cup firmly packed brown sugar
2 tablespoons cornstarch
     Dash of ginger
1 cup water
2 tablespoons margarine
1 pound finely chopped, cooked,
     skinned turkey or chicken
¾ cup QUAKER® Oat Bran hot
     cereal, uncooked
⅓ cup plain low-fat yogurt
⅓ cup finely chopped water
     chestnuts, drained
⅓ cup sliced green onions
2 tablespoons lite soy sauce
1 egg white, slightly beaten
1 teaspoon ginger
½ teaspoon salt (optional)

Drain pineapple, reserving juice. In medium saucepan, combine brown sugar, cornstarch and dash of ginger; mix well. Add combined pineapple juice, water, ¼ cup pineapple and margarine; mix well. Bring to a boil over medium-high heat; reduce heat. Simmer about 1 minute, stirring frequently or until sauce is thickened and clear. Set aside.

Heat oven to 400°F. Lightly spray rack of 13×9-inch baking pan with nonstick cooking spray, or oil lightly. Combine turkey, oat bran, yogurt, water chestnuts, onions, soy sauce, egg white, 1 teaspoon ginger, salt and remaining pineapple; mix well. Shape into 1-inch balls. Place on prepared rack. Bake 20 to 25 minutes or until light golden brown. Serve with pineapple sauce.

Makes 2 dozen

Nutrients per serving (⅛th of recipe):			
Calories	240	Cholesterol	45 mg
Fat	6 g	Sodium	240 mg

Shanghai Party Pleasers

CHEDDAR–RICE PATTIES

2 cups cooked rice
1 cup (4 ounces) shredded
   low-fat Cheddar cheese
½ cup minced onion
3 tablespoons all-purpose flour
½ teaspoon salt
¼ teaspoon ground black pepper
3 egg whites
⅛ teaspoon cream of tartar
   Nonstick cooking spray
   Apple wedges (optional)
   Low-fat sour cream (optional)

Combine rice, cheese, onion, flour, salt, and pepper in medium bowl. Beat egg whites with cream of tartar in small bowl until stiff but not dry. Fold beaten egg whites into rice mixture. Coat large skillet with nonstick cooking spray and place over medium heat until hot. Spoon 2 to 3 tablespoons batter into skillet for each patty; push batter into diamond shape using spatula. Cook patties, turning once, until golden brown on both sides. Serve warm with apple wedges or sour cream.

Makes 4 servings, about 1 dozen

Nutrients per serving (3 patties):

Calories	233	Cholesterol	18 mg
Fat	6 g	Sodium	550 mg

Favorite recipe from **USA Rice Council**

Cheddar-Rice Patties

BANANA–RASPBERRY SMOOTHIE

**2 ripe, medium DOLE®
    Bananas, peeled
1½ cups DOLE® Pure & Light
    Country Raspberry Juice,
    chilled
1 cup frozen vanilla yogurt,
    softened
1 cup DOLE® Fresh or frozen
    Raspberries**

Place all ingredients in blender. Process
until smooth.   *Makes 2 to 3 servings*

Nutrients per serving:

Calories	196	Cholesterol	7 mg
Fat	2 g	Sodium	64 mg

GARDEN VEGETABLE DIP

**1 bunch DOLE® Broccoli
1 head DOLE® Cauliflower
1 pound DOLE® Carrots
½ cup minced onion
2 packages (8 ounces *each*)
    cream cheese, softened
1 teaspoon dill weed
½ teaspoon ground cumin
¼ teaspoon chili powder
⅛ teaspoon salt
10 drops hot pepper sauce
    Vegetable dippers: broccoli
    and cauliflower florettes;
    carrot, celery and cucumber
    slices; bell pepper strips;
    mushroom slices; cherry
    tomatoes**

Banana-Raspberry Smoothie

Break broccoli and cauliflower into
florettes. Mince 1 cup of each; reserve
remaining florettes for vegetable dippers.
Mince 1 cup of carrots; slice remaining
for dippers. In food processor fitted with
metal blade, combine minced broccoli,
cauliflower, carrots, onion, cream cheese
and seasonings; process until smooth.
Refrigerate dip 1 hour, or overnight, in
covered serving bowl. Serve with
vegetable dippers and crackers.

Makes 5½ cups dip

Nutrients per serving (1 tablespoon dip):

Calories	19	Cholesterol	6 mg
Fat	2 g	Sodium	19 mg

PARTY HAM SANDWICHES

¾ cup plain nonfat yogurt
1 tablespoon chopped fresh chives
1 teaspoon dill mustard
1 loaf party rye or pumpernickel bread
   Leaf lettuce, washed, torn and well drained
1 ARMOUR® Lower Salt Ham Nugget (about 1¾ pounds), shaved
1 small cucumber, thinly sliced
12 cherry tomatoes, cut in half

Combine yogurt, chives and mustard in small bowl. Arrange bread slices on serving tray; spread evenly with yogurt mixture. Layer lettuce, ham, cucumber slice and tomato half on top of each bread slice. Garnish serving tray with lettuce and green onions, if desired.

Makes 24 sandwiches

Nutrients per serving (1 sandwich):

Calories	101	Cholesterol	16 mg
Fat	3 g	Sodium	413 mg

DOUBLE STRAWBERRY COCONUT PUNCH

2 cans (12 ounces each) frozen DOLE® Pine-Orange Banana Juice concentrate, thawed
4 cups DOLE® Fresh or frozen Strawberries, divided
1 can (15 ounces) real cream of coconut
4 ripe, medium DOLE® Bananas, peeled
1 pint vanilla ice cream, softened
1 cup flaked coconut (optional)

Reconstitute juice according to directions in large punch bowl. Place 2 cups strawberries, cream of coconut and bananas in blender. Process until smooth; stir into juice in punch bowl. Purée remaining strawberries in blender. Swirl into punch along with ice cream. Top with coconut, if desired.

Makes 25 servings

Nutrients per serving (6 ounces):

Calories	130	Cholesterol	5 mg
Fat	5 g	Sodium	23 mg

SPICY ZUCCHINI AND BACON CANAPÉS

1 (4-ounce) carton low-fat cottage cheese, well drained
2 green onions, finely chopped
½ tablespoon finely chopped jalapeño peppers
½ teaspoon MRS. DASH®, Original Blend
2 medium zucchini, cut into ¼-inch slices
8 slices ARMOUR® Lower Salt Bacon, cooked crisp and crumbled
2 tablespoons finely chopped red pepper *or* 6 cherry tomatoes, quartered

Combine cottage cheese, green onions, jalapeño and seasoning in small bowl. Mound cottage cheese mixture evenly on top of zucchini slices; sprinkle with bacon. Top with sprinkle of red pepper or cherry tomato quarter. Garnish with fresh chives or small sprig of parsley, if desired. *Makes 22 to 24 canapés*

Nutrients per serving (1 canapé):

Calories	17	Cholesterol	2 mg
Fat	1 g	Sodium	66 mg

Top to bottom: Spicy Zucchini and Bacon Canapés, Party Ham Sandwiches

STEAMED MUSSELS IN WHITE WINE

⅓ cup Lite WISH-BONE® Italian Dressing
½ cup chopped shallots or onions
3 pounds mussels, well scrubbed
⅔ cup dry white wine
½ cup chopped parsley
¼ cup water
Generous dash crushed red pepper

In large saucepan or stockpot, heat Italian dressing and cook shallots over medium heat, stirring occasionally, 2 minutes or until tender. Add remaining ingredients. Bring to a boil, then simmer, covered, 4 minutes or until mussel shells open. *(Discard any unopened shells.)* Serve, if desired, with Italian or French bread. *Makes 6 servings*

Nutrients per serving:

Calories	74	Cholesterol	18 mg
Fat	1 g	Sodium	378 mg

Steamed Mussels in White Wine

PEPPERED PECANS

3 tablespoons margarine or butter
3 cloves garlic, minced
1½ teaspoons TABASCO® Pepper Sauce
½ teaspoon salt
3 cups pecan halves

Preheat oven to 250°F. In small skillet, melt butter. Add garlic, TABASCO® sauce and salt; cook 1 minute. Toss pecans with butter mixture; spread in single layer on baking sheet. Bake 1 hour or until pecans are crisp; stir occasionally. *Makes 3 cups*

Nutrients per serving (1 tablespoon):

Calories	50	Cholesterol	0 mg
Fat	5 g	Sodium	30 mg

PICKLE ROLL–EM–UPS

1 package (6 ounces) sliced ham
1 container (8 ounces) soft cream cheese
8 medium-sized CLAUSSEN® Whole Kosher Dill Pickles

Spread one side of each ham slice with one tablespoon cream cheese. Place one pickle on edge of each ham slice. Roll ham slice around pickle; press edges to seal. Cover and refrigerate one hour. To serve, cut each pickle into six slices. *Makes 48 appetizers*

Nutrients per serving (1 appetizer):

Calories	20	Cholesterol	5 mg
Fat	2 g	Sodium	215 mg

Mediterranean Appetizer

MEDITERRANEAN APPETIZER

1 container (8 ounces) Light
     PHILADELPHIA BRAND®
     Pasteurized Process Cream
     Cheese Product, softened
2 teaspoons red wine vinegar
1 clove garlic, minced
½ teaspoon dried oregano leaves,
     crushed
½ teaspoon lemon pepper
     seasoning
24 lahvosh crackers (3 inches in
     diameter) or 4 pita bread
     rounds, split
1½ cups finely torn spinach
1 tomato, chopped
4 ounces **CHURNY® ATHENOS®**
     Feta Cheese, crumbled
½ cup Greek ripe olives, pitted,
     chopped

Stir cream cheese product, vinegar,
garlic and seasonings in small bowl until
well blended.

Spread crackers with cream cheese
mixture. Top with remaining ingredients.
Makes 8 servings

Prep time: 20 minutes

Nutrients per serving:

Calories	180	Cholesterol	30 mg
Fat	10 g	Sodium	620 mg

Two Cheese Pesto Dip

TWO CHEESE PESTO DIP

1 cup light sour cream
½ cup light mayonnaise
½ cup finely chopped fresh
    parsley
¼ cup finely chopped walnuts
1 clove garlic, minced
1½ teaspoons dried basil *or*
    3 tablespoons fresh minced
    basil
½ cup (2 ounces) SARGENTO®
    Preferred Light Fancy
    Shredded Mozzarella Cheese
2 tablespoons SARGENTO®
    Grated Parmesan Cheese

Combine all ingredients. Cover and
refrigerate several hours or overnight.
Serve with assorted fresh vegetable
dippers. *Makes 2 cups*

Nutrients per serving (1 tablespoon):			
Calories	24	Cholesterol	1 mg
Fat	2 g	Sodium	36 mg

SPINACH RICOTTA PIE

4 cups chopped spinach
½ cup chopped onion
1 package (8 ounces) Light
    PHILADELPHIA BRAND®
    Neufchatel Cheese, softened
¾ cup low-fat ricotta cheese
½ teaspoon dried basil leaves,
    crushed
½ teaspoon dried oregano leaves,
    crushed
¼ teaspoon salt
⅛ teaspoon garlic powder
⅛ teaspoon pepper
¾ cup chopped tomato
2 tablespoons KRAFT® 100%
    Grated Parmesan Cheese

Heat oven to 350°F. Place spinach and
onions in small saucepan. Cover; cook
5 minutes or until tender. Beat cheeses
and seasonings in small mixing bowl at
medium speed with electric mixer until
well blended. Stir in spinach mixture;
spread into 9-inch pie plate. Bake 15 to
20 minutes or until thoroughly heated.
Top with remaining ingredients. Serve
with crisp rye crackers or bagel chips.
Makes 10 to 12 servings

Prep time: 15 minutes
Cook time: 20 minutes

Nutrients per serving:			
Calories	90	Cholesterol	20 mg
Fat	6 g	Sodium	190 mg

ITALIAN BREAD PIZZA

1 large loaf Italian bread
1½ cups (6 ounces) shredded lower salt Monterey Jack cheese, divided
1 (16-ounce) jar prepared no salt added, no sugar, no fat pasta sauce
1½ tablespoons dried Italian seasoning
12 ounces ARMOUR® Lower Salt Ham, thinly sliced
1 (20-ounce) can pineapple rings, well drained
8 thin green pepper rings
8 thin red pepper rings

Slice bread lengthwise in half. Toast cut sides under broiler until lightly browned. Sprinkle ¼ cup of the cheese on each half; broil again about 1 to 2 minutes, or until cheese is melted. Combine pasta sauce and seasoning in small saucepan; cook over medium heat until hot. Spoon sauce evenly over bread halves; top evenly with ham and pineapple rings. Place green and red pepper rings alternately on top. Sprinkle each half with ½ cup of remaining cheese; place on baking sheet. Broil 4 to 5 inches from heat source about 4 to 6 minutes, or until cheese is melted. Cut each half into 6 pieces. Garnish with parsley, if desired. *Makes 12 servings*

Nutrients per serving:

Calories	253	Cholesterol	29 mg
Fat	6 g	Sodium	482 mg

FROSTY FRUIT SHAKE

1 can (6 ounces) *or* ¾ cup DOLE® Pineapple Juice, chilled
1 cup DOLE® Fresh or frozen Strawberries
1 ripe, medium DOLE® Banana, peeled
Ice cubes

Place all ingredients in blender. Process until smooth. Pour into tall glass.
Makes 1 serving

Nutrients per serving:

Calories	253	Cholesterol	0 mg
Fat	1 g	Sodium	5 mg

Italian Bread Pizza

Strawberry Watermelon Slush

STRAWBERRY WATERMELON SLUSH

1 pint fresh strawberries,
cleaned and hulled
(about ¾ pound)
2 cups seeded and cubed
watermelon
⅓ cup sugar
⅓ cup vodka (optional)
¼ cup REALEMON® Lemon
Juice from Concentrate
2 cups ice cubes

In blender container, combine all
ingredients except ice; blend well.
Gradually add ice, blending until
smooth. Serve immediately. Garnish
as desired.   *Makes about 1 quart*

Nutrients per serving (1 cup):

Calories	110	Cholesterol	0 mg
Fat	1 g	Sodium	6 mg

ORANGE MILK SHAKE

2 cups skim milk
1 package (4-serving size)
JELL-O® Brand Orange
Flavor Sugar Free Gelatin
1 cup vanilla ice milk

Pour milk into blender container. Add
remaining ingredients; cover. Blend at
high speed 30 seconds or until smooth.
Serve at once.   *Makes 4 servings*

Note: For a thicker shake, pour over
crushed ice or add 1 cup crushed ice to
ingredients in blender.

Nutrients per serving:

Calories	100	Cholesterol	10 mg
Fat	2 g	Sodium	150 mg

TOASTED SESAME SEED WAFERS

¼ cup sesame seeds
1½ cups all-purpose flour
¾ teaspoon salt
⅛ teaspoon paprika
Dash garlic powder
½ cup BUTTER FLAVOR
CRISCO®
3 to 4 drops hot red pepper
sauce
4 tablespoons cold water
1 tablespoon 2% milk

Preheat oven to 375°F. Spread sesame
seeds in 8×8×2-inch baking pan. Bake
for 6 to 10 minutes, or until golden
brown. Transfer to small dish; set aside.

In medium bowl combine flour, salt,
paprika and garlic powder. Cut in Butter
Flavor Crisco® until coarse crumbs
form. Stir in 3 tablespoons toasted
sesame seeds.

Combine red pepper sauce and
4 tablespoons water. Sprinkle over flour
mixture 1 tablespoon at a time, mixing
with fork until particles are moistened
and cling together. Form dough into ball.

Roll dough ⅛ inch thick on lightly
floured board. Cut with 2- or 2½-inch
cookie cutter. Transfer cutouts to
ungreased baking sheet. Brush with
milk. Sprinkle lightly with remaining
sesame seeds. Bake for 12 to
15 minutes, or until light golden brown.
Cool. Store in covered container.
        Makes 4 to 4½ dozen wafers

Nutrients per serving (1 wafer):

Calories	31	Cholesterol	trace
Fat	2 g	Sodium	30 mg

ARTICHOKE PUFFS

16 to 20 slices small party rye
    bread
2 tablespoons CRISCO®
    Shortening, melted
1 can (14 ounces) artichoke
    hearts, drained
2 egg whites
⅓ teaspoon salt
¼ cup grated Parmesan cheese
2 tablespoons shredded sharp
    Cheddar cheese
    Dash ground red pepper
    Paprika

Preheat oven to 400°F. Brush bread
slices with melted Crisco® and place on
an ungreased cookie sheet.

Cut artichoke hearts in half; drain on
paper towels. Place an artichoke piece,
cut-side-down, on each bread slice.

Beat egg whites and salt until stiff, not
dry, peaks form. Fold in cheeses and
ground red pepper.

Spoon about 1 measuring teaspoonful of
egg white mixture over each artichoke
piece; sprinkle with paprika.

Bake at 400°F for 10 to 12 minutes or
until golden brown. Serve hot. Garnish
tray with celery leaves and carrot curls, if
desired.   *Makes 16 puffs*

Nutrients per serving (1 puff):

Calories	52	Cholesterol	2 mg
Fat	2 g	Sodium	113 mg

PAN–ROASTED HERBED ALMONDS

1 teaspoon *each* dried thyme,
    oregano and basil
½ teaspoon *each* garlic salt and
    onion powder
¼ teaspoon ground black pepper
2 tablespoons HOLLYWOOD®
    Peanut Oil
¾ pound (about 2 cups) whole
    blanched almonds

In a small bowl, combine seasonings. In
a large skillet, heat oil over low heat; add
almonds and seasonings and cook
slowly, stirring, until almonds are lightly
browned, approximately 10 minutes.
Place mixture on paper towels to absorb
excess oil. Can be served immediately or
at room temperature.   *Makes 2 cups*

Note: As almonds cool, seasonings will
not adhere; however, herb flavor will
remain.

Nutrients per serving (2 tablespoons):

Calories	122	Cholesterol	0 mg
Fat	6 g	Sodium	135 mg

SHERRIED TURKEY COCKTAIL MEATBALLS

2 pounds Turkey Sausage
⅔ cup seasoned bread crumbs
1 bottle (9 ounces) mango
    chutney
1 cup low-fat plain yogurt
⅓ cup dry sherry

Preheat oven to 375°F. In medium bowl combine sausage and bread crumbs. Form mixture into 1-inch balls. Arrange meatballs on two (10×15-inch) baking pans. Bake 25 to 30 minutes or until meatballs are no longer pink in center. In blender or food processor purée chutney until smooth. In small saucepan over low heat, combine chutney, yogurt and sherry; cook until mixture is slightly thickened. *Do not allow mixture to boil.* To serve, combine meatballs and sauce in chafing dish. *Makes 80 meatballs*

Nutrients per serving (1 meatball):

Calories	33	Cholesterol	7 mg
Fat	1 g	Sodium	95 mg

Favorite recipe from **National Turkey Federation**

GONE BANANAS SHAKE

1½ cups skim milk
½ cup Light PHILADELPHIA BRAND® Pasteurized Process Cream Cheese Product
1 large banana, cut into chunks
3 tablespoons chocolate syrup
6 ice cubes

Gradually add milk to cream cheese product in blender or food processor container; cover. Blend until smooth. Add banana and syrup; blend until smooth. Add ice; blend 1 minute.

Makes 4 servings

Prep time: 10 minutes

Nutrients per serving:

Calories	160	Cholesterol	15 mg
Fat	5 g	Sodium	220 mg

EGGPLANT CAVIAR

1 large eggplant, unpeeled
¼ cup chopped onion
2 tablespoons lemon juice
1 tablespoon olive or vegetable oil
1 small clove garlic
½ teaspoon salt
¼ teaspoon TABASCO® Pepper Sauce
Cooked egg white, sieved (optional)
Lemon slice (optional)
Toast points (optional)

Preheat oven to 350°F. Pierce eggplant with fork. Place eggplant in shallow baking dish. Bake 1 hour or until soft, turning once. Trim off ends; slice eggplant in half lengthwise. Place, cut-side-down, in colander and let drain 10 minutes. Scoop out pulp; reserve pulp and peel. In blender or food processor, combine eggplant peel, onion, lemon juice, oil, garlic, salt and TABASCO® sauce. Cover; process until peel is finely chopped. Add eggplant pulp. Cover; process just until chopped. Place in serving dish. Garnish with egg white and lemon slice, if desired. Serve with toast points, if desired. *Makes 1½ cups*

Nutrients per serving (1 tablespoon):

Calories	10	Cholesterol	0 mg
Fat	1 g	Sodium	45 mg

Breakfast and Brunch

Left: Brunch Rice
Right: Irish Soda Bacon Bread
(page 40)

BRUNCH RICE

  1 teaspoon margarine
  ¾ cup shredded carrots
  ¾ cup diced green bell pepper
  ¾ cup (about 3 ounces) sliced
      fresh mushrooms
  6 egg whites, beaten
  2 eggs, beaten
  ½ cup skim milk
  ½ teaspoon salt
  ¼ teaspoon ground black pepper
  3 cups cooked brown rice
  ½ cup (2 ounces) shredded
      Cheddar cheese
  6 corn tortillas, warmed
      (optional)

Heat margarine in large skillet over medium-high heat until hot. Add carrots, green pepper, and mushrooms; cook 2 minutes. Combine egg whites, eggs, milk, salt, and black pepper in small bowl. Reduce heat to medium and pour egg mixture over vegetables. Continue stirring 1½ to 2 minutes. Add rice and cheese; stir to gently separate grains. Heat 2 minutes. Serve immediately or spoon mixture into warmed corn tortillas. *Makes 6 servings*

To Microwave: Heat margarine in 2- to 3-quart microproof baking dish. Add carrots, green pepper, and mushrooms; cover and cook on HIGH (100% power) 4 minutes. Combine egg whites, eggs, milk, salt, and black pepper in small bowl; pour over vegetables. Cook on HIGH 4 minutes, stirring with fork after each minute to cut cooked eggs into small pieces. Stir in rice and cheese; cook on HIGH about 1 minute or until thoroughly heated. Serve immediately or spoon mixture into warmed corn tortillas.

Nutrients per serving:

| Calories | 212 | Cholesterol | 79 mg |
| Fat | 7 g | Sodium | 353 mg |

Favorite recipe from **USA Rice Council**

IRISH SODA BACON BREAD

4 cups all-purpose flour
3 tablespoons sugar
1½ tablespoons low-sodium
    baking powder
1 teaspoon baking soda
6 tablespoons unsalted
    margarine or butter, cold
1 cup golden raisins
6 slices ARMOUR® Lower Salt
    Bacon, cooked crisp and
    crumbled
2 eggs
1½ cups buttermilk

Preheat oven to 375°F. Combine flour, sugar, baking powder and baking soda in large bowl; cut in margarine until mixture resembles coarse crumbs. Stir in raisins and bacon. Beat eggs slightly in small bowl; reserve 1 tablespoon egg. Add buttermilk and remaining eggs to flour mixture; stir to make soft dough.

Turn out onto lightly floured surface; knead about 1 to 2 minutes, or until smooth. Shape dough into round loaf. Spray round 2-quart casserole dish with nonstick cooking spray; place dough in dish. With floured knife, cut a 4-inch cross about ¼ inch deep on top of loaf. Brush loaf with reserved egg.

Bake about 55 to 65 minutes, or until wooden toothpick inserted into center comes out clean. (Cover loaf with foil during last 30 minutes of baking to prevent overbrowning.) Cool on wire rack 10 minutes; remove from dish. Serve with light cream cheese or honey butter, if desired.   *Makes 12 to 15 servings*

Nutrients per serving:

Calories	231	Cholesterol	40 mg
Fat	7 g	Sodium	130 mg

CARROT–ZUCCHINI MUFFINS

1¾ cups QUAKER® Oats (quick or
    old fashioned, uncooked)
1 cup all-purpose flour
½ cup firmly packed brown sugar
1 tablespoon baking powder
¼ teaspoon ground nutmeg
1 cup shredded carrots (about
    2 large)
½ cup shredded zucchini (about
    1 medium)
⅔ cup skim milk
3 tablespoons vegetable oil
2 egg whites, slightly beaten
¼ cup QUAKER® Oats (quick or
    old fashioned, uncooked)
1 tablespoon chopped nuts
1 tablespoon margarine, melted

Heat oven to 400°F. Line 12 medium muffin cups with paper baking cups or spray bottoms only with nonstick cooking spray. Combine 1¾ cups oats, flour, brown sugar, baking powder and nutmeg. Add carrots, zucchini, milk, oil and egg whites, mixing just until moistened. Fill muffin cups almost full. Combine remaining ingredients; sprinkle evenly over batter. Bake 20 to 25 minutes or until golden brown. Serve warm.   *Makes 12 muffins*

Tips: To freeze muffins, place in freezer bag. Seal, label and freeze. To reheat frozen muffins, remove muffins from bag. Microwave at HIGH (100% power) about 30 seconds per muffin.

Nutrients per serving (1 muffin):

Calories	182	Cholesterol	0 mg
Fat	6 g	Sodium	140 mg

OATS 'N FRUIT COFFEE CAKE

¾ cup QUAKER® Oats (quick or old fashioned, uncooked)
2 tablespoons sugar
½ teaspoon ground cinnamon
2 tablespoons liquid vegetable oil margarine
1 cup sugar
¼ cup liquid vegetable oil margarine
⅔ cup skim milk
2 egg whites, slightly beaten
1 teaspoon vanilla
1 cup whole wheat flour
½ cup QUAKER® Oat Bran hot cereal, uncooked
1 teaspoon baking powder
½ cup chopped dried apricots, raisins, dates, prunes or figs

Combine oats, 2 tablespoons sugar and cinnamon. Stir in 2 tablespoons margarine; mix well. Set aside. Heat oven to 350°F. Lightly spray 8- or 9-inch square baking pan with nonstick cooking spray, or oil lightly. Beat 1 cup sugar and ¼ cup margarine until well blended. Add combined milk, egg whites and vanilla; mix well. Add combined whole wheat flour, oat bran and baking powder; mix until well blended. Spread into prepared pan; sprinkle evenly with apricots. Top with reserved oat mixture to cover apricots. Bake 35 to 40 minutes or until wooden toothpick inserted in center comes out clean. Cool completely on wire rack. Wrap securely; store at room temperature.   *Makes 9 servings*

To Microwave: Combine oats, 2 tablespoons sugar and cinnamon. Stir in 2 tablespoons margarine; mix well. Set aside. Beat 1 cup sugar and ¼ cup margarine until well blended. Add combined milk, egg whites and vanilla; mix well. Add combined whole wheat flour, oat bran and baking powder; mix until well blended. Spread into ungreased 8-inch square microwaveable dish; sprinkle evenly with apricots. Top with reserved oat mixture to cover apricots. Microwave at MEDIUM-LOW to MEDIUM (50% power) 6 minutes, rotating dish after 3 minutes. Microwave at HIGH (100% power) 4 to 6 minutes or until center springs back when lightly touched. Cool completely. Wrap securely; store at room temperature.

Nutrients per serving:

Calories	280	Cholesterol	0 mg
Fat	8 g	Sodium	125 mg

CHEESE 'N' APPLE SPREAD

1 package (8 ounces) Light PHILADELPHIA BRAND® Neufchatel Cheese, softened
½ cup KRAFT® FREE® Nonfat Mayonnaise Dressing
½ cup (2 ounces) KRAFT® Light Naturals Shredded Mild Reduced Fat Cheddar Cheese
½ cup finely chopped apple

Blend together neufchatel cheese and dressing. Stir in Cheddar cheese and apple; refrigerate. Serve on toasted bagelette halves.   *Makes 1⅔ cups*

Prep time: 10 minutes plus refrigerating

Nutrients per serving (2 tablespoons):

Calories	82	Cholesterol	5 mg
Fat	3 g	Sodium	420 mg

Double Oat Muffins

ORANGE CHOCOLATE CHIP BREAD

1 cup skim milk
¼ cup orange juice
⅓ cup sugar
1 egg, slightly beaten
1 tablespoon grated fresh orange
    peel
3 cups all-purpose biscuit
    baking mix
½ cup HERSHEY'S®
    MINI CHIPS®
    Semi-Sweet Chocolate

Combine milk, orange juice, sugar, egg
and orange peel in small bowl. Place
baking mix in medium mixing bowl. Stir
milk mixture into baking mix, beating
until well combined, about 1 minute. Stir
in MINI CHIPS®. Pour into greased
9×5×3-inch loaf pan. Bake at 350°F
for 45 to 50 minutes or until cake tester
inserted in center comes out clean. Cool
in pan on wire rack 10 minutes; remove
from pan. Cool completely. Slice and
serve. To store leftovers, wrap in foil or
plastic wrap. *Makes 16 servings*

Nutrients per serving (1 slice):

Calories	161	Cholesterol	17 mg
Fat	5 g	Sodium	274 mg

DOUBLE OAT MUFFINS

2 cups QUAKER® Oat Bran hot
    cereal, uncooked
⅓ cup firmly packed brown sugar
¼ cup all-purpose flour
2 teaspoons baking powder
¼ teaspoon salt (optional)
¼ teaspoon ground nutmeg
    (optional)
1 cup skim milk
2 egg whites, slightly beaten
3 tablespoons vegetable oil
1½ teaspoons vanilla
¼ cup QUAKER® Oats (quick or
    old fashioned, uncooked)
1 tablespoon firmly packed
    brown sugar

Heat oven to 400°F. Line 12 medium
muffin cups with paper baking cups.
Combine oat bran, ⅓ cup brown sugar,
flour, baking powder, salt and nutmeg.
Add combined milk, egg whites, oil and
vanilla, mixing just until moistened. Fill
muffin cups almost full. Combine oats
and remaining 1 tablespoon brown
sugar; sprinkle evenly over batter. Bake
20 to 22 minutes or until golden brown.
Makes 12 muffins

To Microwave: Line 6 microwaveable muffin cups with double paper baking cups. Combine oat bran, ⅓ cup brown sugar, flour, baking powder, salt and nutmeg. Add combined milk, egg whites, oil and vanilla, mixing just until moistened. Fill muffin cups almost full. Combine oats and remaining 1 tablespoon brown sugar; sprinkle evenly over batter. Microwave at HIGH (100%) 2½ to 3 minutes or until wooden toothpick inserted in centers comes out clean. Remove from pan; cool 5 minutes before serving. Line muffin cups with additional double paper baking cups. Repeat procedure with remaining batter.

Tips: To freeze muffins, place in freezer bag. Seal, label and freeze. To reheat frozen muffins, remove muffins from bag. Microwave at HIGH about 30 seconds per muffin.

Nutrients per serving (1 muffin):			
Calories	140	Cholesterol	0 mg
Fat	5 g	Sodium	90 mg

PINEAPPLE–ORANGE SAUCE

1 can (20 ounces) DOLE® Pineapple Chunks, undrained
Juice and zest from 1 DOLE® Orange
1 tablespoon cornstarch
1 tablespoon sugar
1 teaspoon ground ginger

Combine pineapple, ½ cup orange juice and 1 teaspoon orange zest with remaining ingredients in saucepan. Cook and stir until sauce boils and thickens. Cool to room temperature.

Use sauce over frozen yogurt, pancakes or waffles.

Makes 8 servings, about 2 cups

Nutrients per serving (about ¼ cup sauce):			
Calories	64	Cholesterol	0 mg
Fat	trace	Sodium	1 mg

Pineapple-Orange Sauce

BANANA–CINNAMON ROLLS

¼ cup granulated sugar
1 teaspoon ground cinnamon
2 cups KELLOGG'S®
    RAISIN BRAN Cereal
½ cup mashed ripe banana
½ cup milk
1 egg
1 teaspoon vanilla
1¾ cups all-purpose flour
4 teaspoons baking powder
½ teaspoon salt
½ cup cold margarine

Frosting
1½ cups confectioners' sugar
2 tablespoons hot water
1 tablespoon lemon juice
¼ cup sliced almonds (optional)

Combine granulated sugar and cinnamon; set aside.

Combine KELLOGG'S RAISIN BRAN cereal, banana and milk. Let stand 2 minutes or until cereal softens. Add egg and vanilla; beat well.

In large mixing bowl, combine flour, baking powder and salt. Using pastry blender, cut in margarine until mixture resembles coarse crumbs. Add cereal mixture, stirring only until combined.

On lightly floured surface, gently knead dough 10 times. Roll out dough to measure 12×10-inch rectangle. Sprinkle dough with sugar mixture. Starting with long side, roll up dough jelly-roll style. Cut roll into twelve 1-inch pieces. Place, cut-side-down, in greased 13×9-inch pan.

Bake in 400°F oven about 25 minutes or until lightly browned. Invert onto serving plate.

To make frosting, stir together confectioners' sugar, water and lemon juice until smooth. Spread over hot rolls and sprinkle with almonds. Serve warm.

Makes 12 servings

Nutrients per serving (1 roll):

Calories	260	Cholesterol	19 mg
Fat	9 g	Sodium	360 mg

RICE BRAN BUTTERMILK PANCAKES

1 cup rice flour or all-purpose flour
¾ cup rice bran
1 tablespoon sugar
1 teaspoon baking powder
½ teaspoon baking soda
1¼ cups low-fat buttermilk
3 egg whites, beaten
    Nonstick cooking spray
    Fresh fruit or reduced-calorie syrup (optional)

Sift together flour, bran, sugar, baking powder, and baking soda into large bowl. Combine buttermilk and egg whites in small bowl; add to flour mixture. Stir until smooth. Pour ¼ cup batter onto hot griddle coated with nonstick cooking spray. Cook over medium heat until bubbles form on top and underside is lightly browned. Turn to brown other side. Serve with fresh fruit or syrup.

Makes about 10 (4-inch) pancakes

Variation: For Cinnamon Pancakes, add 1 teaspoon ground cinnamon to dry ingredients.

Nutrients per serving (1 pancake):

Calories	99	Cholesterol	119 mg
Fat	2 g	Sodium	1 mg

Favorite recipe from **USA Rice Council**

Rice Bran Buttermilk Pancakes

Peachy Cinnamon Coffeecake

PEACHY CINNAMON COFFEE CAKE

1 package DUNCAN HINES®
   Bakery Style Cinnamon
   Swirl with Crumb Topping
   Muffin Mix
1 can (8¼ ounces) juice pack
   sliced yellow cling peaches
   Water
1 egg

Preheat oven to 400°F. Grease 8-inch
square or 9-inch round pan.

Drain peaches, reserving juice. Add
water to reserved juice to equal ¾ cup
liquid. Chop peaches.

Combine muffin mix, egg and ¾ cup
peach liquid in medium bowl; fold in
peaches. Pour batter into pan. Knead
swirl packet 10 seconds before opening.
Squeeze contents on top of batter and
swirl with knife. Sprinkle topping over
batter.

Bake at 400°F for 28 to 33 minutes for
8-inch pan (or for 20 to 25 minutes for
9-inch pan) or until golden. Serve warm.
Makes 9 servings

Nutrients per serving:

Calories	205	Cholesterol	0 mg
Fat	7 g	Sodium	248 mg

WEEKEND SKILLET BREAKFAST

12 slices LOUIS RICH® Turkey
   Bacon, cut into ½-inch
   pieces
 1 medium potato, peeled and cut
   into small cubes
 2 green onions with tops, thinly
   sliced
½ teaspoon chili powder
 1 carton (8 ounces)
   cholesterol-free egg
   substitute *or* 4 eggs, beaten

Place Turkey Bacon and potato in
nonstick skillet. Cook over medium heat
about 12 minutes, stirring frequently
until potatoes are fork-tender. Stir in
onions and chili powder; pour egg
substitute evenly over mixture. Cover;
reduce heat to low. Cook 5 minutes more
or until mixture is set. Cut into wedges.
Makes 4 servings

Nutrients per serving:

Calories	155	Cholesterol	30 mg
Fat	7 g	Sodium	650 mg

FRUIT & HAM KABOBS

¾ cup pineapple juice
¼ cup packed brown sugar
2 tablespoons unsalted
   margarine or butter
1 ARMOUR® Lower Salt Ham
   Nugget (about 1¾ pounds),
   cut into 1¼-inch cubes
2 large red apples, cored and cut
   into sixths
2 large green apples, cored and
   cut into sixths
1 fresh pineapple, peeled, cored
   and cut into 1-inch chunks
3 kiwifruit, peeled and cut into
   ½-inch slices

Preheat oven to 350°F. Place pineapple juice, brown sugar and margarine in bottom of large casserole dish. Heat in oven until margarine is melted. Thread ham, apples, pineapple and kiwifruit onto 8 to 10 (10-inch) metal or wooden skewers, alternating the ingredients. Place kabobs in warm sauce; turn to coat all sides with sauce. Bake 20 to 25 minutes, or until heated through. Turn kabobs twice during cooking, basting with sauce mixture. Serve over rice and garnish with red grapes, if desired.   *Makes 8 to 10 kabobs*

Nutrients per serving (1 kabob):

Calories	277	Cholesterol	39 mg
Fat	7 g	Sodium	676 mg

Fruit & Ham Kabobs

FIVE–MINUTE FRUIT DIP

½ cup MIRACLE WHIP® FREE®
   Nonfat Dressing
1 container (8 ounces)
   lemon-flavored low-fat
   yogurt

Mix ingredients until well blended; refrigerate. Serve with assorted fruit kabobs.   *Makes 1¼ cups*

Prep time: 5 minutes plus refrigerating

Nutrients per serving (2 tablespoons):

Calories	60	Cholesterol	0 mg
Fat	1 g	Sodium	230 mg

CRANBERRY OAT BRAN MUFFINS

 2 cups flour
 1 cup oat bran
 ½ cup packed brown sugar
 2 teaspoons baking powder
 ½ teaspoon baking soda
 ½ teaspoon salt (optional)
 ½ cup MIRACLE WHIP® LIGHT
    Reduced Calorie Salad
    Dressing
 3 egg whites, slightly beaten
 ½ cup skim milk
 ⅓ cup orange juice
 1 teaspoon grated orange peel
 1 cup coarsely chopped
    cranberries

Preheat oven to 375°F. Line 12 medium muffin cups with paper baking cups or spray with nonstick cooking spray. Mix together dry ingredients. Add combined dressing, egg whites, milk, juice and peel; mix just until moistened. Fold in cranberries. Fill prepared muffin cups almost full. Bake 15 to 17 minutes or until golden brown.

Makes 12 muffins

Nutrients per serving (1 muffin):			
Calories	183	Cholesterol	4 mg
Fat	4 g	Sodium	191 mg

Cranberry Oat Bran Muffins

HAM & FRUIT PANCAKE ROLLS

 2 cups complete pancake mix
 8 ounces ARMOUR® Lower Salt
    Ham, thinly sliced
 8 tablespoons bottled
    fruit-flavored applesauce or
    canned lite cherry fruit
    filling

Prepare pancake mix according to package directions. Spray griddle or large skillet with nonstick cooking spray. Using ⅓ cup measure, pour batter onto hot griddle. Cook as directed on package, making eight 5-inch pancakes. Place 1 ounce of ham on each cooked pancake; top with 1 tablespoon applesauce. Roll up pancake around ham; secure with toothpicks, if needed. Repeat with remaining pancakes. Serve with additional applesauce, if desired.

Makes 8 rolled pancakes

Nutrients per serving (1 pancake):			
Calories	145	Cholesterol	14 mg
Fat	2 g	Sodium	596 mg

Breakfast Burrito

BREAKFAST BURRITO

4 slices LOUIS RICH® Turkey Bacon
2 flour tortillas (7 inches in diameter)
2 tablespoons shredded sharp Cheddar cheese
2 large egg whites
1 tablespoon chopped mild chilies
  Salsa or taco sauce (optional)
  Additional shredded sharp Cheddar cheese (optional)

Cook Turkey Bacon in nonstick skillet over medium-high heat 8 to 10 minutes or until lightly browned.

Place 2 turkey bacon slices on each tortilla; sprinkle each with 1 tablespoon cheese.

Beat egg whites and chilies; add to hot skillet. Cook and stir about 2 minutes or until set.

Divide egg mixture between tortillas. Fold tortillas over filling. Top with salsa and additional cheese, if desired.

Makes 2 burritos

To keep burritos warm: Wrap filled burritos in foil and place in warm oven up to 30 minutes.

Nutrients per serving (1 burrito):			
Calories	220	Cholesterol	25 mg
Fat	9 g	Sodium	470 mg

Ham Breakfast Sandwich

HAM BREAKFAST SANDWICH

1 ounce Neufchâtel or light
    cream cheese, softened
2 teaspoons apricot spreadable
    fruit
2 teaspoons plain nonfat yogurt
6 slices raisin bread
    Lettuce leaves
1 package (6 ounces)
    ECKRICH® Lite Lower
    Salt Ham
3 Granny Smith apple rings

Combine cheese, spreadable fruit and yogurt in small bowl. Spread on bread. To make each sandwich: Place lettuce on 1 slice bread. Top with 2 slices ham, 1 apple ring and another slice of bread.

Makes 3 sandwiches

Nutrients per serving (1 sandwich);

Calories	223	Cholesterol	5 mg
Fat	5 g	Sodium	963 mg

DOUBLE BRAN–LEMON MUFFINS

1 cup 100% wheat bran cereal
½ cup oat bran
    Grated peel of 1 SUNKIST®
    Lemon
½ cup fresh squeezed lemon juice
    (3 SUNKIST® Lemons)
½ cup nonfat milk
1¼ cups all-purpose flour
2 teaspoons baking powder
½ teaspoon baking soda
¼ cup firmly packed brown sugar
2 egg whites
¼ cup honey
¼ cup vegetable oil

In bowl, combine wheat bran cereal, oat bran, lemon peel, lemon juice and milk; let stand 10 minutes. In large bowl, sift together flour, baking powder and baking soda; stir in brown sugar. In small bowl, beat egg whites until foamy; add honey and oil. Stir egg mixture into bran mixture; mix well. Add to dry ingredients all at once; stir just until dry ingredients are moistened. Quickly spoon into 12 paper-lined 2½×1¼-inch muffin cups; fill about ⅞ full. (Or, spray muffin pan with nonstick cooking spray.) Bake at 400°F for 20 to 23 minutes.

Makes 12 muffins

Nutrients per serving (1 muffin):

Calories	153	Cholesterol	0 mg
Fat	5 g	Sodium	138 mg

COUNTRY BREAKFAST CEREAL

3 cups cooked brown rice
2 cups skim milk
½ cup raisins or chopped prunes
1 tablespoon margarine
    (optional)
1 teaspoon ground cinnamon
⅛ teaspoon salt
    Honey or brown sugar
    (optional)
    Fresh fruit (optional)

Combine rice, milk, raisins, margarine, cinnamon, and salt in 2- to 3-quart saucepan. Bring to a boil; stir once or twice. Reduce heat to medium-low; cover and simmer 8 to 10 minutes or until thickened. Serve with honey and fresh fruit.

Makes 6 servings

Nutrients per serving:

Calories	174	Cholesterol	2 mg
Fat	1 g	Sodium	98 mg

Favorite recipe from **USA Rice Council**

Bran-Cherry Bread

APRICOT MUFFINS

1¾ cups all-purpose flour
⅓ cup sugar
¼ teaspoon salt (optional)
1 tablespoon baking powder
2 cups KELLOGG'S®
    COMMON SENSE® Oat Bran
    Cereal, any variety
1½ cups apricot nectar
2 egg whites
¼ cup vegetable oil
½ cup chopped dried apricots

Stir together flour, sugar, salt and baking powder; set aside. In large mixing bowl, combine oat bran cereal, apricot nectar, egg whites and oil until thoroughly mixed. Stir in dried apricots. Add flour mixture, stirring only until just moistened. Divide batter evenly among 12 lightly greased 2½-inch muffin cups. Bake in 400°F oven about 25 minutes or until golden brown. Serve warm.

Makes 12 muffins

Nutrients per serving (1 muffin):

Calories	200	Cholesterol	0 mg
Fat	5 g	Sodium	224 mg

BRAN–CHERRY BREAD

2 cups all-purpose flour
¾ cup sugar, divided
1 tablespoon baking powder
1 teaspoon salt
½ teaspoon ground nutmeg
1½ cups KELLOGG'S®
    CRACKLIN' OAT BRAN®
    Cereal
1¼ cups skim milk
1 egg
2 tablespoons vegetable oil
1 jar (10 ounces) maraschino
    cherries, drained and finely
    chopped
1 cup chopped walnuts, divided
1 tablespoon margarine

Combine flour, ½ cup sugar, baking powder, salt and nutmeg. Set aside.

In large mixing bowl, combine KELLOGG'S CRACKLIN' OAT BRAN cereal and milk. Let stand 10 minutes or until cereal is softened. Add egg and oil. Beat well. Stir in flour mixture. Set aside 2 tablespoons chopped cherries. Fold remaining cherries and ¾ cup nuts into batter. Spread in 9×5×3-inch loaf pan coated with nonstick cooking spray.

Melt margarine in small skillet until bubbly. Remove from heat. Stir in remaining ¼ cup sugar, remaining ¼ cup nuts and reserved cherries. Sprinkle over batter.

Bake at 350°F about 1 hour. Cool in pan on wire rack 10 minutes. Remove from pan. *Makes 1 loaf, 15 slices*

Nutrients per serving (1 slice):

Calories	240	Cholesterol	20 mg
Fat	9 g	Sodium	260 mg

TANGY FRUIT AND NUT MUESLI

1¾ cups water
1⅓ cups QUAKER® Oats (quick or old fashioned, uncooked)
3 cups oranges or tangerines, peeled, seeded and chopped
½ cup chopped dates or raisins
½ cup coarsely chopped nuts
½ teaspoon ground cinnamon

Combine all ingredients; mix well. Cover; refrigerate overnight. Serve cold or hot with milk or yogurt, if desired. For thicker muesli, drain excess liquid before serving or heating in microwave. Store in refrigerator up to 1 week.

Makes 6 servings

Nutrients per serving (½ cup cereal only):

Calories	220	Cholesterol	0 mg
Fat	8 g	Sodium	2 mg

BRUNCH POTATO CASSOULET

2 tablespoons unsalted margarine or butter
2 cups (8 ounces) ARMOUR® Lower Salt Ham cut into ½-inch cubes
2 cups frozen natural potato wedges
1 cup sliced mushrooms
½ cup chopped red onion
½ cup chopped green bell pepper
1 cup frozen speckled butter beans, cooked according to package directions omitting salt and drained
Lower salt cheese (optional)

Preheat oven to 350°F. Melt margarine in large skillet over medium heat. Add ham, potatoes, mushrooms, onion and green bell pepper; cook over medium heat 5 to 6 minutes, or until onion is soft. Stir in cooked beans. Transfer to medium earthenware pot or ovenproof Dutch oven. Bake, covered, 10 to 12 minutes, or until heated through. If desired, sprinkle with lower salt cheese. Broil 4 to 6 inches from heat source 2 to 3 minutes, or until cheese is melted and slightly browned.

Makes 4 to 6 servings

Nutrients per serving:

Calories	161	Cholesterol	19 mg
Fat	7 g	Sodium	391 mg

Brunch Potato Cassoulet

BROWN RICE, MUSHROOM, AND HAM HASH

1 tablespoon olive oil
2 cups (about 8 ounces) sliced
    fresh mushrooms
1 small onion, minced
1 clove garlic, minced
3 cups cooked brown rice
1 cup (6 ounces) diced
    turkey ham
½ cup chopped walnuts (optional)
¼ cup snipped parsley
1 tablespoon white wine vinegar
1 tablespoon Dijon-style mustard
¼ teaspoon ground black pepper

Heat oil in Dutch oven or large saucepan over medium-low heat until hot. Add mushrooms, onion, and garlic; cook until tender. Stir in rice, ham, walnuts, parsley, vinegar, mustard, and pepper; cook, stirring until thoroughly heated.

Makes 8 servings

To Microwave: Combine oil, mushrooms, onion, and garlic in 2- to 3-quart microproof baking dish. Cook on HIGH (100% power) 3 to 4 minutes. Stir in rice, ham, walnuts, parsley, vinegar, mustard, and pepper. Cook on HIGH 3 to 4 minutes, stirring after 2 minutes, or until thoroughly heated.

Nutrients per serving:

Calories	133	Cholesterol	10 mg
Fat	4 g	Sodium	184 mg

Favorite recipe from **USA Rice Council**

NORTHERN CALIFORNIA BANANA BREAD

3 extra-ripe, medium DOLE®
    Bananas, peeled
½ cup margarine, softened
½ cup firmly packed brown sugar
½ cup granulated sugar
1 egg
1 teaspoon vanilla extract
1¼ cups all-purpose flour
⅔ cup oat bran
½ cup whole wheat flour
2 teaspoons baking powder
1 teaspoon ground cinnamon
½ teaspoon salt
1 cup DOLE® Chopped Dates
1 cup DOLE® Chopped
    Almonds, toasted

Place bananas in blender. Process until puréed; use 1½ cups for recipe. Beat margarine and sugars in large bowl until light and fluffy. Beat in 1½ cups puréed bananas, egg and vanilla. Combine all-purpose flour, oat bran, whole wheat flour, baking powder, cinnamon and salt in medium bowl. Beat into banana mixture until blended. Stir in dates and almonds. Pour batter into greased 9×5-inch loaf pan. Bake in 350°F oven 65 minutes or until cake tester inserted in center comes out clean. Cool in pan on wire rack 10 minutes. Remove from pan. Cool completely on wire rack before slicing. To serve, cut loaf into 14 slices, then cut each slice lengthwise in half.

Makes 28 servings

Prep time: 15 minutes
Bake time: 65 minutes

Nutrients per serving:

Calories	163	Cholesterol	10 mg
Fat	7 g	Sodium	96 mg

APPLE STREUSEL COFFEE CAKE

Cake
- ¼ cup **CRISCO® Shortening**
- ½ cup sugar
- 2 egg whites
- 1 teaspoon vanilla
- ¾ cup dry oat bran high fiber hot cereal
- 1 cup chunky applesauce
- 1¼ cups all-purpose flour
- 1½ teaspoons ground cinnamon
- 1 teaspoon baking powder
- ¾ teaspoon baking soda
- ¼ teaspoon salt (optional)
- ¼ teaspoon ground nutmeg

Filling and Topping
- 1 cup chunky applesauce, divided
- ¼ cup sugar
- ¼ teaspoon ground cinnamon

Heat oven to 375°F. Grease 8-inch square pan.

For Cake: Combine Crisco® and ½ cup sugar in medium bowl with fork until blended and crumbly. Add egg whites and vanilla. Beat until fairly smooth. Stir in oat bran, then 1 cup applesauce. Let stand 5 minutes. Combine flour, 1½ teaspoons cinnamon, baking powder, baking soda, salt and nutmeg in another bowl. Stir into oat bran mixture. Spread half of batter in pan.

For Filling and Topping: Spread ¾ cup applesauce over batter. Combine ¼ cup sugar and ¼ teaspoon cinnamon. Sprinkle half over applesauce. Add remaining batter; spread gently and evenly. Top with remaining ¼ cup applesauce. Spread thinly and evenly.

Sprinkle with remaining sugar-cinnamon mixture. Bake at 375°F for 30 to 35 minutes or until top is golden brown and center springs back when touched lightly. Cut in squares. Serve warm.

Makes 9 servings

Nutrients per serving:

Calories	242	Cholesterol	0 mg
Fat	6 g	Sodium	120 mg

PRALINE PANCAKES

- 1½ cups skim milk
- 2 tablespoons margarine, melted
- 2 teaspoons brandy
- 1 teaspoon vanilla extract
- 1 cup all-purpose flour
- 2 tablespoons sugar
- 1 teaspoon baking powder
- ¼ teaspoon salt
- ⅛ teaspoon ground cinnamon
- 1 cup cooked rice, cooled
- ⅓ cup pecans, coarsely chopped
- 4 egg whites, stiffly beaten
- Nonstick cooking spray
- Reduced-calorie syrup (optional)

Combine milk, margarine, brandy, vanilla, flour, sugar, baking powder, salt, and cinnamon in large bowl; stir until smooth. Stir in rice and pecans. Fold in beaten egg whites. Pour scant ¼ cup batter onto hot griddle coated with nonstick cooking spray. Cook over medium heat until bubbles form on top and underside is lightly browned. Turn to brown other side. Serve warm drizzled with syrup. *Makes 6 servings*

Nutrients per serving:

Calories	252	Cholesterol	1 mg
Fat	9 g	Sodium	387 mg

Favorite recipe from **USA Rice Council**

BREAKFAST SAUSAGE BAKE

2 tablespoons margarine
1 pound fresh mushrooms, finely chopped
1 cup dry fine bread crumbs
1 package (1 pound)
    LOUIS RICH® Turkey Breakfast Sausage, thawed
1 red or green pepper, chopped
3 tablespoons chopped fresh parsley *or* 1 tablespoon dried parsley flakes
¼ teaspoon ground red pepper
2 cartons (8 ounces each) cholesterol-free egg substitute *or* 8 eggs, beaten

Preheat oven to 350°F. Melt margarine in large nonstick skillet over medium-high heat. Add mushrooms. Cook and stir about 10 minutes or until mixture boils and moisture evaporates. Remove from heat; stir in bread crumbs. Spray 13×9-inch baking dish with nonstick cooking spray. Press mushroom mixture onto bottom of prepared baking dish to form crust.

In same nonstick skillet, cook sausage over medium heat about 12 minutes, breaking sausage apart into small pieces and stirring frequently until lightly browned. Remove from heat.

Stir in chopped red pepper, parsley and ground red pepper. Spread sausage mixture over crust; pour egg substitute evenly over mixture. Bake 25 to 30 minutes or until mixture is set.

Makes 12 servings

Note: For 6 servings, use half of the ingredients; prepare and bake as above in 9-inch pie plate.

Nutrients per serving:

Calories	140	Cholesterol	20 mg
Fat	6 g	Sodium	370 mg

RICE CRÊPES

1 carton (8 ounces) egg substitute*
⅔ cup evaporated skim milk
1 tablespoon margarine, melted
½ cup all-purpose flour
1 tablespoon granulated sugar
1 cup cooked rice
    Nonstick cooking spray
2½ cups fresh fruit (strawberries, raspberries, blueberries, or other favorite fruit)
    Low-sugar fruit spread (optional)
    Light sour cream (optional)
1 tablespoon confectioners' sugar for garnish (optional)

Combine egg substitute, milk, and margarine in small bowl. Stir in flour and granulated sugar until smooth and well blended. Stir in rice; let stand 5 minutes. Heat 8-inch nonstick skillet or crêpe pan; coat with nonstick cooking spray. Spoon ¼ cup batter into pan.

Lift pan off heat; quickly tilt pan in rotating motion so that bottom of pan is completely covered with batter. Place pan back on heat and continue cooking until surface is dry, about 45 seconds. Turn crêpe over and cook 15 to 20 seconds; set aside. Continue with remaining crêpe batter. Place waxed paper between crêpes. Spread each crêpe with your favorite filling: strawberries, raspberries, blueberries, fruit spread, or sour cream.

Roll up and sprinkle with confectioners' sugar for garnish.   *Makes 10 crêpes*

*Substitute 8 egg whites or 4 eggs for 8 ounces egg substitute, if desired.

Nutrients per serving (1 crêpe):

Calories	111	Cholesterol	1 mg
Fat	2 g	Sodium	152 mg

Favorite recipe from **USA Rice Council**

Rice Crêpes

BREAKFAST IN A CUP

3 cups cooked rice
1 cup (4 ounces) shredded Cheddar cheese, divided
1 can (4 ounces) diced green chilies
1 jar (2 ounces) diced pimientos, drained
⅓ cup skim milk
2 eggs, beaten
½ teaspoon ground cumin
½ teaspoon salt
½ teaspoon ground black pepper Nonstick cooking spray

Combine rice, ½ cup cheese, chilies, pimientos, milk, eggs, cumin, salt, and pepper in large bowl. Divide mixture evenly into 12 muffin cups coated with nonstick cooking spray. Sprinkle with remaining ½ cup cheese. Bake at 400°F for 15 minutes or until set.

Makes 12 servings

Tip: Breakfast Cups may be stored in the freezer in freezer bags or tightly sealed containers. To reheat frozen Breakfast Cups, microwave each cup on HIGH (100% power) 1 minute.

Nutrients per serving (1 cup):

Calories	123	Cholesterol	45 mg
Fat	4 g	Sodium	368 mg

Favorite recipe from **USA Rice Council**

Breakfast in a Cup

BACON MORNING MUFFINS

12 slices LOUIS RICH® Turkey
    Bacon, cut into ¼-inch
    pieces
1¼ cups all-purpose flour
 1 cup quick-cooking oats,
    uncooked
 2 teaspoons baking powder
 ½ cup skim milk
 ⅓ cup honey
 ¼ cup corn oil
 2 large egg whites

Combine Turkey Bacon, flour, oats and
baking powder in large mixing bowl.
Combine remaining ingredients; add to
bacon mixture. Stir just until moistened
(batter will be lumpy). Spray 12 (2½-
inch) muffin cups with nonstick cooking
spray or line with paper bake cups.
Spoon batter into muffin cups. Bake in
400°F oven 15 minutes. Refrigerate or
freeze leftover muffins.

Makes 12 muffins

Nutrients per serving (1 muffin):

Calories	185	Cholesterol	10 mg
Fat	8 g	Sodium	260 mg

BANANA BRAN LOAF

 1 cup mashed ripe bananas
    (about 2 large)
 ½ cup sugar
 ⅓ cup liquid vegetable oil
    margarine
 ⅓ cup skim milk
 2 egg whites
1¼ cups all-purpose flour
 1 cup QUAKER® Oat Bran hot
    cereal, uncooked
 2 teaspoons baking powder
 ½ teaspoon baking soda

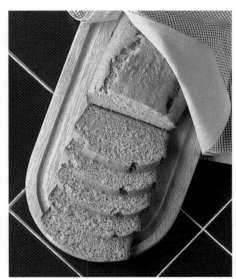

Banana Bran Loaf

Heat oven to 350°F. Lightly spray
8×4-inch or 9×5-inch loaf pan with
nonstick cooking spray, or oil lightly.
Combine bananas, sugar, margarine,
milk and egg whites; mix well. Add
combined flour, oat bran, baking powder
and baking soda; mix just until
moistened. Pour into prepared pan. Bake
55 to 60 minutes or until wooden
toothpick inserted in center comes out
clean. Cool 10 minutes in pan; remove to
wire rack. Cool completely.

Makes 16 servings

Tips: To freeze bread slices; layer waxed
paper between each slice of bread. Wrap
securely in foil or place in freezer bag.
Seal, label and freeze.

To reheat bread slices; unwrap frozen
bread slices and wrap in paper towel.
Microwave at HIGH (100%) about 30
seconds for each slice, or until warm.

Nutrients per serving (1 slice):

Calories	130	Cholesterol	0 mg
Fat	4 g	Sodium	110 mg

Brunch Quesadillas with Fruit Salsa

BRUNCH QUESADILLAS WITH FRUIT SALSA

1 pint fresh strawberries, hulled
and diced
1 fresh ripe Anjou pear, cored
and diced
1 tablespoon chopped fresh
cilantro
1 tablespoon honey
1 cup (4 ounces) SARGENTO®
Preferred Light Fancy
Shredded Mozzarella Cheese
4 flour tortillas (8 inches in
diameter)
2 teaspoons light margarine,
melted
2 tablespoons light sour cream

To make Fruit Salsa, combine
strawberries, pear, cilantro and honey in
medium bowl; set aside.

Sprinkle 2 tablespoons cheese on one
half of each tortilla. Top with ⅓ cup
salsa (drain and discard any liquid that
has formed from the fruit) and another
2 tablespoons cheese. Fold tortillas in
half. Brush top of each folded tortilla
with some of the melted margarine.

Grill folded tortillas, greased-side-down,
in dry preheated skillet until light golden
brown and crisp, about 2 minutes. Brush
tops with remaining melted margarine;
turn and brown other sides. Remove to
serving plate or platter. Cut each tortilla
in half. Serve with remaining Fruit Salsa.
Garnish with sour cream. Serve
immediately.   *Makes 4 servings*

Nutrients per serving:

Calories	278	Cholesterol	14 mg
Fat	9 g	Sodium	264 mg

MEXICAN EGG MUFFIN

1 large egg
2 teaspoons water
1 teaspoon chopped green onion
1 teaspoon diet margarine
½ English muffin, toasted
4 teaspoons prepared salsa
1 slice BORDEN® Lite-line® Process Cheese Product, any flavor, cut into triangles*

In small bowl, beat egg, water and onion. In small skillet, melt margarine; add egg mixture. Cook and stir until egg is set. Spoon egg mixture onto muffin; top with salsa then Lite-line® slice. Place on baking sheet; broil until Lite-line® slice begins to melt. Garnish as desired.

Makes 1 serving

*"½ the calories" 8% milkfat product

Nutrients per serving:

Calories	220	Cholesterol	226 mg
Fat	10 g	Sodium	614 mg

PAPAYA MUFFINS

1½ cups whole wheat flour
1 tablespoon baking powder
½ teaspoon salt
1½ cups KELLOGG'S® ALL-BRAN® Cereal
1¼ cups skim milk
¼ cup honey
¼ cup vegetable oil
1 tablespoon dark molasses
1 egg
¾ cup chopped fresh papaya
2 teaspoons finely chopped crystallized ginger

Stir together flour, baking powder and salt. Set aside. Measure KELLOGG'S ALL-BRAN cereal and milk into large mixing bowl. Let stand 2 minutes or until cereal is softened. Add honey, oil, molasses and egg. Beat well. Stir in papaya and ginger.

Add flour mixture, stirring only until combined. Portion batter evenly into 12 greased 2½-inch muffin pan cups.

Bake at 400°F about 25 minutes or until muffins are golden brown. Serve warm.

Makes 12 muffins

Nutrients per serving (1 muffin):

Calories	160	Cholesterol	19 mg
Fat	6 g	Sodium	314 mg

Mexican Egg Muffin

Top to bottom: Cheese Danish, Belgian Waffle Dessert (page 64)

CHEESE DANISH

1 tablespoon sugar
1 teaspoon ground cinnamon
5 flour tortillas (6 or 7 inches in diameter)
  Nonstick cooking spray
1 cup cold skim milk
1 package (4-serving size) JELL-O® Vanilla Flavor Sugar Free Instant Pudding and Pie Filling
1 container (8 ounces) light pasteurized process cream cheese product
2 cups thawed COOL WHIP® LITE® Whipped Topping
1 square BAKER'S® Semi-Sweet Chocolate

Heat oven to 350°F.

Mix sugar and cinnamon. Spray tortillas with nonstick cooking spray. Sprinkle each tortilla with scant ½ teaspoon sugar-cinnamon mixture. Turn tortillas over; repeat process. Cut each tortilla into 4 wedges. Stand rounded edge of each tortilla wedge in bottom of muffin cup by curling in sides. Bake 10 minutes or until lightly browned and crispy. Cool.

Pour milk into large mixing bowl. Add pudding mix. Beat at low speed with electric mixer until well blended, 1 to 2 minutes. Beat in cream cheese product at medium speed until smooth. Gently stir in whipped topping. Refrigerate at least 1 hour.

To serve, fill each tortilla shell with scant 3 tablespoons cheese mixture using pastry bag or spoon. Place chocolate in small plastic sandwich bag or self-closing bag. Microwave on HIGH (100%) about 1 minute or until chocolate is melted. Fold top of bag tightly; snip off one corner (about ⅛ inch). Hold bag tightly at top; drizzle chocolate through opening over prepared Danish. Refrigerate until chocolate sets, about 5 minutes. *Makes 20 Danish*

Note: Freeze any leftover Danish. Thaw in refrigerator as needed.

Nutrients per serving (1 Danish):

Calories	90	Cholesterol	5 mg
Fat	4 g	Sodium	180 mg

RAINBOW TROUT BREAKFAST FILLETS

½ cup all-purpose flour
1½ teaspoons paprika
1 teaspoon ground thyme
¼ teaspoon salt
  Dash pepper
4 CLEAR SPRINGS® Brand Idaho Rainbow Trout fillets (4 ounces each)
1 egg, beaten
1 tablespoon olive oil

Combine flour, paprika, thyme, salt and pepper on waxed paper; set aside. Dip each trout fillet in egg; coat with seasoned flour mixture. Sauté trout in oil in large skillet over medium-high heat 1 to 2 minutes per side or until fish flakes easily with fork. Serve with fruit and garnish as desired.

Makes 4 servings

Nutrients per serving:

Calories	240	Cholesterol	115 mg
Fat	9 g	Sodium	179 mg

BELGIAN WAFFLE DESSERT

2¼ cups cold 2% low-fat milk
1 package (4-serving size)
    JELL-O® Vanilla Flavor
    Sugar Free Instant Pudding
    and Pie Filling
2 tablespoons lemon juice
1 teaspoon grated lemon peel
1 cup thawed COOL WHIP®
    LITE® Whipped Topping
1 pint (about 2 cups)
    strawberries, quartered
½ pint (about 1 cup) raspberries
½ pint (about 1 cup) blueberries
    or blackberries
10 small frozen Belgian or regular
    waffles, toasted

Pour milk into large mixing bowl. Add pudding mix, lemon and peel. Beat with wire whisk until well blended, 1 to 2 minutes. Gently stir in whipped topping. Refrigerate.

Mix fruit in bowl; refrigerate.

To serve, spoon about 3 tablespoons pudding mixture on each dessert plate. Top each with waffle, additional 2 tablespoons pudding mixture and scant ½ cup fruit. Assemble desserts as needed. Store leftover pudding mixture and fruit in refrigerator.

Makes 10 waffles

Nutrients per serving (1 waffle):

Calories	170	Cholesterol	5 mg
Fat	5 g	Sodium	310 mg

PINEAPPLE–ALMOND DATE BREAD

1 cup DOLE® Sliced Almonds
¾ cup sugar
½ cup margarine, softened
1 egg
1 can (8¼ ounces) DOLE®
    Crushed Pineapple
1 tablespoon grated DOLE®
    Orange peel
2 cups all-purpose flour
1 teaspoon baking powder
1 teaspoon baking soda
¼ teaspoon ground nutmeg
1 cup DOLE® Chopped Dates

Toast ¾ cup almonds; reserve remaining ¼ cup for topping. Beat sugar and margarine in large bowl until light and fluffy. Beat in egg until blended. Stir in undrained pineapple and orange peel. Combine flour, baking powder, baking soda and nutmeg in medium bowl. Beat into pineapple mixture until blended. Stir in ¾ cup toasted almonds and dates. Pour batter into well-greased 9×5-inch loaf pan. Sprinkle remaining ¼ cup untoasted almonds on top. Bake in 350°F oven 55 to 60 minutes or until cake tester inserted in center comes out clean. Cool in pan on wire rack 10 minutes. Remove from pan. Cool completely on wire rack before slicing. To serve, cut loaf into 14 slices, then cut each slice lengthwise in half.

Makes 28 servings

Prep time: 15 minutes
Bake time: 60 minutes

Nutrients per serving:

Calories	147	Cholesterol	10 mg
Fat	7 g	Sodium	83 mg

LEMON–GLAZED PEACH MUFFINS

1 cup all-purpose flour
3 tablespoons sugar
2 teaspoons baking powder
½ teaspoon salt
½ teaspoon pumpkin pie spice
1 can (16 ounces) sliced cling
    peaches in light syrup
1 cup KELLOGG'S®
    ALL-BRAN® Cereal
½ cup skim milk
1 egg white
2 tablespoons vegetable oil
    Lemon Sauce (recipe follows)

Stir together flour, sugar, baking powder, salt and pumpkin pie spice. Set aside. Drain peaches, reserving ⅓ cup syrup. Set aside 8 peach slices; chop remaining peach slices. In large bowl measure cereal, milk and ⅓ cup reserved syrup. Stir to combine. Let stand 2 minutes or until cereal is softened. Add egg white and oil. Beat well. Stir in chopped peaches. Add flour mixture, stirring only until dry ingredients are moistened. Divide batter evenly among 8 lightly greased 2½-inch muffin cups. Place 1 peach slice over top of each muffin. Bake at 400°F for 25 minutes or until golden brown. Serve warm with lemon sauce. *Makes 8 muffins*

LEMON SAUCE

⅓ cup sugar
2 tablespoons cornstarch
1½ cups cold water
1 teaspoon grated lemon peel
1 tablespoon lemon juice

Combine sugar and cornstarch in 2-quart saucepan. Add water, stirring until smooth. Cook over medium heat, stirring constantly, until mixture boils.

Continue cooking and stirring 3 minutes longer. Remove from heat; stir in lemon peel and juice. Serve hot over warm peach muffins.

Nutrients per serving (1 muffin plus 3 tablespoons sauce):

Calories	210	Cholesterol	1 mg
Fat	4 g	Sodium	355 mg

RICE BRAN GRANOLA CEREAL

2 cups uncooked old-fashioned
    rolled oats
1 cup crisp rice cereal
¾ cup rice bran
¾ cup raisins
⅓ cup slivered almonds
1 tablespoon ground cinnamon
⅓ cup honey
1 tablespoon margarine, melted
    Nonstick cooking spray

Combine oats, cereal, bran, raisins, almonds, and cinnamon in large bowl; stir in honey and margarine. Spread mixture on baking sheet coated with nonstick cooking spray. Bake in preheated 350°F oven for 8 to 10 minutes. Let cool. Serve as a topping for yogurt and/or fresh fruit. Store in a tightly covered container.
Makes 10 (½-cup) servings

Tip: Can be served as a cereal (with milk), or as a snack.

Nutrients per serving (½ cup cereal only):

Calories	199	Cholesterol	0 mg
Fat	7 g	Sodium	57 mg

Favorite recipe from **USA Rice Council**

65

Soups and Breads

*Left: Golden Tomato Soup
Right: Touch of Honey Bread
(page 68)*

GOLDEN TOMATO SOUP

 4 teaspoons reduced-calorie
    margarine
 1 cup chopped onion
 2 cloves garlic, coarsely chopped
 ½ cup chopped carrot
 ¼ cup chopped celery
 8 medium tomatoes, blanched,
    peeled, seeded, chopped
 6 cups chicken broth
 2 tablespoons uncooked rice
 2 tablespoons tomato paste
 1 tablespoon Worcestershire
    sauce
 ¼ to ½ teaspoon black pepper
 ½ teaspoon dried thyme
 5 drops hot pepper sauce

Melt margarine in large Dutch oven over medium-high heat. Add onion and garlic; cook and stir 1 to 2 minutes or until tender. Add carrot and celery; cook 7 to 9 minutes or until tender, stirring frequently. Stir in tomatoes, broth, rice, tomato paste, Worcestershire sauce, pepper, thyme and hot pepper sauce. Reduce heat to low; cook about 30 minutes, stirring frequently.

Remove from heat. Let cool about 10 minutes. In food processor or blender, process soup in small batches until smooth. Return soup to Dutch oven; simmer 3 to 5 minutes or until heated through. Garnish as desired.

Makes 8 servings

Nutrients per serving:

Calories	91	Cholesterol	1 mg
Fat	2 g	Sodium	641 mg

Favorite recipe from **Florida Tomato Committee**

SOUPS AND BREADS

TOUCH OF HONEY BREAD

2½ to 3 cups all-purpose flour,
    divided
1 cup QUAKER® Oat Bran hot
    cereal, uncooked
1 package quick-rise yeast
½ teaspoon salt
1¼ cups water
2 tablespoons honey
2 tablespoons margarine

In large mixer bowl, combine 1 cup flour, oat bran, yeast and salt. Heat water, honey and margarine until very warm (120° to 130°F). Add to dry ingredients; beat at low speed of electric mixer until moistened. Increase speed to medium; continue beating 3 minutes. Stir in enough remaining flour to form a stiff dough. Lightly spray bowl with nonstick cooking spray, or oil lightly. Turn dough out onto lightly floured surface. Knead 8 to 10 minutes or until dough is smooth and elastic. Place in prepared bowl, turning once to coat surface of dough. Cover; let rise in warm place (80° to 85°F) 30 minutes or until doubled in size.

Lightly spray 8×4-inch loaf pan with nonstick cooking spray, or oil lightly. Punch down dough. Roll into 15×7-inch rectangle. Starting at narrow end, roll up dough tightly. Pinch ends and seam to seal; place, seam-side-down, in prepared pan. Cover; let rise in warm place 30 minutes or until doubled in size. Heat oven to 375°F. Bake 35 to 40 minutes or until golden brown. Remove from pan; cool on wire rack at least 1 hour before slicing. *Makes 16 servings*

Nutrients per serving (1 slice):

| Calories | 120 | Cholesterol | 0 mg |
| Fat | 2 g | Sodium | 85 mg |

EASY POPPY SEED YEAST BREAD

2 packages (¼ ounce each)
    active dry yeast
1 cup warm water (105° to 110°F)
1½ cups (12-ounce can) *undiluted*
    CARNATION® Evaporated
    Lowfat Milk
3 tablespoons margarine,
    softened
3 tablespoons granulated sugar
2 teaspoons salt
¼ cup poppy seed, divided
5 to 5½ cups all-purpose flour,
    divided
1 egg white
1 tablespoon water

In large mixer bowl, dissolve yeast in warm water. Add evaporated lowfat milk, margarine, sugar, salt and *3 tablespoons* poppy seed. Gradually add *3 cups* flour, beating on medium speed until almost smooth (about 1 minute). Add *remaining* 2 to 2½ cups flour to form a stiff dough. Use spatula to push dough down off beater stems. (Dough will be sticky). Cover bowl; let rise in warm draft-free place (80° to 85°F) for 30 minutes. Stir for 2 minutes. Divide dough equally into 2 greased 8½×4½×2½-inch loaf pans. (Flour hands for easier handling.) Push dough into corners and pat tops until smooth. In small bowl, combine egg white and water; brush tops of loaves. Sprinkle with *remaining 1* tablespoon poppy seed. Let dough rise for 25 minutes. Bake at 375°F for 20 to 30 minutes or until loaves are brown and sound hollow when tapped. Remove from pans; cool completely on wire rack. *Makes 2 loaves*

Nutrients per serving (½-inch slice):

| Calories | 195 | Cholesterol | 2 mg |
| Fat | 3 g | Sodium | 330 mg |

68

QUICK 'N EASY CORN AND PEPPER CHOWDER

1 tablespoon margarine
1 cup coarsely chopped green or red bell pepper
1 cup chopped onion
3½ cups (16-ounce package) frozen, whole-kernel corn
1 cup chicken broth
4 ounces (¾ cup) cooked, lean ham (95% fat free), cubed
½ teaspoon ground cumin
¼ teaspoon ground white pepper
3 cups (two 12-ounce cans) *undiluted* CARNATION® Evaporated Lowfat Milk, divided
⅓ cup plus 1 tablespoon all-purpose flour

In large saucepan, melt margarine; sauté pepper and onion over medium heat for 5 minutes, or until tender. Stir in corn, broth, ham, cumin and white pepper. Cook for an additional 5 minutes, stirring occasionally, until corn is cooked. Pour *½ cup* evaporated lowfat milk into medium bowl; whisk in flour until well blended. Add *remaining* 2½ cups evaporated lowfat milk; mix well. Slowly pour into saucepan. Increase heat to medium-high; cook, stirring constantly, for 5 minutes until mixture comes to a boil and thickens slightly. Boil for 1 minute. If a thinner chowder is desired, add additional chicken broth.

Makes 6 cups, 6 servings

Nutrients per serving:

Calories	213	Cholesterol	15 mg
Fat	6 g	Sodium	355 mg

VEGETABLE AND HAM SOUP

2 tablespoons unsalted margarine or butter
1 medium onion, coarsely chopped
2½ cups (10 ounces) ARMOUR® Lower Salt Ham cut into ½-inch cubes
1 package (16 ounces) frozen mixed vegetables
1 large potato, peeled and diced
2½ tablespoons no-salt-added chicken flavor instant bouillon
2 teaspoons MRS. DASH®, Original Blend
Pepper to taste

Melt margarine in Dutch oven over medium heat. Add onion; sauté until tender. Add remaining ingredients and 5 cups water. Bring to boil over medium-high heat. Reduce heat to simmer. Cook, uncovered, for 30 minutes, or until potato is tender. Garnish with carrot curls and fresh chives, if desired.

Makes 6 to 8 servings

To Microwave: Place margarine and onion in 10-inch microwave-safe tube pan. Cover with vented plastic wrap; cook on HIGH (100%) power about 2 to 3 minutes, or until onion is tender. Add remaining ingredients and 5 cups water. Cover with vented plastic wrap. Cook on HIGH power for 10 minutes, or until boiling. Reduce power to MEDIUM-HIGH (70%) power; continue cooking for 30 minutes, or until potato is tender. Garnish as above.

Nutrients per serving:

Calories	157	Cholesterol	18 mg
Fat	6 g	Sodium	334 mg

Crusty Oval Rolls

CRUSTY OVAL ROLLS

   1 **package active dry yeast**
1⅓ **cups warm water (105° to 115°F)**
   1 **tablespoon honey**
   1 **tablespoon shortening, melted,**
      cooled
   1 **teaspoon salt**
3¼ **to 4 cups bread flour, divided**
  ¼ **cup cold water**
   1 **teaspoon cornstarch**

In large bowl, combine yeast and warm water; stir to dissolve yeast. Stir in honey, shortening, salt and 2½ cups flour; beat until very elastic. Stir in enough of the remaining flour to make dough easy to handle.

Turn out onto floured surface. Knead 15 minutes or until dough is smooth and elastic, adding as much remaining flour as needed to prevent sticking. Shape dough into ball. Place in large, greased bowl; turn dough once to grease surface. Cover with towel; let rise in warm place (85°F) until doubled, about 1 hour.

Punch dough down; knead briefly on floured surface. Cover; let rest 10 minutes. Divide dough into 10 equal pieces; shape each piece into ball. Starting at center and working toward opposite ends, roll each ball on floured surface with palms of hands into tapered oval. Place, evenly spaced, on 2 greased baking sheets. Cover; let rise in warm place until almost doubled, about 25 minutes.

In small saucepan, combine cold water and cornstarch. Bring to a boil over high heat, stirring constantly. Boil until thickened and clear, about 2 minutes; cool slightly. Brush risen rolls with warm cornstarch mixture. Slash each roll lengthwise with sharp knife about ½ inch deep and about ½ inch from each end.

Preheat oven to 375°F. Bake 30 to 35 minutes or until rolls are golden brown and sound hollow when tapped. Remove to wire racks to cool.　　*Makes 10 rolls*

Nutrients per serving (1 roll):			
Calories	180	Cholesterol	0 mg
Fat	2 g	Sodium	214 mg

WILD RICE SOUP

⅓ **cup chopped carrot**
⅓ **cup chopped celery**
⅓ **cup chopped onion**
2 **teaspoons margarine or butter**
1⅓ **cups cooked wild rice**
1 **jar (12 ounces) HEINZ®**
    HomeStyle Turkey Gravy
1½ **cups skim milk**
2 **tablespoons dry sherry**

Sauté vegetables in margarine in 2-quart saucepan over medium-high heat until tender. Stir in rice, gravy and milk. Reduce heat to low. Simmer 5 minutes. Stir in sherry.

Makes 4 servings, about 4 cups

Nutrients per serving (about 1 cup):			
Calories	164	Cholesterol	7 mg
Fat	4 g	Sodium	645 mg

SOUTHWESTERN BEEF STEW

- 1 tablespoon vegetable oil
- 1¼ pounds well-trimmed beef tip roast, cut into 1-inch pieces
- ½ cup coarsely chopped onion
- 1 large clove garlic, minced
- 1½ teaspoons dried oregano leaves
- 1 teaspoon ground cumin
- ½ teaspoon *each* crushed red pepper and salt
- 4 medium tomatoes, chopped and divided (about 4 cups)
- ½ cup water
- 1 can (4 ounces) whole green chilies
- 1 tablespoon cornstarch
- ¼ cup sliced green onion tops

Heat oil in Dutch oven over medium-high heat. Add beef pieces, onion and garlic; cook and stir until beef is browned. Pour off drippings. Combine oregano, cumin, red pepper and salt; sprinkle over beef. Add 3 cups of the tomatoes and the water, stirring to combine. Reduce heat; cover tightly and simmer 1 hour and 55 minutes or until beef is tender, stirring occasionally. Drain green chilies; reserve liquid. Cut chilies into ½-inch pieces; add to beef mixture. Combine cornstarch and reserved liquid; gradually stir into stew and cook, uncovered, until thickened. Stir in remaining tomatoes; garnish with green onion tops. *Makes 4 servings*

Nutrients per serving:

Calories	250	Cholesterol	85 mg
Fat	8 g	Sodium	546 mg

Favorite recipe from **National Live Stock and Meat Board**

Southwestern Beef Stew

CORN BREAD

¼ cup CRISCO® Shortening
¼ cup sugar
2 egg whites
1 cup all-purpose flour
1 cup yellow cornmeal
4 teaspoons baking powder
½ teaspoon salt (optional)
1¼ cups skim milk

Heat oven to 425°F. Grease 9-inch square pan.

Cream Crisco® and sugar with fork in medium bowl until blended. Add egg whites. Beat until fairly smooth.

Combine flour, cornmeal, baking powder and salt (if used) in separate bowl. Add to shortening mixture alternately with milk. Stir until dry ingredients are just moistened. Pour into prepared pan.

Bake at 425°F for 20 minutes or until light golden brown around edges. Cut in squares. Serve warm.

Makes 9 servings

Nutrients per serving:

Calories	190	Cholesterol	0 mg
Fat	6 g	Sodium	220 mg

BASIL–VEGETABLE SOUP

1 package (9 ounces) frozen cut green beans
1 can (15 ounces) cooked cannellini beans, undrained
3 medium carrots, cut into thin slices
3 medium zucchini or yellow squash, cut into thin slices
2 quarts beef broth
2 cloves garlic, minced
  Salt and pepper to taste
2 to 3 ounces uncooked vermicelli or spaghetti
½ cup tightly packed fresh basil leaves, finely chopped
  Grated Romano cheese

Combine beans, carrots, zucchini, broth and garlic in Dutch oven. Bring to a boil over high heat. Reduce heat to low. Cover; simmer until carrots are tender. Season to taste with salt and pepper. Add vermicelli; bring to a boil over high heat. Reduce heat to low. Simmer until pasta is tender, yet firm. (If desired, pasta may be cooked separately, then added to soup just before serving.) Add basil; continue to simmer until basil is completely tender. Sprinkle with cheese.

Makes 10 to 12 servings

Nutrients per serving:

Calories	110	Cholesterol	trace
Fat	1 g	Sodium	585 mg

NAVY BEAN SOUP

2 tablespoons vegetable oil
1 cup chopped leeks
1½ cups (6 ounces) ARMOUR®
   Lower Salt Ham cut into
   ½-inch cubes
1 cup uncooked navy beans,
   soaked overnight and
   drained
1 tablespoon chopped jalapeño
   peppers

Heat oil in 3-quart saucepan over
medium heat. Add leeks; sauté 3 to
5 minutes or until tender. Stir in ham,
beans and peppers; add enough water to
just cover beans. Bring to a boil over
high heat. Reduce heat to low. Cover;
simmer 1 to 1½ hours or until beans are
tender. *Makes 4 servings*

Nutrients per serving:

Calories	282	Cholesterol	21 mg
Fat	10 g	Sodium	420 mg

Meatball & Vegetable Soup

MEATBALL & VEGETABLE SOUP

1 pound lean ground beef
½ cup fresh bread crumbs
   (1 slice)
⅓ cup chopped onion
1 egg, slightly beaten
4 teaspoons WYLERS® or
   STEERO® Beef-Flavor
   Instant Bouillon
⅛ teaspoon garlic powder
6 cups water
1 (28-ounce) can whole
   tomatoes, undrained and
   broken up
½ teaspoon black pepper
2 cups frozen hash brown
   potatoes
1 cup frozen peas and carrots

In bowl, combine meat, crumbs, onion,
egg, *1 teaspoon* bouillon and garlic
powder; mix well. Shape into 1-inch
meatballs. In Dutch oven, brown
meatballs; pour off fat. Add water,
tomatoes, pepper and remaining
3 teaspoons bouillon. Bring to a boil;
reduce heat. Simmer, uncovered,
20 minutes. Stir in vegetables; cook
15 minutes or until tender, stirring
occasionally. Refrigerate leftovers.
   Makes 10 servings, about 2½ quarts

Nutrients per serving:

Calories	201	Cholesterol	49 mg
Fat	10 g	Sodium	378 mg

73

West Coast Bouillabaisse

WEST COAST BOUILLABAISSE

1 cup sliced onions
2 stalks celery, cut diagonally
    into slices
2 cloves garlic, minced
1 tablespoon vegetable oil
4 cups chicken broth
1 can (28 ounces) tomatoes with
    juice, cut up
1 can (6½ ounces) minced clams
    with juice
½ cup dry white wine
1 teaspoon Worcestershire sauce
½ teaspoon dried thyme, crushed
¼ teaspoon bottled hot pepper
    sauce
1 bay leaf
1 cup frozen cooked bay shrimp,
    thawed
1 can (6½ ounces) STARKIST®
    Tuna, drained and broken
    into chunks
  Salt and pepper to taste
6 slices lemon
6 slices French bread

In a Dutch oven sauté onions, celery and garlic in oil for 3 minutes. Stir in broth, tomatoes with juice, clams with juice, wine, Worcestershire, thyme, hot pepper sauce and bay leaf. Bring to a boil; reduce heat. Simmer for 15 minutes. Stir in shrimp and tuna; cook for 2 minutes to heat. Remove bay leaf. Season with salt and pepper. Garnish with lemon slices and serve with bread.

Makes 6 servings

Nutrients per serving:			
Calories	212	Cholesterol	70 mg
Fat	6 g	Sodium	1146 mg

BRAN PITA BREAD

1 package active dry yeast
1¼ cups warm water (110° to
    115°F)
1½ cups KELLOGG'S®
    ALL-BRAN® Cereal
1½ cups all-purpose flour, divided
½ teaspoon salt
¼ cup vegetable oil
1 cup whole wheat flour

In large bowl of electric mixer, dissolve yeast in warm water, about 5 minutes. Add KELLOGG'S ALL-BRAN cereal, mixing until combined. On low speed, beat in 1 cup of the all-purpose flour, the salt and oil. Beat on high speed 3 minutes, scraping sides of bowl.

Using dough hook on electric mixer or by hand, stir in whole wheat flour. Continue kneading with mixer on low speed or by hand 5 minutes longer or until dough is smooth and elastic. Add the remaining ½ cup all-purpose flour, if needed, to make soft dough.

Divide dough into 12 portions. Roll each portion between floured hands into a very smooth ball. Cover with plastic wrap or a damp cloth; let rest 10 minutes.

On a well-floured surface, lightly roll one piece of dough at a time into 6-inch round, turning dough over once. Do not stretch, puncture or crease dough. Keep unrolled dough covered while rolling each dough piece. Place 2 rounds of dough at a time on ungreased baking sheet.

Bake in 450°F oven about 4 minutes or until dough is puffed and slightly firm. Turn with a spatula; continue baking about 2 minutes or until lightly browned; cool. Repeat with remaining dough. Cut in half and fill with a vegetable or meat filling.   *Makes 12 servings*

Nutrients per serving (2 pita bread halves):

Calories	160	Cholesterol	0 mg
Fat	5 g	Sodium	210 mg

CHICKEN & RICE GUMBO

- **1 (46-fluid ounce) can COLLEGE INN® Chicken Broth**
- **1 pound boneless chicken, cut in bite-size pieces**
- **1 (17-ounce) can whole kernel sweet corn, drained**
- **1 (14½-ounce) can stewed tomatoes, undrained and chopped**
- **1 (10-ounce) package frozen okra, thawed and chopped**
- **½ cup uncooked rice**
- **1 teaspoon ground black pepper**

In large saucepan, over medium-high heat, heat chicken broth, chicken, corn, tomatoes, okra, rice and pepper until mixture comes to a boil. Reduce heat; simmer, uncovered, 20 minutes or until chicken and rice are cooked.

Makes 10 servings

Nutrients per serving:

Calories	150	Cholesterol	19 mg
Fat	2 g	Sodium	699 mg

Bran Pita Bread

CHICKEN NOODLE SOUP

1 (46-fluid ounce) can
    COLLEGE INN® Chicken
    Broth
½ pound boneless chicken, cut in
    bite-size pieces
1½ cups uncooked medium egg
    noodles
1 cup sliced carrots
½ cup chopped onion
⅓ cup sliced celery
1 teaspoon dried dill weed
¼ teaspoon ground black pepper

In large saucepan, over medium-high heat, heat chicken broth, chicken, noodles, carrots, onion, celery, dill and pepper until mixture comes to a boil. Reduce heat; simmer, uncovered, 20 minutes or until chicken and noodles are cooked. *Makes 8 servings*

Nutrients per serving:

Calories	88	Cholesterol	19 mg
Fat	2 g	Sodium	579 mg

SPICY ONION BREAD

2 tablespoons instant minced
    onion
⅓ cup water
1½ cups biscuit baking mix
1 egg, slightly beaten
½ cup milk
½ teaspoon TABASCO® Pepper
    Sauce
2 tablespoons butter, melted
½ teaspoon caraway seeds
    (optional)

Preheat oven to 400°F. Soak instant minced onion in water 5 minutes. Combine biscuit mix, egg, milk and

TABASCO® sauce and stir until blended. Stir in onion. Turn into greased 8-inch pie plate. Brush with melted butter. Sprinkle with caraway seeds. Bake 20 to 25 minutes or until golden brown.

Makes 8 servings

Nutrients per serving:

Calories	139	Cholesterol	43 mg
Fat	7 g	Sodium	310 mg

PICANTE ONION SOUP

3 cups thinly sliced onions
1 clove garlic, minced
¼ cup butter or margarine
2 cups tomato juice
1 can (10½ ounces) condensed
    beef broth
1 soup can water
½ cup PACE® Picante Sauce
1 cup unseasoned croutons
    (optional)
1 cup (4 ounces) shredded
    Monterey Jack cheese
    (optional)
    Additional PACE® Picante
    Sauce

Cook onions and garlic in butter in 3-quart saucepan over medium-low heat about 20 minutes, stirring frequently, until onions are tender and golden brown. Stir in tomato juice, broth, water and ½ cup picante sauce; bring to a boil over high heat. Reduce heat to low. Simmer, uncovered, 20 minutes. Ladle soup into bowls and sprinkle with croutons and cheese. Serve with additional picante sauce.

Makes 6 servings

Nutrients per serving:

Calories	119	Cholesterol	trace
Fat	8 g	Sodium	1051 mg

Picante Onion Soup

Speedy Turkey Sausage Soup

SPEEDY TURKEY SAUSAGE SOUP

8 cups water
1 can (14½ ounces) stewed
    tomatoes, undrained
1 package (10 ounces) frozen
    chopped spinach
2 carrots, sliced
1 medium onion, chopped
2 teaspoons instant beef bouillon
    or 2 bouillon cubes
¼ teaspoon black pepper
1 package (1 pound)
    LOUIS RICH® Turkey
    Breakfast Sausage, thawed
1 cup uncooked elbow macaroni
    or other small-size pasta
    Grated Parmesan cheese
    (optional)

Bring water, tomatoes, spinach, carrots,
onion, bouillon and pepper to a full boil
in large saucepan. Drop bite-size pieces
of uncooked sausage into boiling soup
mixture to form "dumplings," stirring
occasionally. Stir in macaroni. Simmer

10 minutes or until macaroni is tender.
Ladle into serving bowls and sprinkle
with Parmesan cheese, if desired.
Refrigerate or freeze unused portions.

Makes 10 servings

Nutrients per serving:

Calories	145	Cholesterol	35 mg
Fat	3 g	Sodium	670 mg

CHILLED PEAR HELENE SOUP

4 pears, peeled, cored, cubed
1 can (12 ounces) pear nectar
1 container (8 ounces) Light
    PHILADELPHIA BRAND®
    Pasteurized Process Cream
    Cheese Product
½ cup champagne
½ pint raspberries

Place pears in blender or food processor
container; cover. Blend until smooth.
Add nectar, cream cheese product and
champagne; blend until smooth. Pour
into medium bowl; cover. Refrigerate.

When ready to serve, place raspberries
in blender or food processor container;
cover. Blend until smooth. Strain.

Spoon soup into individual serving
bowls. Spoon approximately
2 tablespoons raspberry purée at
intervals onto each serving. Pull wooden
pick through purée making decorative
design as desired. Garnish with
additional raspberries and fresh mint
leaves, if desired.

Makes 4 to 6 servings

Prep time: 10 minutes plus
refrigerating

Nutrients per serving:

Calories	200	Cholesterol	20 mg
Fat	7 g	Sodium	220 mg

THREE–BEAN CHILI

1 can (16 ounces) tomatoes, cut
    into bite-size pieces
1 jar (12 ounces) HEINZ®
    HomeStyle Brown Gravy
1 tablespoon chili powder
1 can (15 ounces) chili beans in
    chili gravy
1 can (15 ounces) garbanzo
    beans, drained
1 can (15 ounces) pinto or
    kidney beans, drained
1 can (4 ounces) chopped green
    chilies
   Plain nonfat yogurt or light
    dairy sour cream, sliced
    green onions and/or
    shredded low-fat Cheddar
    cheese (optional)

Combine tomatoes, gravy and chili
powder in 3-quart saucepan. Bring to a
boil over high heat. Stir in beans and
chilies. Reduce heat to low. Cover;
simmer 15 minutes, stirring occasionally.
Serve with desired toppings.

Makes 6 servings, about 6½ cups

Nutrients per serving (about 1 cup):			
Calories	281	Cholesterol	0 mg
Fat	4 g	Sodium	1135 mg

CHEDDAR–ONION
CASSEROLE BREAD

2½ cups flour
  1 tablespoon baking powder
  ½ teaspoon salt
  ½ cup HELLMANN'S® or
    BEST FOODS® Light
    Reduced Calorie Mayonnaise
  2 cups (8 ounces) shredded
    Cheddar cheese
  ½ cup minced green onions
  ¾ cup milk
  1 egg

Preheat oven to 425°F. Grease 1½-
quart casserole dish. In large bowl,
combine flour, baking powder and salt.
Stir in mayonnaise until mixture
resembles coarse crumbs. Add cheese
and green onions; toss. In small bowl,
beat milk and egg. Stir into cheese
mixture just until moistened. Spoon into
prepared casserole dish.

Bake 35 to 45 minutes or until wooden
toothpick inserted into center comes
out clean. Cut into wedges; serve
immediately.

Makes 1 loaf, 12 wedges

Nutrients per serving (1 wedge):			
Calories	214	Cholesterol	43 mg
Fat	10 g	Sodium	301 mg

SAVORY LENTIL SOUP

1 cup uncooked lentils
3 cups (12 ounces) ARMOUR®
    Lower Salt Ham cut into
    small cubes
1 (14½-ounce) can no-salt-added
    stewed tomatoes
1 small onion, chopped
½ cup chopped celery
1 teaspoon hot pepper sauce
1 teaspoon MRS. DASH®,
    Original Blend

Wash lentils; remove any grit or broken
shells. Combine all ingredients in large
covered kettle; stir in 4 cups water. Bring
to boil over medium-high heat, stirring
often. Reduce heat to simmer. Cover and
cook for 1 hour, or until lentils are tender
and soup is thick. Garnish with celery
leaves, if desired.   *Makes 6 servings*

Nutrients per serving:			
Calories	220	Cholesterol	28 mg
Fat	3 g	Sodium	537 mg

Chunky Ham Stew

CHUNKY HAM STEW

1 medium onion, chopped
2 stalks celery, sliced
2 carrots, sliced
4 cups low-sodium chicken broth
2 cups (8 ounces) ARMOUR®
   Lower Salt Ham cut into
   ½-inch cubes
1 tablespoon MRS. DASH®,
   Original Blend
1 cup frozen peas
2 tablespoons cornstarch

Combine onion, celery, carrots, broth, ham and seasoning in Dutch oven. Cover and cook over medium-high heat for 20 minutes, or until carrots are almost tender. Stir in peas. Mix ¼ cup water and cornstarch and add to stew. Stir constantly until stew comes to a boil and thickens. If desired, garnish with celery leaves.   *Makes 4 to 6 servings*

To Microwave: Combine ingredients as directed above in 10-inch microwave-safe tube pan. Cover with vented plastic wrap. Cook on HIGH (100%) power for 10 minutes. Stir; rotate pan. Continue cooking, covered, on HIGH power about 10 to 15 minutes, or until carrots are almost tender. Stir in peas. Mix ¼ cup water and cornstarch; stir into stew. Cook, covered, on HIGH power about 2 to 3 minutes, or until stew comes to a boil and thickens, stirring 3 times during cooking. Garnish as above.

Nutrients per serving:

Calories	131	Cholesterol	19 mg
Fat	3 g	Sodium	410 mg

DILLY CHEESE MUFFINS

2 cups all-purpose flour
1 tablespoon sugar
1 tablespoon baking powder
2 teaspoons dried dill weed
1 teaspoon onion powder
½ teaspoon salt
¼ teaspoon freshly ground black
   pepper
1 cup creamed small curd
   cottage cheese
¾ cup milk
¼ cup margarine or butter,
   melted
1 egg, beaten

Preheat oven to 400°F. Grease or paper-line 12 (2½-inch) muffin cups. In large bowl, combine flour, sugar, baking powder, dill weed, onion powder, salt and pepper. In small bowl, combine cottage cheese, milk, margarine and egg until blended. Stir into flour mixture just until moistened. Spoon into muffin cups. Bake 20 to 25 minutes or until golden and wooden toothpick inserted in centers comes out clean. Remove from pan.
                    Makes 12 muffins

Nutrients per serving (1 muffin):

Calories	149	Cholesterol	22 mg
Fat	6 g	Sodium	302 mg

QUICK DELI TURKEY SOUP

 1 can (13¾ ounces)
    ready-to-serve chicken broth
 1 can (14½ ounces) stewed
    tomatoes, undrained
 1 small zucchini, cut up
    (about 1 cup)
 ¼ teaspoon dried basil leaves
 ½ pound BUTTERBALL® Deli
    Turkey Breast, cubed
 ½ cup cooked chili-mac pasta or
    macaroni

Combine broth, tomatoes with juice,
zucchini and basil in large saucepan.
Bring to a boil over high heat. Reduce
heat to medium; simmer 10 minutes or
until zucchini is tender. Stir in turkey
and pasta. Continue heating until turkey
is hot.   *Makes 4 servings*

Nutrients per serving:

Calories	152	Cholesterol	40 mg
Fat	3 g	Sodium	537 mg

HEARTY CHICKEN AND RICE SOUP

10 cups chicken broth
 1 medium onion, chopped
 1 cup sliced celery
 1 cup sliced carrots
 ¼ cup snipped parsley
 ½ teaspoon cracked black pepper
 ½ teaspoon dried thyme leaves
 1 bay leaf
1½ cups chicken cubes (about
    ¾ pound)
 2 cups cooked rice
 2 tablespoons lime juice
    Lime slices for garnish

Combine broth, onion, celery, carrots,
parsley, pepper, thyme, and bay leaf in
Dutch oven. Bring to a boil over high
heat. Stir once or twice. Reduce heat to
low. Simmer, uncovered, 10 to 15
minutes. Add chicken; simmer,
uncovered, 5 to 10 minutes or until
chicken is cooked. Remove and discard
bay leaf. Stir in rice and lime juice just
before serving. Garnish with lime slices.
             Makes 8 servings

Nutrients per serving:

Calories	184	Cholesterol	23 mg
Fat	4 g	Sodium	1209 mg

Favorite recipe from **USA Rice Council**

Hearty Chicken and Rice Soup

ONION FLATBREAD

2⅓ cups warm water (105° to
       115°F), divided
  ½ cup plus 3 tablespoons honey,
       divided
1½ packages active dry yeast
  6 tablespoons olive oil, divided
  3 cups whole wheat flour
  ⅓ cup cornmeal
  2 tablespoons coarse salt
  3 to 4 cups all-purpose flour,
       divided
  2 large red onions, thinly sliced
  1 cup red wine vinegar
       Additional cornmeal
  1 cup grated Parmesan cheese
       Freshly ground black pepper
          to taste

In large bowl, combine ⅓ cup water and
3 tablespoons honey in large bowl;
sprinkle yeast over water. Let stand about
15 minutes until bubbly. Add remaining
2 cups water, 3 tablespoons olive oil,
whole wheat flour and cornmeal. Mix
until well blended. Stir in salt and 2
cups all-purpose flour. Gradually stir in
enough remaining flour until mixture
clings to sides of bowl.

Turn out onto lightly floured surface.
Knead in enough remaining flour to
make a smooth and satiny dough, about
10 minutes. Divide dough in half. Place
each half in large, lightly greased bowl;
turn over to grease surface. Cover; let
rise in warm place (85°F) until doubled.
Meanwhile, combine onions, vinegar and
remaining ½ cup honey. Marinate at
least 1 hour.

Grease 2 (12-inch) pizza pans; sprinkle
with additional cornmeal. Stretch and pat
out dough on pans; create valleys with
fingertips. Cover; let rise in warm place
(85°F) until doubled, about 1 hour. Drain
onions; scatter over dough. Sprinkle with
remaining 3 tablespoons olive oil and
cheese; season with pepper.

Preheat oven to 400°F. Bake 25 to
30 minutes or until flatbread is crusty
and golden. Cut each flatbread into 8
wedges. Serve warm.

Makes 2 flatbreads, 16 wedges

Nutrients per serving (1 wedge):

Calories	296	Cholesterol	5 mg
Fat	8 g	Sodium	916 mg

Favorite recipe from *The Times-Picayune*

POTATO–CHEESE CALICO SOUP

  1 pound potatoes, peeled and
       thinly sliced
  1 cup sliced onion
2½ cups chicken broth
  ½ cup low-fat milk
  1 cup sliced mushrooms
  ½ cup diced red bell pepper
  ½ cup sliced green onions
  1 cup (4 ounces) finely shredded
       Wisconsin Asiago Cheese
       Salt and black pepper
  2 tablespoons chopped parsley

In 3-quart saucepan, combine potatoes,
1 cup onion and broth. Bring to boil.
Reduce heat to low. Cover; cook until
potatoes are tender, about 10 minutes.
Pour into blender container; blend until
smooth. Return to saucepan. Stir in
milk, mushrooms, bell pepper and green
onions. Bring to simmer over medium-
low heat. Add cheese, a few tablespoons
at a time, stirring to melt. Season with
salt and black pepper. Sprinkle with
parsley.   *Makes 6 servings, 6 cups*

Nutrients per serving (1 cup):

Calories	151	Cholesterol	9 mg
Fat	4 g	Sodium	526 mg

Favorite recipe from **Wisconsin Milk
Marketing Board** © 1992

VEGETABLE DINNER ROLLS

2 cups all-purpose flour
1 cup whole wheat flour
2 cups KELLOGG'S®
    BRAN FLAKES Cereal
2 tablespoons sugar
½ teaspoon salt
1 teaspoon herb-spice seasoning
1 package active dry yeast
1 cup water
2 tablespoons margarine
2 egg whites
1 cup shredded zucchini
½ cup shredded carrots
¼ cup sliced green onions
2 teaspoons sesame seed
    (optional)

In small bowl, stir together flours. In large electric mixer bowl, combine KELLOGG'S BRAN FLAKES cereal, 1 cup of the flour mixture, sugar, salt, seasoning and yeast. Set aside.

Heat water and margarine until warm (115° to 120°F). Add to cereal mixture with egg whites. Beat on low speed with electric mixer 30 seconds or until thoroughly combined. Increase speed to high and beat 3 minutes longer, scraping bowl frequently. Mix in vegetables.

By hand, stir in enough remaining flour to make sticky dough. Cover loosely. Let rise in warm place (80° to 85°F) until double in volume. Stir down batter. Portion evenly into 12 (2½-inch) muffin pan cups coated with nonstick cooking spray. Sprinkle with sesame seed, if desired. Let rise in warm place until double in volume. Bake at 400°F about 17 minutes or until golden brown. Serve warm.   *Makes 12 rolls*

Nutrients per serving (1 roll):

Calories	170	Cholesterol	0 mg
Fat	2 g	Sodium	156 mg

CREOLE–FLAVORED BEEF SOUP

3 to 4 pounds beef shank cross
    cuts
4 cups water
1 can (28 ounces) crushed
    tomatoes
1 cup sliced celery
1 large onion, chopped
2 cloves garlic, minced
2 beef bouillon cubes
½ teaspoon salt
¼ teaspoon *each* ground black
    pepper and ground red
    pepper
2 cups chopped cabbage
1 green bell pepper, chopped
¼ cup fresh lemon juice
2 cups cooked rice

Place beef shank cross cuts, water, tomatoes, celery, onion, garlic, bouillon cubes, salt and black and red peppers in Dutch oven. Bring to a boil; reduce heat and simmer, covered, 2 hours, stirring occasionally. Remove shanks; cool slightly. Cut meat from bone into small pieces. Skim fat from broth. Return meat to Dutch oven; add cabbage and green pepper. Continue to simmer, covered, 30 minutes or until meat and vegetables are tender. Stir in lemon juice. To serve, spoon about ¼ cup cooked rice into each serving.   *Makes 8 servings*

Prep time: 30 minutes
Cook time: 2 hours and 45 minutes

Nutrients per serving:

Calories	241	Cholesterol	44 mg
Fat	5 g	Sodium	582 mg

Favorite recipe from **National Live Stock and Meat Board**

Zesty Tomato Turkey Soup

JALAPEÑO–BACON CORN BREAD

4 slices bacon
¼ cup minced green onions with tops
2 jalapeño peppers, stemmed, seeded and minced
1 cup yellow cornmeal
1 cup all-purpose flour
2½ teaspoons baking powder
½ teaspoon baking soda
½ teaspoon salt
1 egg
¾ cup plain yogurt
¾ cup low-fat milk
¼ cup butter or margarine, melted
½ cup (2 ounces) shredded Cheddar cheese

Preheat oven to 400°F. Cook bacon in skillet until crisp; drain on paper towels. Pour 2 tablespoons of the bacon drippings into 9-inch cast-iron skillet or 9-inch square baking pan. Crumble bacon into small bowl; add green onions and peppers.

Combine cornmeal, flour, baking powder, baking soda and salt in large bowl. Beat egg slightly in medium bowl; add yogurt and whisk until smooth. Whisk in milk and butter. Pour liquid mixture into dry ingredients; stir just until moistened. Stir in bacon mixture. Pour into skillet; sprinkle with cheese. Bake 20 to 25 minutes or until wooden toothpick inserted in center comes out clean. Cut into wedges or squares; serve hot.   *Makes 9 to 12 servings*

Nutrients per serving:

Calories	165	Cholesterol	27 mg
Fat	8 g	Sodium	335 mg

ZESTY TOMATO TURKEY SOUP

2 slices bacon
¼ cup chopped onion
1 small clove garlic, minced
2 cans (12 ounces each) cocktail vegetable juice
1 can (8 ounces) stewed tomatoes, undrained, cut up
1 cup (5 ounces) diced cooked BUTTERBALL® Turkey
⅓ cup chopped seeded cucumber
¼ cup chopped green bell pepper
1 teaspoon chicken bouillon granules
1 teaspoon Worcestershire sauce
½ teaspoon sugar

Cook bacon in large saucepan over medium-high heat until crisp; break into pieces and set aside. In drippings, sauté onion and garlic until tender. Add remaining ingredients including reserved bacon. Bring to a boil over high heat. Reduce heat to low; simmer 5 minutes or until hot.   *Makes 4 servings*

To Microwave: Cut bacon into 1-inch pieces. Cook bacon in 2-quart microwave-safe casserole on HIGH (100%) 2½ to 3 minutes, stirring once. Remove bacon and set aside. In drippings, cook onion and garlic on HIGH 2 minutes, stirring once. Add remaining ingredients including reserved bacon. Cook on HIGH 7 to 8 minutes or until hot, stirring twice.

Nutrients per serving:

Calories	127	Cholesterol	27 mg
Fat	3 g	Sodium	912 mg

Cottage Herb Rolls

COTTAGE HERB ROLLS

1 package active dry yeast
¼ cup warm water
2½ cups unsifted flour
¼ cup sugar
1 teaspoon dried oregano leaves
1 teaspoon salt
½ cup cold margarine or butter
1 cup BORDEN® or
    MEADOW GOLD® Cottage
    Cheese
1 egg, beaten
    Melted margarine or butter

Dissolve yeast in warm water. In large bowl, combine flour, sugar, oregano and salt; mix well. Cut in margarine until mixture resembles coarse cornmeal. Blend in cheese, egg and yeast mixture. Turn onto well-floured surface; knead. Shape into ball; place in well-greased bowl. Brush top with melted margarine.

Cover; let rise until doubled. Punch down; shape as desired. Brush with melted margarine; cover. Let rise again until nearly doubled. Bake in preheated 375°F oven 12 to 15 minutes. Serve warm. *Makes 1½ to 2 dozen rolls*

Nutrients per serving:

Calories	102	Cholesterol	10 mg
Fat	5 g	Sodium	174 mg

ASPARAGUS AND SURIMI SEAFOOD SOUP

3 cans (10½ ounces *each*)
    low-sodium chicken broth
    (about 4 cups)
2 thin slices fresh ginger
2 cups (about ¾ pound)
    diagonally sliced asparagus
    (½ inch long)
¼ cup sliced green onions,
    including part of green tops
3 tablespoons rice vinegar or
    white wine vinegar
¼ teaspoon crushed red pepper
8 to 12 ounces crab-flavored
    SURIMI Seafood legs or
    chunks, cut diagonally

Bring chicken broth and ginger to a boil in a large saucepan. Add asparagus, green onions, vinegar and crushed red pepper. Simmer 5 minutes or until the asparagus is crisp-tender. Add Surimi Seafood and simmer 5 minutes longer or until seafood is hot. Remove and discard ginger. Serve hot. *Makes 4 servings*

Nutrients per serving:

Calories	136	Cholesterol	18 mg
Fat	3 g	Sodium	784 mg

Favorite recipe from **Surimi Seafood Education Center**

SEAFOOD CORN CHOWDER

1 tablespoon margarine
1 cup chopped onions
½ cup chopped green bell pepper
½ cup chopped red bell pepper
⅓ cup chopped celery
1 tablespoon all-purpose flour
1 can (10½ ounces) low-sodium
 chicken broth
2 cups skim milk
1 can (12 ounces) evaporated
 skim milk
8 to 12 ounces crab-flavored
 SURIMI Seafood chunks
2 cups fresh or frozen whole
 kernel corn
½ teaspoon black pepper
½ teaspoon paprika

Melt margarine in large saucepan over medium heat. Add onions, peppers and celery. Cook, uncovered, over moderate heat 4 to 5 minutes or until vegetables are soft. Add flour to vegetable mixture; cook and stir constantly 2 minutes. Gradually add chicken broth and bring to a boil. Add milk, evaporated milk, Surimi Seafood, corn, black pepper and paprika. Heat, stirring occasionally, 5 minutes or until chowder is hot. Serve.

Makes 6 servings

Nutrients per serving:

Calories	217	Cholesterol	17 mg
Fat	3 g	Sodium	630 mg

Favorite recipe from **Surimi Seafood Education Center**

Left to right: Seafood Corn Chowder, Asparagus and Surimi Seafood Soup

CUBAN BLACK BEAN & HAM SOUP

1 cup uncooked black beans, soaked overnight and drained
1 slice (2 ounces) ARMOUR® Lower Salt Ham
½ cup chopped green bell pepper
1 medium onion, finely chopped
2 teaspoons MRS. DASH®, Original Blend
1 teaspoon garlic powder
1 teaspoon ground cumin
¼ teaspoon black pepper
1½ cups (6 ounces) ARMOUR® Lower Salt Ham cut into ¾-inch cubes

Cuban Black Bean & Ham Soup

Combine beans, ham slice, green pepper, onion and seasonings in medium saucepan; add enough water to just cover beans. Bring to boil; reduce heat, cover and simmer about 1½ to 2 hours, or until beans are tender and most of liquid is absorbed. Add ham cubes. Cook 10 minutes, or until ham cubes are heated through. Remove ham slice before serving. Serve over rice, if desired. *Makes 4 servings*

Nutrients per serving:			
Calories	244	Cholesterol	28 mg
Fat	4 g	Sodium	489 mg

SAVORY FRENCH BREAD

1 large loaf French bread
¼ cup butter or margarine, softened
¼ teaspoon TABASCO® Pepper Sauce
½ teaspoon dried basil leaves
½ teaspoon dried dill weed
½ teaspoon chopped chives
¼ teaspoon garlic powder
¼ teaspoon paprika

Preheat oven to 400°F. Slice bread diagonally, but do not cut through bottom crust of loaf. In small bowl mix remaining ingredients. Spread between bread slices; wrap bread in aluminum foil and heat in oven for 15 to 20 minutes. Serve warm.

Makes 6 to 8 servings

Nutrients per serving:			
Calories	216	Cholesterol	17 mg
Fat	7 g	Sodium	390 mg

Chicken Cilantro Bisque

CHICKEN CILANTRO BISQUE

6 ounces boneless, skinless chicken breasts, cut into chunks
2½ cups low-sodium chicken broth
½ cup cilantro leaves
½ cup sliced green onions
¼ cup sliced celery
1 large clove garlic, minced
½ teaspoon ground cumin
⅓ cup all-purpose flour
1½ cups (12-ounce can) *undiluted* CARNATION® Evaporated Skimmed Milk
Fresh ground black pepper to taste

In large saucepan, combine chicken, broth, cilantro, green onions, celery, garlic and cumin. Heat to boiling; reduce heat and boil gently, covered, for 15 minutes. Pour soup into blender container. Add flour. Cover and blend, starting at low speed, until smooth. Pour mixture back into saucepan. Cook over medium heat, stirring constantly, until mixture comes to a boil and thickens. Remove from heat. Gradually stir in milk. Reheat just to serving temperature. Do not boil. Season with pepper to taste. Garnish as desired.

Makes about 4 servings

Nutrients per serving:			
Calories	176	Cholesterol	28 mg
Fat	2 g	Sodium	608 mg

Entrées

Left: Sunday Super Stuffed Shells
Right: Ginger Spicy Chicken (page 92)

SUNDAY SUPER STUFFED SHELLS

- **3 cloves fresh garlic**
- **2 tablespoons olive oil**
- **¾ pound ground veal**
- **¾ pound ground pork**
- **1 package (10 ounces) frozen chopped spinach, cooked, drained and squeezed dry**
- **1 cup parsley, finely chopped**
- **1 cup bread crumbs**
- **2 eggs, beaten**
- **3 cloves fresh garlic, minced**
- **3 tablespoons grated Parmesan cheese**
   Salt to taste
- **1 package (12 ounces) uncooked jumbo pasta shells, cooked, rinsed and drained**
- **3 cups spaghetti sauce**
   Sautéed zucchini slices (optional)

Cook and stir 3 whole garlic cloves in hot oil in large skillet over medium heat until garlic is browned. Discard garlic. Add veal and pork. Cook until lightly browned, stirring to separate meat; drain fat. Set aside.

Combine spinach, parsley, bread crumbs, eggs, minced garlic and cheese in large bowl; blend well. Season to taste with salt. Add cooled meat mixture; blend well. Fill shells with stuffing.

Spread about 1 cup spaghetti sauce over bottom of greased 12×8-inch pan. Arrange shells in pan. Pour remaining sauce over shells. Cover with foil. Bake in preheated 375°F oven 35 to 45 minutes or until bubbly. Serve with zucchini. Garnish as desired.

Makes 9 to 12 servings

Nutrients per serving:

Calories	290	Cholesterol	81 mg
Fat	10 g	Sodium	428 mg

Favorite recipe from **The Fresh Garlic Association**

Scallop Kabobs

Remove chicken; keep warm. Add pepper strips, pineapple with juice, picante sauce, cilantro and ginger to skillet. Cook, stirring frequently, 5 to 7 minutes or until peppers are tender and sauce is thickened. Return chicken to skillet and heat through.

Makes 4 servings

Nutrients per serving:

Calories	256	Cholesterol	73 mg
Fat	10 g	Sodium	284 mg

GINGER SPICY CHICKEN

Salt
2 whole chicken breasts, split, skinned and boned
2 tablespoons vegetable oil
1 medium-size red bell pepper, cut into 2×¼-inch strips
1 medium-size green bell pepper, cut into 2×¼-inch strips
1 can (8 ounces) pineapple chunks in juice, undrained
½ cup PACE® Picante Sauce
2 tablespoons chopped cilantro *or* parsley
2 to 3 teaspoons grated fresh ginger *or* ¾ to 1 teaspoon ground ginger

Lightly salt chicken breasts. Heat oil in large skillet over medium heat. Add chicken; cook about 5 minutes on each side or until light brown and tender.

SCALLOP KABOBS

¼ cup REALEMON® Lemon Juice from Concentrate
2 tablespoons vegetable oil
1 teaspoon dried oregano leaves
½ teaspoon dried basil leaves
1 clove garlic, finely chopped
⅛ teaspoon salt
1 pound sea scallops
8 ounces fresh mushrooms
2 small zucchini, cut into chunks
2 small onions, cut into wedges
½ red, yellow or green bell pepper, cut into bite-size pieces
Additional REALEMON® Brand

In shallow dish, combine ReaLemon® brand, oil and seasonings; add scallops. Cover; marinate in refrigerator 2 hours, stirring occasionally. Remove scallops from marinade; discard marinade. Divide scallops and vegetables equally among 8 skewers. Grill or broil as desired, until scallops are opaque, basting frequently with additional ReaLemon® brand. Refrigerate leftovers.

Makes 8 kabobs

Nutrients per serving (2 kabobs):

Calories	213	Cholesterol	37 mg
Fat	8 g	Sodium	255 mg

SAUCY PORK AND PEPPERS

2 fresh limes
¼ cup 62%-less-sodium soy sauce
4 cloves garlic, crushed
1 teaspoon dried oregano leaves
½ teaspoon dried thyme leaves
    Dash cayenne pepper
2 to 3 fresh parsley sprigs
1 bay leaf
1 pound pork tenderloin, cut
    into 1-inch cubes
1 tablespoon olive oil
1 teaspoon firmly packed brown
    sugar
2 medium onions, each cut into
    8 pieces
2 medium tomatoes, each cut
    into 8 pieces and seeded
1 large red bell pepper, cut into
    8 pieces
1 large green bell pepper, cut
    into 8 pieces

Remove peel from limes using vegetable peeler. Squeeze juice from limes. In small bowl, combine lime juice and peel, soy sauce, garlic, oregano leaves, thyme leaves, cayenne pepper, parsley and bay leaf; blend well. Place pork cubes in plastic bag or nonmetal bowl. Pour marinade mixture over pork, turning to coat. Seal bag or cover dish; marinate at least 2 hours or overnight in refrigerator, turning pork several times.

Remove lime peel, parsley sprigs and bay leaf from marinade; discard. Remove pork from marinade, reserving marinade. Drain pork well. Heat oil in large skillet over high heat. Add brown sugar; stir until sugar is brown and bubbly. Add pork cubes; cook and stir about 5 minutes or until pork is browned. Reduce heat to low. Add onions, tomatoes, peppers and reserved marinade; simmer 10 to 15 minutes or until pork is tender.

Makes 4 servings

Nutrients per serving:

Calories	243	Cholesterol	79 mg
Fat	8 g	Sodium	547 mg

Favorite recipe from **National Pork Producers Council**

Saucy Pork and Peppers

ORIENTAL SEAFOOD STIR–FRY

½ **cup water**
3 **tablespoons REALEMON®
    Lemon Juice from
    Concentrate**
3 **tablespoons soy sauce**
1 **tablespoon firmly packed
    brown sugar**
1 **tablespoon cornstarch**
2 **ounces fresh pea pods**
¾ **cup sliced fresh mushrooms**
¾ **cup diced red bell pepper**
1 **medium onion, cut into wedges**
1 **tablespoon vegetable oil**
½ **pound imitation crab blend,
    flaked
    Shredded napa (Chinese
    cabbage), angel hair pasta
    or rice noodles**

Combine water, ReaLemon® brand, soy
sauce, sugar and cornstarch in small
bowl. In large skillet or wok, over
medium-high heat, cook and stir
vegetables in oil until tender-crisp;
remove. Add soy mixture; over medium
heat, cook and stir until slightly

Oriental Seafood Stir-Fry

thickened. Add vegetables and crab
blend; heat through. Serve with napa,
pasta or rice noodles. Refrigerate
leftovers.   *Makes 4 servings*

Nutrients per serving:

Calories	151	Cholesterol	11 mg
Fat	4 g	Sodium	1266 mg

GREEK LAMB SAUTÉ WITH MOSTACCIOLI

½ **of (1-pound) package
    CREAMETTE® Mostaccioli,
    uncooked**
1 **tablespoon olive or
    vegetable oil**
1 **medium green bell pepper,
    chopped**
1 **medium onion, chopped**
1 **medium eggplant, peeled,
    seeded and cut into 1-inch
    cubes**
2 **cloves garlic, minced**
½ **pound lean boneless lamb, cut
    into ¾-inch cubes**
2 **tomatoes, peeled, seeded and
    chopped**
¼ **teaspoon ground nutmeg**
¼ **cup grated Parmesan cheese**

Prepare Creamette® Mostaccioli
according to package directions; drain.
In large skillet, heat oil. Add green
pepper, onion, eggplant and garlic; cook
and stir until tender-crisp. Add lamb;
cook until tender. Stir in tomatoes and
nutmeg; cook until heated through.
Toss meat mixture with hot cooked
mostaccioli and Parmesan cheese. Serve
immediately. Refrigerate leftovers.
                    Makes 8 servings

Nutrients per serving:

Calories	205	Cholesterol	29 mg
Fat	5 g	Sodium	82 mg

BLACK PEPPER PATTIES

1 package (about 1 pound)
  LOUIS RICH® Fresh Ground
  Turkey
1 teaspoon instant chicken
  bouillon
¼ teaspoon dried thyme leaves
1 teaspoon coarse ground black
  pepper

Sauce
  1 large tomato, chopped
  ½ cup plain nonfat yogurt
  1 tablespoon chopped fresh
    parsley

Mix turkey, bouillon and thyme in bowl.
Shape into four 4-inch patties. Sprinkle
pepper on patties (about ⅛ teaspoon per
side), lightly pressing pepper into turkey.
Cook turkey in nonstick skillet over
medium heat about 12 minutes or until
no longer pink, turning occasionally.

Meanwhile, mix sauce ingredients in
small bowl. Serve cold sauce over turkey
patties. *Makes 4 servings*

Nutrients per serving (1 patty):

Calories	190	Cholesterol	75 mg
Fat	8 g	Sodium	315 mg

PORK LOIN ROULADE

4 boneless center pork loin
  slices, about 1 pound
½ red bell pepper, cut into strips
½ green bell pepper, cut into
  strips
1 tablespoon vegetable oil
⅔ cup orange juice
⅔ cup bottled barbecue sauce
1 tablespoon prepared
  Dijon-style mustard

Pork Loin Roulade

Place cutlets between 2 pieces of plastic
wrap. Pound with a mallet to about
¼-inch thickness. Place several red and
green pepper strips crosswise on each
pork portion; roll up jelly-roll style.
Secure rolls with wooden toothpicks.

In a large heavy skillet, brown the pork
rolls in hot oil. Drain fat from pan.
Combine remaining ingredients and add
to skillet. Bring mixture to boiling;
reduce heat. Cover and simmer 10 to
12 minutes or until pork is tender.
Remove toothpicks and serve.

Makes 4 servings

Nutrients per serving:

Calories	255	Cholesterol	72 mg
Fat	10 g	Sodium	530 mg

Favorite recipe from **National Pork
Producers Council**

APPLESAUCE– STUFFED TENDERLOIN

2 pork tenderloins (about
    1 pound each), trimmed
¼ cup dry vermouth *or* apple
    juice
    Nonstick cooking spray
⅔ cup chunky applesauce
¼ cup finely chopped dry-roasted
    peanuts
¼ teaspoon salt
¼ teaspoon finely crushed fennel
    seed
⅛ teaspoon black pepper

Using sharp knife, form a "pocket" in each pork tenderloin by cutting a lengthwise slit down center of each almost to, but not through, bottom of each tenderloin. Place in nonmetal baking dish. Pour vermouth in pockets and over tenderloins; cover dish. Marinate about 1 hour at room temperature.

Heat oven to 375°F. Spray 15×10-inch jelly-roll pan or shallow baking pan with nonstick cooking spray. In small bowl, combine applesauce, peanuts, salt, fennel seed and pepper; blend well. Spoon mixture into pocket in each tenderloin. Secure stuffed pockets with toothpicks. Place stuffed tenderloins in prepared pan. Roast at 375°F for about 30 minutes, or until meat thermometer registers 155°F. Let stand 5 to 10 minutes before slicing.

Makes 8 servings

Nutrients per serving:

Calories	179	Cholesterol	79 mg
Fat	6 g	Sodium	131 mg

Favorite recipe from **National Pork Producers Council**

BAKED TOMATOES FLORENTINE

1 cup sliced fresh mushrooms
    (optional)
1 tablespoon finely chopped
    onion
¼ cup water
1 cup BORDEN® Lite-line®
    Protein Fortified Skim Milk
3 tablespoons flour
2 teaspoons WYLER'S® or
    STEERO® Chicken-Flavor
    Instant Bouillon
6 slices BORDEN® Lite-line®
    Process Cheese Product, any
    flavor, cut into small pieces*
2 cups cubed cooked chicken
    (breast meat)
1 (10-ounce) package frozen
    chopped spinach or
    broccoli, thawed and well
    drained
4 large tomatoes, tops cut off and
    insides scooped out

Preheat oven to 350°F. In small saucepan, cook mushrooms, if desired, and onion in water until tender; drain. In small saucepan, combine milk, flour and bouillon; over low heat, cook and stir until thickened. Add Lite-line® pieces; cook and stir until melted. In medium bowl, combine mushroom mixture, chicken, spinach and ¾ *cup* sauce; stuff tomatoes. Arrange in baking dish; cover and bake 15 to 20 minutes or until hot. Over low heat, heat remaining sauce with 1 to 2 tablespoons water. Spoon over tomatoes before serving. Garnish as desired. Refrigerate leftovers.

Makes 4 servings

*"½ the calories" 8% milkfat version

Nutrients per serving:

Calories	290	Cholesterol	71 mg
Fat	6 g	Sodium	1053 mg

Applesauce-Stuffed Tenderloin

Easy Tuna Melt

EASY TUNA MELT

1 (3½-ounce) can solid white
    water-pack tuna, drained
2 teaspoons reduced-calorie
    salad dressing
1 teaspoon dill pickle relish
1 English muffin, split and
    toasted
2 tomato slices
2 slices BORDEN® Lite-line®
    Process Cheese Product, any
    flavor*

Combine tuna, salad dressing and relish.
Top each muffin half with tomato slice,
then half the tuna mixture and Lite-line®
slice. Broil or heat in microwave oven
until Lite-line® slice begins to melt.
Refrigerate leftovers.

Makes 2 servings

*"½ the calories" 8% milkfat version

Nutrients per serving:

Calories	193	Cholesterol	34 mg
Fat	7 g	Sodium	833 mg

CHICKEN BREASTS FLORENTINE

6 boneless skinless chicken
    breast halves (about
    1½ pounds)
1 package (10 ounces) frozen
    chopped spinach, thawed,
    squeezed dry
1 jar (2½ ounces) sliced
    mushrooms, drained
½ cup chopped onion
½ cup shredded low-fat
    mozzarella cheese
½ cup low-fat ricotta cheese
⅛ teaspoon black pepper
1 jar (12 ounces) HEINZ®
    HomeStyle Chicken Gravy
½ teaspoon dried thyme leaves,
    crushed

Place chicken breasts in lightly greased
13×9-inch baking pan. Combine
spinach, mushrooms, onion, cheeses and
pepper in medium bowl. Spoon spinach
mixture on top of chicken breasts.
Combine gravy and thyme; spoon over
spinach and chicken. Cover; bake in
375°F oven 40 to 45 minutes.

Makes 6 servings

To Microwave: Place chicken breasts
in 13×9-inch microwave-safe baking
dish. Combine spinach, mushrooms,
onion, cheeses and pepper in medium
bowl. Spoon spinach mixture on top of
chicken breasts. Combine gravy and
thyme; spoon over spinach and chicken.
Cover dish with waxed paper. Microwave
at HIGH (100%) 18 to 20 minutes or
until chicken is no longer pink,
rearranging halfway through cooking.

Nutrients per serving:

Calories	227	Cholesterol	77 mg
Fat	7 g	Sodium	573 mg

BARBECUE BACON MEATLOAF

2 packages (1 pound each) LOUIS RICH® Ground Turkey
12 slices LOUIS RICH® Turkey Bacon, diced
1 cup quick-cooking oats, uncooked
1 medium onion, finely chopped
½ cup barbecue sauce
2 large egg whites
1 tablespoon Worcestershire sauce

Mix all ingredients in a large bowl. Press meat mixture into ungreased 9×5-inch loaf pan. Top with additional barbecue sauce, if desired. Bake at 375°F for 1 hour 15 minutes. Allow to stand 10 minutes before slicing.

Makes 10 servings

Note: Meatloaf ingredients can be combined a day ahead and refrigerated. Bake at 375°F for 1½ hours.

Nutrients per serving:

Calories	215	Cholesterol	70 mg
Fat	9 g	Sodium	525 mg

DAD'S FAVORITE TURKEY KABOBS

3 ears corn, cut into 1-inch pieces
2 medium zucchini, cut into ¾-inch pieces
2 red bell peppers, cut into 1-inch cubes
2 Turkey Tenderloins (about 1 pound), cut into 1-inch cubes
⅓ cup reduced-calorie Italian salad dressing
Additional reduced-calorie Italian salad dressing

Dad's Favorite Turkey Kabobs

In medium saucepan over high heat, blanch corn in boiling water about 1 to 2 minutes. Remove corn from saucepan and plunge into cold water.

In large glass bowl, place corn, zucchini, peppers, turkey and ⅓ cup dressing; cover and refrigerate 1 to 2 hours.

Drain turkey and vegetables, discarding marinade. Alternately thread turkey cubes and vegetables on skewers, leaving ½-inch space between turkey and vegetables.

On outdoor charcoal grill, cook kabobs 18 to 20 minutes, brushing with additional dressing. Turn skewers after first 10 minutes.

Makes 4 servings, 8 kabobs

Nutrients per serving (2 kabobs):

Calories	218	Cholesterol	70 mg
Fat	4 g	Sodium	381 mg

Favorite recipe from **National Turkey Federation**

Orange Roughy with Cucumber Relish

ORANGE ROUGHY WITH CUCUMBER RELISH

   1 can (11 ounces) mandarin
      oranges, drained
   1 small cucumber, peeled,
      seeded, finely chopped
  ⅓ cup HEINZ® Distilled White
      Vinegar
   1 green onion, minced
   1 tablespoon snipped fresh dill
      or 1 teaspoon dried dill weed
      Nonstick cooking spray
   4 orange roughy fillets (about
      5 ounces *each*)
      Dill sprigs

Reserve 8 orange sections for garnish;
coarsely chop remaining sections and
combine with cucumber, vinegar, onion
and dill. Spray broiler pan with nonstick
cooking spray; place fish on pan. Spoon
1 tablespoon liquid from cucumber
mixture over each fillet. Broil, 3 to
4 inches from heat source, 8 to 10
minutes or until fish tests done. To serve,
spoon cucumber relish on top of fish.
Garnish with reserved orange sections
and dill sprigs.   *Makes 4 servings*

Nutrients per serving:			
Calories	229	Cholesterol	28 mg
Fat	10 g	Sodium	95 mg

HERB–MARINATED CHUCK STEAK

  ¼ cup chopped onion
   2 tablespoons *each* chopped
      parsley and white vinegar
   1 tablespoon vegetable oil
   2 teaspoons Dijon-style mustard
   1 clove garlic, minced
  ½ teaspoon dried thyme leaves
   1 pound boneless beef chuck
      shoulder steak, cut 1 inch
      thick

Combine onion, parsley, vinegar, oil,
mustard, garlic and thyme. Place beef
chuck shoulder steak in plastic bag; add
onion mixture, spreading evenly over
both sides. Close bag securely; marinate
in refrigerator 6 to 8 hours (or overnight,
if desired), turning at least once. Pour off
marinade; discard. Place steak on rack
in broiler pan so surface of meat is 3 to
5 inches from heat source. Broil about
16 minutes for rare and about 18 minutes
for medium, turning once. Carve steak
diagonally across the grain into thin
slices. Garnish as desired.

Makes 4 servings

Nutrients per serving:			
Calories	216	Cholesterol	85 mg
Fat	10 g	Sodium	94 mg

Favorite recipe from **National Live Stock
and Meat Board**

MESQUITE GRILLED TURKEY TENDERLOINS

1 cup mesquite chips
2 pounds Turkey Breast Tenderloins
Pepper to taste
Caribbean Salsa (recipe follows)

In small bowl cover mesquite chips with water; soak for 2 hours. Preheat charcoal grill for direct-heat cooking. Drain water from mesquite chips; add chips to hot coals. Sprinkle tenderloins with pepper; grill 8 to 10 minutes on each side until tenderloins are no longer pink in center and register 170°F on meat thermometer. Allow to stand 10 minutes before serving.

To serve, slice tenderloins into ½-inch medallions and arrange on serving plate. Top with Caribbean Salsa.

Makes 8 servings

CARIBBEAN SALSA

2 cups (¼-inch) mango cubes
½ cup peeled, seeded (¼-inch) cucumber cubes
¼ cup chopped fresh cilantro or parsley
2 tablespoons finely chopped green onion
½ jalapeño pepper, seeded and finely chopped
3 tablespoons fresh lime juice
1½ teaspoons firmly packed brown sugar
1 teaspoon minced fresh ginger
Dash black pepper

In medium-size bowl combine mango, cucumber, cilantro, green onion, jalapeño pepper, lime juice, brown sugar, ginger and black pepper. Cover and refrigerate at least one hour to allow flavors to blend.

Nutrients per serving:

Calories	163	Cholesterol	70 mg
Fat	2 g	Sodium	79 mg

Favorite recipe from **National Turkey Federation**

Mesquite Grilled Turkey Tenderloins

RHUBARB PORK LOIN

1 boneless pork loin roast
   (3 pounds), rolled
1 clove garlic, cut into 8 to
   10 slivers
1 teaspoon dried rosemary,
   crushed
4 stalks rhubarb, sliced (about
   2 cups)
¼ cup plus 2 tablespoons honey
¼ cup cider vinegar
6 whole cloves
½ teaspoon salt
½ teaspoon dry mustard
2 to 3 drops red food coloring
   (optional)

Preheat oven to 350°F. Place pork roast in roasting pan. Cut 8 to 10 slits in surface of pork and insert garlic slivers. Rub entire surface of roast with rosemary. Insert meat thermometer so bulb is centered in thickest part, not resting in fat. Roast 1 hour.

Meanwhile, combine remaining ingredients in small, heavy saucepan. Bring to a boil over high heat. Reduce heat to low. Simmer 10 minutes. Remove and discard whole cloves. Pour rhubarb sauce over pork; continue to roast, basting often, for about 45 minutes or until roast reaches an internal temperature of 155°F. Let stand 10 minutes to allow internal temperature to rise to 160°F. Carve into thin slices. Heat rhubarb sauce remaining in roasting pan; serve with pork. Garnish as desired. *Makes 10 servings*

Nutrients per serving:			
Calories	208	Cholesterol	61 mg
Fat	9 g	Sodium	162 mg

Favorite recipe from **National Pork Producers Council**

CHICKEN CRIMINI

1 package (1½ pounds)
   PERDUE® Fit 'n Easy fresh
   skinless and boneless pick of
   the chick
½ teaspoon ground thyme
   Salt and ground black pepper
   to taste
1½ tablespoons olive oil
¼ pound wild mushrooms, such
   as crimini, shiitake or
   oyster, thinly sliced
¼ cup reduced-sodium beef broth
3 tablespoons Marsala wine
1 tablespoon grated Parmesan
   cheese
2 tablespoons minced fresh
   parsley
1 lemon, thinly sliced (optional)

Place chicken pieces between sheets of plastic wrap. Pound chicken with meat mallet until slightly flattened. Season with thyme, salt and pepper and set aside. In large, nonstick skillet over medium heat, heat oil. Add mushrooms and sauté 1 to 2 minutes. With slotted spoon, remove mushrooms and set aside. Add chicken to skillet and cook about 5 minutes on each side or until lightly browned. Remove chicken and keep warm.

With wooden spatula or spoon, stir beef broth and wine into skillet, scraping bottom to incorporate browned bits into pan juices. Return chicken to skillet; top with mushrooms. Sprinkle with Parmesan and spoon pan juices over all. Reduce heat to low; cover skillet and simmer 5 to 10 minutes until chicken is cooked through. To serve, sprinkle with parsley and garnish with lemon slices, if desired. *Makes 6 servings*

Nutrients per serving:			
Calories	181	Cholesterol	81 mg
Fat	7 g	Sodium	103 mg

GRILLED SUMMER FISH

1¼ pounds fish fillets (such as cod, blue fish, haddock, sole)
1 medium green bell pepper, seeded and chopped
1 medium tomato, cored and chopped
¼ cup chopped green onions
1 tablespoon chopped fresh dill
½ teaspoon salt
2 tablespoons lemon juice
1 cup (4 ounces) shredded Jarlsberg cheese

Grease 12×18-inch piece of heavy-duty aluminum foil. Place fish fillets in center of foil. Combine vegetables and place over fish. Sprinkle with dill and salt; drizzle with lemon juice. Top with Jarlsberg cheese. Fold up sides of foil, crimping to make a tight seal on top and ends. Place foil packet on top of hot barbecue grill. Grill for 25 minutes. Carefully open packet; if fish is still translucent in the middle, reseal and grill for an additional 5 to 10 minutes.

Makes 4 servings

To Microwave: In microwave-safe baking dish, assemble ingredients as above. Cover; microwave at HIGH (100%) for 7 minutes. Fish is done when it flakes easily when tested with fork near center. If necessary, continue cooking on HIGH for an additional minute. Let stand, covered, for 5 minutes.

To Bake: In large baking dish, assemble ingredients as above. Bake, uncovered, in 375°F oven for 20 minutes, or until fish flakes with fork and cheese is browned.

Nutrients per serving:

Calories	230	Cholesterol	92 mg
Fat	8 g	Sodium	429 mg

Favorite recipe from **Norseland Foods, Inc.**

SPAGHETTI PIZZA DELUXE

1 package (7 ounces) CREAMETTE® Spaghetti, uncooked
½ cup skim milk
1 egg, beaten
  Nonstick cooking spray
½ pound lean ground beef
1 medium onion, chopped
1 medium green bell pepper, chopped
2 cloves garlic, minced
1 can (15 ounces) tomato sauce
1 teaspoon Italian seasoning
1 teaspoon salt-free herb seasoning
¼ teaspoon black pepper
2 cups sliced fresh mushrooms
2 cups shredded part-skim mozzarella cheese

Prepare Creamette® Spaghetti as package directs; drain. In medium bowl, blend milk and egg; add spaghetti and toss to coat. Spray 15×10-inch jelly-roll pan with nonstick cooking spray. Spread spaghetti mixture evenly in prepared pan. In large skillet, cook beef, onion, green pepper and garlic until beef is no longer pink; drain. Add tomato sauce and seasonings; simmer 5 minutes. Spoon meat mixture evenly over spaghetti. Top with mushrooms and cheese. Bake in 350°F oven for 20 minutes. Let stand 5 minutes before cutting. Refrigerate leftovers.

Makes 8 servings

Note: To reduce sodium, substitute no-salt-added tomato sauce.

Nutrients per serving:

Calories	267	Cholesterol	76 mg
Fat	9 g	Sodium	499 mg

Turkey and Rice Quiche

MICROWAVED LEMON–APPLE FISH ROLLS

4 sole, cod or red snapper fillets (1 pound)
   Grated peel of 1 SUNKIST® Lemon, divided
1 teaspoon dried dill weed, divided
¾ cup plus 2 tablespoons apple juice, divided
   Juice of ½ SUNKIST® Lemon
2 tablespoons finely minced onion
1 tablespoon unsalted margarine
1 tablespoon all-purpose flour
1 tablespoon chopped parsley

Sprinkle fish with half the lemon peel and half the dill. Roll up each fillet; place, seam-side-down, in 8-inch round microwave-safe dish. Combine ¾ cup apple juice, lemon juice, onion, remaining lemon peel and dill; pour over fish. Dot with margarine. Cover dish loosely with plastic wrap. Microwave at HIGH power (100%) for 3 minutes. Uncover; spoon cooking liquid over fish. Cook, covered, 3 to 4 minutes longer, until fish flakes easily with fork. Remove fish to serving dish; let stand, covered, while making sauce.

Pour cooking liquid from fish into small microwave-safe bowl. Gradually blend remaining 2 tablespoons apple juice into flour; stir into cooking liquid. Microwave at HIGH power, uncovered, 3 to 4 minutes (stirring twice), until sauce boils and slightly thickens. Add parsley; spoon over fish. *Makes 4 servings*

Nutrients per serving:

Calories	164	Cholesterol	55 mg
Fat	4 g	Sodium	94 mg

TURKEY AND RICE QUICHE

3 cups cooked rice, cooled to room temperature
1½ cups chopped cooked turkey
1 medium tomato, seeded and finely diced
¼ cup sliced green onions
¼ cup finely diced green pepper
1 tablespoon chopped fresh basil *or* 1 teaspoon dried basil
½ teaspoon seasoned salt
⅛ to ¼ teaspoon ground red pepper
½ cup skim milk
3 eggs, beaten
   Nonstick cooking spray
½ cup (2 ounces) shredded Cheddar cheese
½ cup (2 ounces) shredded mozzarella cheese

Combine rice, turkey, tomato, onions, green pepper, basil, salt, ground red pepper, milk, and eggs in 13×9-inch pan coated with nonstick cooking spray. Top with cheeses. Bake at 375°F for 20 minutes or until knife inserted near center comes out clean. To serve, cut quiche into 8 squares; cut each square diagonally into 2 triangles. Garnish as desired.

Makes 8 servings, 16 triangles

Nutrients per serving (2 triangles):

Calories	231	Cholesterol	111 mg
Fat	7 g	Sodium	527 mg

Favorite recipe from **USA Rice Council**

Baja Fish and Rice Bake

BAJA FISH AND RICE BAKE

   3 tablespoons vegetable oil
   ¾ cup chopped onion
   ½ cup chopped celery
   1 clove garlic, minced
   ½ cup uncooked rice
3½ cups (two 14½-ounce cans)
       CONTADINA® Stewed
       Tomatoes, cut up, with juice
   1 teaspoon lemon pepper
       seasoning
   ½ teaspoon salt
   ⅛ teaspoon cayenne pepper
   1 pound fish fillets (any firm
       white fish)
   ¼ cup finely chopped fresh
       parsley
       Lemon slices (optional)

Heat oil in large skillet over medium heat; sauté onion, celery and garlic. Stir in rice; sauté about 5 minutes, or until rice browns slightly. Add tomatoes and juice, lemon pepper, salt and cayenne pepper. Place fish fillets in bottom of

12×7½×2-inch baking dish. Spoon rice mixture over fish. Cover with foil; bake in preheated 400°F oven for 45 to 50 minutes or until rice is tender. Allow to stand 5 minutes before serving. Sprinkle with parsley. Garnish with lemon slices, if desired.

Makes 6 servings

To Microwave: Combine onion, celery and garlic in microwave-safe bowl. Microwave at HIGH power (100%) for 3 minutes. Stir in rice, tomatoes and juice, lemon pepper, salt and cayenne pepper. Microwave at HIGH power for an additional 5 minutes. Place fish fillets in 12×7½×2-inch microwave-safe baking dish. Spoon tomato mixture over fish. Cover tightly with plastic wrap, turning up corner to vent. Microwave at HIGH power for 20 to 25 minutes or until rice is tender. Allow to stand 5 minutes before serving. Serve as above.

Nutrients per serving:

Calories	241	Cholesterol	38 mg
Fat	8 g	Sodium	580 mg

CHICKEN WITH PINEAPPLE SALSA

1 can (20 ounces) DOLE®
     Crushed Pineapple in Juice
4 boneless skinless chicken
     breast halves
1 large clove garlic, pressed
1 teaspoon ground cumin
     Salt and black pepper to taste
1 tablespoon vegetable oil
½ cup minced DOLE® Red Bell
     Pepper
¼ cup minced DOLE® Green Bell
     Pepper
1 tablespoon minced DOLE®
     Green Onion
2 teaspoons minced cilantro
2 teaspoons minced fresh or
     canned jalapeño chilies
1 teaspoon lime zest

Drain pineapple; reserve juice.

Rub chicken with garlic; sprinkle with cumin, salt and black pepper. In 12-inch skillet, sauté chicken in hot oil over medium-high heat until browned; turn once. Add ½ cup pineapple juice to chicken. Reduce heat. Cover; simmer 7 to 10 minutes.

For salsa, in medium bowl, combine pineapple, remaining reserved juice and remaining ingredients.

Cut each breast into slices. Serve chicken with salsa. Garnish as desired.

Makes 4 servings

Prep time: 5 minutes
Cook time: 15 minutes

Nutrients per serving:

Calories	262	Cholesterol	68 mg
Fat	5 g	Sodium	81 mg

FIESTA TURKEY PIE

1 package (about 1 pound)
     LOUIS RICH® Fresh Ground
     Turkey
1 cup salsa
1 can (8 ounces) refrigerated
     crescent dinner rolls
¼ cup shredded sharp Cheddar
     cheese

Preheat oven to 450°F. Cook turkey in nonstick skillet over medium heat about 10 minutes or until turkey is no longer pink, stirring to break turkey into small pieces. Stir in salsa.

Press crescent roll dough onto bottom, up side and on rim of 9-inch pie plate to form crust. Spread turkey mixture evenly over crust; sprinkle with cheese. Bake 18 to 20 minutes or until crust is browned. *Makes 6 to 8 servings*

Nutrients per serving:

Calories	196	Cholesterol	35 mg
Fat	10 g	Sodium	413 mg

Chicken with Pineapple Salsa

BUTTERFLIED EYE ROUND ROAST

1 beef eye round roast (3 pounds)
¼ cup *each* red wine vinegar and
    water
2 tablespoons olive oil
2 cloves garlic, minced
1 tablespoon chopped fresh
    thyme *or* 1 teaspoon dried
    thyme leaves
½ teaspoon crushed red pepper

Butterfly beef eye round roast by cutting horizontally through the center (parallel to surface of meat) the length and width of roast. Do not cut through opposite side of roast. Open meat and lay flat. Combine vinegar, water, oil, garlic, thyme and red pepper. Place beef roast in plastic bag; add vinegar mixture, turning to coat roast. Close bag securely; marinate in refrigerator 6 to 8 hours (or overnight, if desired), turning roast occasionally.

Remove roast from marinade; reserve marinade. Place beef on rack in broiler pan so surface of meat is 5 to 7 inches from heat source. Broil 20 to 25 minutes to desired doneness (rare or medium), turning and basting with reserved marinade occasionally. Tent with foil and allow roast to stand 10 to 15 minutes in warm place before carving. Carve roast into thin slices. *Makes 12 servings*

Note: A beef eye round roast will yield 4 (3-ounce) cooked servings per pound.

Nutrients per serving (3 ounces cooked beef):

Calories	172	Cholesterol	59 mg
Fat	7 g	Sodium	53 mg

Favorite recipe from **National Live Stock and Meat Board**

Butterflied Eye Round Roast

WISCONSIN TUNA CAKES WITH LEMON–DILL SAUCE

1 can (12½ ounces) STARKIST®
Tuna, drained and finely
flaked
¾ cup seasoned bread crumbs
¼ cup minced green onions
2 tablespoons chopped drained
pimento
1 egg
½ cup low-fat milk
½ teaspoon grated lemon peel
2 tablespoons margarine or
butter

Lemon-Dill Sauce
¼ cup chicken broth
1 tablespoon lemon juice
¼ teaspoon dried dill weed

Hot steamed shredded
zucchini and carrots
Lemon slices

In large bowl, toss together tuna, bread
crumbs, onions and pimento. In small
bowl, beat together egg and milk; stir in
lemon peel. Stir into tuna mixture; toss
until moistened. With lightly floured
hands, shape into eight 4-inch patties.

In large nonstick skillet, melt margarine.
Fry patties, a few at a time, until golden
brown on both sides, about 3 minutes
per side. Place on ovenproof platter in
300°F oven until ready to serve.

For Lemon-Dill Sauce, in small
saucepan, heat broth, lemon juice and
dill. Serve tuna cakes with zucchini and
carrots; spoon sauce over cakes.
Garnish with lemon slices.

Makes 4 servings

Nutrients per serving (2 patties plus 1 tablespoon sauce):			
Calories	278	Cholesterol	85 mg
Fat	10 g	Sodium	576 mg

*Wisconsin Tuna Cakes with
Lemon-Dill Sauce*

CHICKEN & VEGETABLE MEDLEY

4 skinned boneless chicken
breast halves (1 pound)
1 tablespoon vegetable oil
½ cup water
2 teaspoons WYLER'S® or
STEERO® Chicken-Flavor
Instant Bouillon *or*
2 Chicken-Flavor Bouillon
Cubes
½ teaspoon dried thyme leaves,
crushed
¼ teaspoon onion powder
1 cup *each* thin strips carrots,
red pepper, yellow squash
and zucchini

In large skillet, brown chicken in oil.
Add water, bouillon, thyme, onion
powder and carrots. Cover; simmer
10 minutes. Add remaining vegetables;
cover and cook 5 to 10 minutes longer or
until tender. Refrigerate leftovers.

Makes 4 servings

Nutrients per serving:			
Calories	216	Cholesterol	80 mg
Fat	7 g	Sodium	513 mg

LASAGNA

1 cup chopped onions
3 cloves garlic, minced
2 tablespoons CRISCO®
   PURITAN® Oil
1 pound extra lean ground beef
2 cans (14½ ounces *each*)
   no-salt-added stewed
   tomatoes
1 can (6 ounces) no-salt-added
   tomato paste
2 teaspoons dried basil leaves
1 teaspoon dried oregano leaves
½ teaspoon sugar
¼ teaspoon black pepper
2 cups low-fat cottage cheese
½ cup grated Parmesan cheese,
   divided
¼ cup chopped parsley
8 ounces wide lasagna noodles
1 cup (4 ounces) shredded
   low-moisture part-skim
   mozzarella cheese, divided

Sauté onions and garlic in Crisco®
Puritan® Oil in large skillet on medium
heat until soft. Push to one side of
skillet. Add ground beef. Cook, stirring
well, to crumble beef. Drain, if
necessary. Add tomatoes. Break into
smaller pieces. Add tomato paste, basil,
oregano, sugar and pepper. Simmer
30 minutes. Combine cottage cheese,
¼ cup Parmesan cheese and parsley.
Set aside.

Cook lasagna noodles 7 minutes in
unsalted boiling water. Drain well. Heat
oven to 350°F. Place thin layer of meat
sauce in 13×9×2-inch pan. Add, in
layers, half the noodles, half the cottage
cheese mixture, 2 tablespoons Parmesan
cheese, ⅓ cup mozzarella and thin
layer of sauce. Repeat noodle and
cheese layers. Top with remaining sauce
and remaining ⅓ cup mozzarella. Bake
at 350°F for 45 minutes. Let stand 15
minutes before serving. Cut into 3×4-
inch rectangles. *Makes 12 servings*

Nutrients per serving:

Calories	270	Cholesterol	55 mg
Fat	10 g	Sodium	300 mg

CHICKEN PICANTE

½ cup medium-hot chunky taco
   sauce
¼ cup Dijon-style mustard
2 tablespoons fresh lime juice
3 whole chicken breasts, split,
   skinned and boned
2 tablespoons butter or
   margarine
   Chopped cilantro for garnish
   Plain nonfat yogurt

Combine taco sauce, mustard and lime
juice in large bowl. Add chicken, turning
to coat. Cover; marinate in refrigerator at
least 30 minutes.

Melt butter in large skillet over medium
heat until foamy. Remove chicken from
marinade; reserve marinade. Add
chicken to skillet; cook about 10 minutes
or until brown on both sides. Add
marinade; cook about 5 minutes or until
chicken is tender and marinade glazes
chicken. Remove chicken to serving
platter. Boil marinade over high heat
1 minute; pour over chicken. Garnish
with cilantro. Serve with yogurt.

Makes 6 servings

Nutrients per serving:

Calories	194	Cholesterol	73 mg
Fat	8 g	Sodium	329 mg

Favorite recipe from **National Broiler
Council**

Chicken Picante

Herb Marinated Chicken Breasts

of broiler pan. Broil 4 to 6 minutes on each side or until tender, brushing frequently with dressing mixture.

Makes 6 servings

Prep time: 15 minutes plus refrigerating
Cook time: 12 minutes

Nutrients per serving:

Calories	170	Cholesterol	55 mg
Fat	7 g	Sodium	110 mg

HERB MARINATED CHICKEN BREASTS

¾ cup MIRACLE WHIP® Salad
   Dressing
¼ cup dry white wine
2 garlic cloves, minced
2 tablespoons finely chopped
   green onion
2 teaspoons dried basil leaves,
   crushed
1 teaspoon dried thyme leaves,
   crushed
6 boneless skinless chicken
   breast halves (about
   1¾ pounds)

Stir together salad dressing, wine and seasonings. Pour dressing mixture over chicken. Cover; refrigerate several hours or overnight. Drain, reserving dressing mixture. Place chicken on greased rack

SPAGHETTI AND BACON TOSS

1 small zucchini, sliced
4 green onions, chopped
1 (8-ounce) carton plain nonfat
   yogurt
½ cup canned white sauce
¼ cup skim milk
8 ounces uncooked spaghetti,
   cooked according to
   package directions omitting
   salt and drained
1 (12-ounce) package ARMOUR®
   Lower Salt Bacon slices,
   cooked crisp and crumbled
1 large fresh tomato, seeded and
   chopped

Spray medium saucepan with nonstick cooking spray; place over medium heat. Add zucchini and green onions; sauté until tender. Combine yogurt, white sauce and milk in small bowl; add to vegetables. Cook until heated through and mixture steams. Toss warm spaghetti with bacon; top with sauce. Garnish each serving with chopped tomato.

Makes 4 to 6 servings

Nutrients per serving:

Calories	289	Cholesterol	19 mg
Fat	10 g	Sodium	485 mg

NO–FUSS TUNA QUICHE

1 unbaked 9-inch deep dish
pastry shell
1½ cups low-fat milk
3 extra large eggs
⅓ cup chopped green onions
1 tablespoon chopped drained
pimiento
1 teaspoon dried basil, crushed
½ teaspoon salt
1 can (6½ ounces) STARKIST®
Tuna, drained and flaked
½ cup (2 ounces) shredded
low-fat Cheddar cheese
8 spears (4 inches each) broccoli

Preheat oven to 450°F. Bake pastry shell for 5 minutes; remove to rack to cool. *Reduce oven temperature to 325°F.* For filling, in large bowl whisk together milk and eggs. Stir in onions, pimiento, basil and salt. Fold in tuna and cheese. Pour into prebaked pastry shell. Bake at 325°F for 30 minutes.

Meanwhile, in a saucepan steam broccoli spears over simmering water for 5 minutes. Drain; set aside. After 30 minutes, arrange broccoli spears, spoke-fashion, over quiche. Bake for an additional 25 to 35 minutes, or until a knife inserted 2 inches from center comes out clean. Let stand for 5 minutes. Cut into 8 wedges, centering a broccoli spear in each wedge.

Makes 8 servings

Note: If desired, 1 cup chopped broccoli may be added to the filling before baking.

Prep time: 20 minutes

Nutrients per serving:

Calories	226	Cholesterol	95 mg
Fat	10 g	Sodium	461 mg

No-Fuss Tuna Quiche

Beef Cubed Steaks Provençale

TURKEY BURGERS

1 **pound ground fresh turkey**
¼ **cup BENNETT'S® Chili Sauce**
1 **teaspoon WYLER'S® or
    STEERO® Chicken-Flavor
    Instant Bouillon**

Combine ingredients; shape into patties.
Grill, broil or pan-fry as desired.
Refrigerate leftovers.

Makes 4 servings

Nutrients per serving:

Calories	172	Cholesterol	75 mg
Fat	7 g	Sodium	510 mg

BEEF CUBED STEAKS PROVENÇALE

2 **cloves garlic, minced**
½ **teaspoon dried basil leaves**
¼ **teaspoon black pepper**
4 **lean beef cubed steaks (about
    4 ounces each)**
1½ **teaspoons olive oil**
2 **small zucchini, thinly sliced**
6 **cherry tomatoes, cut in half**
1½ **teaspoons grated Parmesan
    cheese**
  Salt (optional)

Combine garlic, basil and pepper; divide
mixture in half. Press one half of
seasoning mixture evenly into both sides
of beef cubed steaks; set aside. Heat oil
and remaining seasoning mixture in
large nonstick skillet over medium heat.
Add zucchini; cook and stir 3 minutes.
Add tomatoes; continue cooking 1
minute, stirring frequently. Remove
vegetables to platter; sprinkle with
cheese and keep warm. Increase heat to
medium-high. Add 2 of the steaks to
same pan; panbroil to desired doneness,
3 to 4 minutes, turning once. Repeat
with remaining 2 steaks. Season steaks
with salt, if desired. Serve with reserved
vegetables; garnish as desired.

Makes 4 servings

Nutrients per serving:

Calories	223	Cholesterol	81 mg
Fat	10 g	Sodium	60 mg

Favorite recipe from **National Live Stock
and Meat Board**

"GRILLED" TUNA WITH VEGETABLES IN HERB BUTTER

4 pieces heavy-duty aluminum
   foil, each 12×18 inches
1 can (12½ ounces) STARKIST®
   Tuna, drained and broken
   into chunks
1 cup slivered red or green bell
   peppers
1 cup slivered yellow squash or
   zucchini
1 cup pea pods, cut crosswise
   into halves
1 cup slivered carrots
4 green onions, cut into 2-inch
   slices
3 tablespoons butter or
   margarine, melted
1 tablespoon lemon or lime juice
1 clove garlic, minced
2 teaspoons dried tarragon,
   crushed
1 teaspoon dried dill weed
   Salt and pepper to taste
   (optional)

On each piece of foil mound tuna, bell peppers, squash, pea pods, carrots and onions. For herb butter: In a small bowl stir together butter, lemon juice, garlic, tarragon and dill weed. Drizzle over tuna and vegetables. Sprinkle with salt and pepper. Fold edges of each foil square together to make packets.

"Grilled" Tuna with Vegetables in Herb Butter

To grill: Place foil packets about 4 inches above hot coals. Grill for 10 to 12 minutes, or until heated through, turning packets over halfway through grill time.

To bake: Place foil packets on a baking sheet. Bake in preheated 450°F oven for 15 to 20 minutes, or until heated through.

To serve: Cut an "X" on top of each packet; peel back the foil.

Makes 4 servings

Nutrients per serving:			
Calories	235	Cholesterol	70 mg
Fat	9 g	Sodium	519 mg

115

FAST BEEF ROAST WITH MUSHROOM SAUCE

- **1 boneless beef rib eye roast (about 2 pounds)**
- **2 tablespoons vegetable oil**
- **4 cups water**
- **1 can (10¾ ounces) condensed beef broth**
- **1 cup dry red wine**
- **2 cloves garlic, minced**
- **1 teaspoon dried marjoram leaves**
- **4 black peppercorns**
- **3 whole cloves**
  Mushroom Sauce (recipe follows)

Tie roast with heavy string at 2-inch intervals. Heat oil in Dutch oven over medium-high heat. Cook roast until evenly browned. Pour off drippings. Add water, broth, wine, garlic, marjoram,

peppercorns and cloves; bring to a boil. Reduce heat to medium-low. Cover; simmer 15 minutes per pound. Check temperature with instant-read thermometer; temperature should be 130°F for rare. *Do not overcook.* Remove roast to serving platter; reserve cooking liquid. Cover roast tightly with plastic wrap or foil; allow to stand 10 minutes before carving (temperature will continue to rise about 10°F to 140°F for rare). Prepare Mushroom Sauce. Remove strings from roast. Carve into thin slices and top with Mushroom Sauce. Serve with assorted vegetables, if desired. *Makes 6 to 8 servings*

Note: A boneless beef rib eye roast will yield three to four 3-ounce cooked servings per pound.

MUSHROOM SAUCE

- **1 tablespoon butter**
- **1 cup sliced fresh mushrooms**
- **1 cup beef cooking liquid, strained**
- **1½ teaspoons cornstarch**
- **¼ teaspoon salt**
- **2 dashes pepper**
- **1 tablespoon thinly sliced green onion tops**

Melt butter in medium saucepan over medium-high heat. Add mushrooms; cook and stir 5 minutes. Remove and reserve. Add cooking liquid, cornstarch, salt and pepper to pan. Bring to a boil; cook and stir until thickened, 1 to 2 minutes. Remove from heat. Stir in reserved mushrooms and green onion.

Fast Beef Roast with Mushroom Sauce

Nutrients per serving (includes 3 tablespoons sauce):			
Calories	188	Cholesterol	59 mg
Fat	8 g	Sodium	327 mg

Favorite recipe from **National Live Stock and Meat Board**

Pepper-Chicken Fettucini Toss

PEPPER–CHICKEN FETTUCINI TOSS

- **1 package (1 pound) CREAMETTE® Fettucini, uncooked**
- **¼ cup olive or vegetable oil**
- **3 whole boneless skinless chicken breasts, cut into strips (about 18 ounces)**
- **2 large red bell peppers, cut into strips**
- **2 large yellow bell peppers, cut into strips**
- **1 medium green bell pepper, cut into strips**
- **1 medium onion, cut into chunks**
- **2 cups sliced fresh mushrooms**
- **1 teaspoon salt-free herb seasoning**
- **2 tablespoons grated Parmesan cheese**

Prepare Creamette® Fettucini according to package directions; drain. In large skillet, heat oil; add chicken, peppers, onion, mushrooms and seasoning. Cook and stir over medium heat until chicken is cooked through, 8 to 10 minutes. Add hot cooked fettucini and Parmesan cheese; toss to coat. Serve immediately. Refrigerate leftovers.

Makes 12 servings

Nutrients per serving:			
Calories	264	Cholesterol	36 mg
Fat	7 g	Sodium	33 mg

Sweet and Spicy Pork Tenderloin

SINGING SHRIMP WITH PINEAPPLE

1 medium DOLE® Fresh Pineapple

Singing Spice
¼ teaspoon *each*: ground allspice, ground anise seed (optional), ground cinnamon, ground cloves, ground ginger and crushed red pepper flakes

1 pound large shrimp, peeled and deveined
½ teaspoon salt
1 onion, cut into wedges
1 clove garlic, pressed
1 large DOLE® Red Bell Pepper, seeded, sliced
1 teaspoon vegetable oil
¾ cup water
1½ teaspoons cornstarch
2 tablespoons chopped cilantro, divided
2 tablespoons chopped fresh mint leaves, divided

Twist crown from pineapple. Cut pineapple in half lengthwise. Refrigerate half for another use, such as salads. Cut fruit from shell with knife. Cut fruit crosswise into thin slices.

Combine spices in cup. Sprinkle half of spice mixture over shrimp. Sprinkle shrimp with salt.

In 10-inch nonstick skillet, sauté onion, garlic and bell pepper in oil over medium-high heat until tender.

Blend water and cornstarch in cup. Stir cornstarch mixture and remaining spice mixture into skillet.

Arrange shrimp on top of vegetables. Reduce heat. Cover; simmer 5 to 7 minutes or until shrimp are opaque, stirring occasionally. Remove shrimp to serving plate with slotted spoon.

Add pineapple to vegetables in skillet with 1 tablespoon *each* cilantro and mint. Stir until heated through. Serve with shrimp. Sprinkle with remaining cilantro and mint.   *Makes 4 servings*

Prep time: 10 minutes
Cook time: 15 minutes

Nutrients per serving:

Calories	270	Cholesterol	157 mg
Fat	3 g	Sodium	270 mg

SWEET AND SPICY PORK TENDERLOIN

2 teaspoons dried tarragon leaves
½ teaspoon dried thyme leaves
⅛ to ½ teaspoon black pepper
¼ teaspoon cayenne pepper
Dash salt
1 pound pork tenderloin, trimmed and cut crosswise into ½-inch pieces
2 tablespoons margarine, melted
1½ tablespoons honey

In small bowl, combine tarragon, thyme, peppers and salt; blend well. Brush both sides of each pork tenderloin piece with margarine; sprinkle both sides with seasoning mixture. Arrange tenderloin pieces on broiler pan. Broil 5 to 6 inches from heat source for 2 minutes per side. Remove from broiler. Brush top side of each piece with honey. Broil for an additional minute. Place pork pieces on serving plate.   *Makes 4 servings*

Nutrients per serving:

Calories	219	Cholesterol	79 mg
Fat	10 g	Sodium	158 mg

Favorite recipe from **National Pork Producers Council**

119

SAUCY STUFFED PEPPERS

6 medium green peppers
1¼ cups water
2 cups low-sodium tomato juice, divided
1 can (6 ounces) tomato paste
1 teaspoon dried oregano leaves, crushed, divided
½ teaspoon dried basil leaves, crushed
½ teaspoon garlic powder, divided
1 pound lean ground chuck
1½ cups QUAKER® Oats (quick or old fashioned, uncooked)
1 medium tomato, chopped
¼ cup chopped carrot
¼ cup chopped onion

Heat oven to 350°F. Cut peppers lengthwise in half. Remove membrane and seeds; set aside. In large saucepan, combine water, 1 cup tomato juice, tomato paste, ½ teaspoon oregano, basil and ¼ teaspoon garlic powder. Simmer 10 to 15 minutes.

Combine beef, oats, remaining 1 cup tomato juice, ½ teaspoon oregano and ¼ teaspoon garlic powder with tomato, carrot and onion; mix well. Fill each pepper half with about ⅓ cup meat mixture. Place in 13×9-inch glass baking dish; pour sauce evenly over peppers. Bake 45 to 50 minutes.

Makes 12 servings

Nutrients per serving:

Calories	170	Cholesterol	30 mg
Fat	9 g	Sodium	140 mg

PAELLA

1 tablespoon olive oil
½ pound chicken breast cubes
1 cup uncooked long-grain white rice*
1 medium onion, chopped
1 clove garlic, minced
1½ cups chicken broth*
1 can (8 ounces) stewed tomatoes, chopped, reserving liquid
½ teaspoon paprika
⅛ to ¼ teaspoon ground red pepper
⅛ teaspoon ground saffron
½ pound medium shrimp, peeled and deveined
1 small red pepper, cut into strips
1 small green pepper, cut into strips
½ cup frozen green peas

Heat oil in Dutch oven over medium-high heat until hot. Add chicken and stir until browned. Add rice, onion, and garlic. Cook, stirring, until onion is tender and rice is lightly browned. Add broth, tomatoes, tomato liquid, paprika, ground red pepper, and saffron. Bring to a boil over high heat; stir. Reduce heat to low; cover and simmer 10 minutes. Add shrimp, pepper strips, and peas. Cover and simmer 10 minutes or until rice is tender and liquid is absorbed.

Makes 6 servings

*If using medium grain rice, use 1¼ cups broth; if using parboiled rice, use 1¾ cups broth.

Nutrients per serving:

Calories	253	Cholesterol	82 mg
Fat	4 g	Sodium	392 mg

Favorite recipe from **USA Rice Council**

STUFFED CHICKEN BREASTS

4 boneless, skinless chicken
   breast halves (about
   1 pound), pounded to
   ¼-inch thickness
½ teaspoon ground black pepper,
   divided
¼ teaspoon salt
1 cup cooked brown rice (cooked
   in chicken broth)
¼ cup minced tomato
¼ cup (1 ounce) finely shredded
   mozzarella cheese
3 tablespoons toasted rice bran*
   (optional)
1 tablespoon chopped fresh basil
   Nonstick cooking spray

Season insides of chicken breasts with
¼ teaspoon pepper and salt. Combine
rice, tomato, cheese, bran, basil, and
remaining ¼ teaspoon pepper. Spoon
rice mixture on top of chicken breasts;
fold over and secure sides with wooden
toothpicks soaked in water. Wipe off
outsides of chicken breasts with paper
towel.

Coat a large skillet with nonstick cooking
spray and place over medium-high heat
until hot. Cook stuffed chicken breasts
1 minute on each side or just until
golden brown. Transfer chicken to
shallow baking pan. Bake at 350°F for
8 to 10 minutes.   *Makes 4 servings*

*To toast rice bran, spread on baking
sheet and bake at 325°F for 7 to 8
minutes.

Nutrients per serving:

Calories	223	Cholesterol	79 mg
Fat	5 g	Sodium	337 mg

Favorite recipe from **USA Rice Council**

LINGUINE PRIMAVERA

2 tablespoons olive or
   vegetable oil
2 tablespoons lemon juice
1 medium red pepper, cut into
   strips
1 large onion, chopped
1 package (8 ounces) fresh
   mushrooms, sliced
½ pound lean fully cooked ham,
   cut into julienne strips
1 package (10 ounces) frozen
   peas, thawed
1 package (6 ounces) frozen
   snow peas, thawed
1 can (5 ounces) evaporated
   skimmed milk
½ cup shredded Provolone
   cheese, divided
½ of (1-pound) package
   CREAMETTE® Linguine
   Freshly ground black pepper

In large skillet, heat olive oil and lemon
juice. Add red pepper, onion and
mushrooms; cook until tender-crisp. Add
ham, peas, milk and ¼ cup cheese; heat
through, stirring frequently. Keep warm.
Prepare Creamette® Linguine according
to package directions; drain. Combine
hot cooked linguine and vegetable
mixture; toss to coat. Top with remaining
¼ cup cheese. Serve immediately with
freshly ground black pepper. Refrigerate
leftovers.   *Makes 8 servings*

Nutrients per serving:

Calories	273	Cholesterol	22 mg
Fat	8 g	Sodium	493 mg

121

Salads

Left: Sesame Pork Salad
Right: Melon Cooler Salad (page 124)

SESAME PORK SALAD

    3 cups cooked rice
1½ cups slivered cooked pork*
    ¼ pound fresh snow peas,
        trimmed and julienned
    1 medium cucumber, peeled,
        seeded, and julienned
    1 medium red pepper, julienned
    ½ cup sliced green onions
    2 tablespoons sesame seeds,
        toasted (optional)
    ¼ cup chicken broth
    3 tablespoons rice or white wine
        vinegar
    3 tablespoons soy sauce
    1 tablespoon peanut oil
    1 teaspoon sesame oil

Combine rice, pork, snow peas, cucumber, pepper, onions, and sesame seeds in large bowl. Combine broth, vinegar, soy sauce, and oils in small jar with lid. Pour over rice mixture; toss lightly. Serve at room temperature or slightly chilled.   *Makes 6 servings*

*Substitute 1½ cups slivered cooked chicken for pork, if desired.

Nutrients per serving:

Calories	269	Cholesterol	32 mg
Fat	8 g	Sodium	867 mg

Favorite recipe from **USA Rice Council**

Salade Niçoise

MELON COOLER SALAD

½ cup frozen lemonade or
    limeade concentrate, thawed
1 package (8 ounces) Light
    PHILADELPHIA BRAND®
    Neufchatel Cheese, softened
4 cups assorted melon balls

Place lemonade concentrate and
neufchatel cheese in blender or food
processor container; cover. Blend until
smooth. Spoon melon balls into parfait
glasses or individual bowls; top with
cream cheese mixture.

Makes 8 servings

Nutrients per serving:

Calories	140	Cholesterol	25 mg
Fat	7 g	Sodium	125 mg

SALADE NIÇOISE

2 cans (6½ ounces each) tuna in
    water, drained, flaked
8 new potatoes, cooked, sliced
½ pound green beans, cooked
½ pound yellow wax beans,
    cooked
8 radishes, sliced
    Niçoise or pitted ripe olives
    (optional)
    Torn assorted greens
    Herb Dressing (recipe follows)

Arrange tuna, potatoes, beans, radishes,
olives and greens on serving platter or
individual plates. Serve with Herb
Dressing. *Makes 8 servings*

HERB DRESSING

¼ cup fresh basil leaves
1 tablespoon fresh parsley,
    stemmed
1 small shallot
1 container (8 ounces) Light
    PHILADELPHIA BRAND®
    Pasteurized Process Cream
    Cheese Product
⅓ cup skim milk
3 tablespoons white wine vinegar
½ teaspoon salt
½ teaspoon black pepper

Place basil, parsley and shallot in
blender or food processor container;
cover. Process until chopped. Add
remaining ingredients; blend until
smooth.

Prep time: 35 minutes

Nutrients per serving:

Calories	190	Cholesterol	94 mg
Fat	7 g	Sodium	500 mg

QUICK BACON–POTATO SALAD

4 medium potatoes, peeled and cut into ½-inch cubes
¼ cup water
12 slices LOUIS RICH® Turkey Bacon
¾ cup reduced-calorie salad dressing or mayonnaise
1 teaspoon prepared mustard
¼ teaspoon garlic powder
½ small cucumber, diced
½ small onion, chopped

Combine potatoes and water in 2-quart microwave-safe casserole; cover. Microwave at HIGH (100%) 9 to 11 minutes or until tender, stirring halfway through cooking.

Meanwhile, cut turkey bacon into ½-inch pieces. Cook in nonstick skillet over medium heat 8 to 10 minutes or until lightly browned. Combine salad dressing, mustard and garlic powder in large bowl. Add potatoes, turkey bacon and remaining ingredients. Chill before serving.   *Makes 6 servings*

Nutrients per serving:

Calories	210	Cholesterol	25 mg
Fat	9 g	Sodium	450 mg

ORANGE SALAD WITH CINNAMON DRESSING

8 oranges, peeled, sliced
4 cups torn assorted greens
Cinnamon Dressing (recipe follows)

Orange Salad with Cinnamon Dressing

Arrange orange slices and greens on individual salad plates. Serve with Cinnamon Dressing. Garnish with orange peel, if desired.

Makes 8 servings

CINNAMON DRESSING

1 package (8 ounces) Light PHILADELPHIA BRAND® Neufchatel Cheese, softened
⅓ cup orange juice
1 tablespoon honey
1½ teaspoons grated orange peel
½ teaspoon ground cinnamon

Place ingredients in blender or food processor container; cover. Blend until smooth.

Prep time: 20 minutes

Nutrients per serving:

Calories	160	Cholesterol	40 mg
Fat	7 g	Sodium	120 mg

CHEF'S SALAD

1 package (4-serving size)
   JELL-O® Brand Lemon
   Flavor Sugar Free Gelatin
¼ teaspoon salt
¾ cup boiling water
½ cup cold water
   Ice cubes
1 tablespoon vinegar
2 teaspoons reduced-calorie
   French dressing
¼ teaspoon Worcestershire sauce
⅛ teaspoon white pepper
¾ cup chopped tomato
½ cup finely shredded lettuce
2 tablespoons chopped scallions
2 tablespoons chopped radishes
½ cup slivered cooked turkey
   breast
½ cup slivered Swiss cheese

Completely dissolve gelatin and salt in boiling water. Combine cold water and ice cubes to make 1¼ cups. Add to gelatin, stirring until slightly thickened. Remove any unmelted ice. Stir in vinegar, dressing, Worcestershire sauce and pepper. Chill until slightly thickened.

Stir in vegetables, turkey and cheese. Spoon into 3 individual plastic containers or dishes. Chill until firm, about 2 hours.

Makes 3½ cups, 3 entrée servings

Nutrients per serving:

Calories	100	Cholesterol	30 mg
Fat	4 g	Sodium	330 mg

Chef's Salad

CHUNKY CUCUMBER DILL DRESSING

1 cup peeled, chopped
   cucumber, divided
¾ cup plus 2 tablespoons nonfat
   plain yogurt
3 tablespoons fresh dill, chopped
2 teaspoons sugar
2 teaspoons lemon juice
⅛ teaspoon black pepper

In blender or food processor, blend ½ cup cucumber with remaining ingredients. Stir in remaining ½ cup cucumber. Refrigerate or serve over green salad or chicken salad.

Makes about 6 servings

Nutrients per serving (2 tablespoons):

Calories	31	Cholesterol	1 mg
Fat	trace	Sodium	71 mg

Favorite recipe from **The Sugar Association, Inc.**

Ham Tortellini Salad

HAM TORTELLINI SALAD

1 (7- to 8-ounce) package cheese-filled spinach tortellini
3 cups (12 ounces) ARMOUR® Lower Salt Ham cut into ¾-inch cubes
½ cup sliced green onions
10 cherry tomatoes, cut in half
1 cup bottled low-sodium, creamy buttermilk or reduced-calorie zesty Italian salad dressing
Leaf lettuce or butterhead lettuce, washed and drained
¼ cup finely chopped red bell pepper

Cook tortellini according to package directions omitting salt; drain and run under cold water to cool. Combine all ingredients *except* leaf lettuce and red pepper in large bowl. Toss until well blended. Serve on lettuce-lined salad plates. Sprinkle with red pepper. Serve immediately. *Makes 6 servings*

Nutrients per serving:

Calories	165	Cholesterol	39 mg
Fat	4 g	Sodium	545 mg

CHUNKY CHICKEN SALSA SALAD

1 clove garlic, minced
½ pound boneless, skinless
    chicken breasts
1 can (16 ounces) California
    cling peach slices in juice or
    extra light syrup
½ teaspoon chili powder
¼ teaspoon *each* ground cumin
    and seasoned salt
1 head iceberg lettuce, rinsed
    and crisped
1 box (10½ ounces) frozen corn,
    cooked, drained and cooled
1 cup cherry tomatoes, halved
½ cup *each* sliced green onions
    and minced cilantro
1 can (4 ounces) diced green
    chilies, drained

Bring 2 cups water to a boil; add garlic. Poach chicken breasts in water, 10 to 15 minutes, until cooked through. Drain, cool and shred chicken breasts. Drain peach slices, reserving ¼ cup liquid; save remainder for other uses. Cut peach slices in half and set aside. Blend reserved peach liquid with chili powder, cumin and seasoned salt for dressing. Set aside. Cut lettuce into chunks. Toss together lettuce chunks, shredded chicken, reserved peach slices, corn, cherry tomatoes, green onions, cilantro and diced green chilies. Drizzle salad with dressing and toss well just before serving.   *Makes 4 servings*

Nutrients per serving:

Calories	202	Cholesterol	33 mg
Fat	1 g	Sodium	196 mg

Favorite recipe from **California Cling Peach Advisory Board**

LEMON GINGER SAUCE

½ cup MIRACLE WHIP® FREE®
    Nonfat Dressing
2 tablespoons lemon juice
1½ tablespoons firmly packed
    brown sugar
1 teaspoon grated lemon peel
1 teaspoon ground ginger

Mix together ingredients until well blended; refrigerate. Serve over fresh fruit.   *Makes ½ cup*

Prep time: 5 minutes plus refrigerating

Nutrients per serving (2 tablespoons):

Calories	70	Cholesterol	1 mg
Fat	trace	Sodium	422 mg

CREAMY FRUIT MOLD

1 package (0.3 ounces)
    sugar-free lime flavor gelatin
1 cup boiling water
1 cup PET® Light Evaporated
    Skimmed Milk
2 cups cut-up fresh fruit*

Dissolve gelatin in boiling water. Cool slightly to prevent milk from curdling. Stir in evaporated skimmed milk. Chill until the consistency of unbeaten egg whites. Stir in fruit. Pour into an 8-inch square pan or a 5-cup mold. Chill until firm. Garnish with additional fruit.
    Makes 7 servings

*Suggested fresh fruit: apples, Bing cherries, oranges, peaches or strawberries.

Nutrients per serving:

Calories	51	Cholesterol	1 mg
Fat	0 g	Sodium	77 mg

Lemon Ginger Sauce

Springtime Vegetable Slaw

SPRINGTIME VEGETABLE SLAW

- 1 pound shredded DOLE® Cabbage
- 1 cup grated DOLE® Carrots
- ½ cup DOLE® Broccoli florettes, chopped
- ½ cup halved cherry tomatoes
- ½ cup sliced DOLE® Celery
- ½ cup peeled, seeded, diced cucumber
- 1 cup chopped parsley
- ⅓ cup olive oil
- 2 tablespoons vinegar
- 1 tablespoon Dijon-style mustard
- 1 teaspoon garlic salt

Combine cabbage, carrots, broccoli, tomatoes, celery and cucumber in large salad bowl. Whisk together remaining ingredients for dressing. Pour over vegetables; toss to coat well.

Makes 10 servings

Nutrients per serving:

Calories	87	Cholesterol	0 mg
Fat	7 g	Sodium	147 mg

APPLE SALAD

⅓ cup MIRACLE WHIP® FREE®
  Nonfat Dressing
1 tablespoon apple juice
2 teaspoons peanut butter
⅛ teaspoon ground cinnamon
2 small apples, chopped
1 can (8 ounces) pineapple
  chunks, drained
½ cup *each* KRAFT® Miniature
  Marshmallows and grapes

Mix dressing, juice, peanut butter and
cinnamon until well blended. Stir in
remaining ingredients; refrigerate.

Makes 3½ cups

Prep time: 10 minutes plus
refrigerating

Nutrients per serving (½ cup):

Calories	100	Cholesterol	0 mg
Fat	1 g	Sodium	160 mg

ORIENTAL GINGER DRESSING

½ cup pineapple juice
1 tablespoon sugar
2 tablespoons cider vinegar
1 tablespoon soy sauce
1 teaspoon fresh ginger, grated
½ teaspoon sesame oil

Combine all ingredients in jar with tight-
fitting lid. Cover and shake vigorously
until combined. Chill and shake again
before serving. Serve over green salad,
chicken salad or pasta salad.

Makes 4 servings

Nutrients per serving (2 tablespoons):

Calories	38	Cholesterol	0 mg
Fat	1 g	Sodium	258 mg

Favorite recipe from **The Sugar
Association, Inc.**

CITRUS CHEESE SALAD

½ cup BORDEN® Lite-line® or
  VIVA® Lowfat Cottage
  Cheese
1 slice BORDEN® Lite-line®
  Process Cheese Product, any
  flavor, cut into small pieces*
2 tablespoons chopped
  cucumber
½ fresh grapefruit, pared and
  sectioned
  Lettuce leaf

In small bowl, combine cottage cheese,
Lite-line® pieces and cucumber. On
salad plate, arrange grapefruit on
lettuce. Top with cheese mixture.
Refrigerate leftovers.

Makes 1 serving

*"½ the calories" 8% milkfat version

Nutrients per serving:

Calories	200	Cholesterol	15 mg
Fat	3 g	Sodium	714 mg

Citrus Cheese Salad

WARM TURKEY SALAD

1 medium DOLE® Fresh
    Pineapple
4 ounces green beans or
    broccoli, steamed
2 DOLE® Carrots, slivered or
    sliced
½ cup slivered jicama or radishes
½ cup slivered DOLE® Red Bell
    Pepper
    DOLE® Salad Greens
    Salt and pepper to taste
2 turkey cutlets (½ pound)
1 tablespoon vegetable oil
    Lite Honey Mustard Dressing
    (recipe follows)

Twist crown from pineapple. Cut pineapple in half lengthwise. Refrigerate half for another use, such as fruit salads. Cut remaining half in half lengthwise. Remove fruit from shells with knife. Cut each quarter into 4 spears. Arrange pineapple, green beans, carrots, jicama and red bell pepper on 2 dinner plates lined with salad greens, leaving space for sautéed turkey. Lightly salt and pepper turkey. In medium skillet, brown turkey on both sides in oil. Cover; simmer 5 to 7 minutes. Add 1 tablespoon water if needed. Remove from skillet. Cut turkey crosswise into 4 or 5 slices. Arrange on salad plates with pineapple and vegetables. Serve with Lite Honey Mustard Dressing. *Makes 2 servings*

LITE HONEY MUSTARD DRESSING

¼ cup cholesterol-free
    reduced-calorie mayonnaise
1 to 2 tablespoons pineapple
    juice or orange juice
1 teaspoon honey
1 teaspoon Dijon-style mustard
¼ teaspoon dried tarragon,
    crumbled

Combine all ingredients in small bowl.

Nutrients per serving:			
Calories	267	Cholesterol	30 mg
Fat	10 g	Sodium	233 mg

Warm Turkey Salad

LIGHT PASTA SALAD

½ cup MIRACLE WHIP®
    LIGHT Reduced Calorie
    Salad Dressing
½ cup KRAFT® "Zesty" Italian
    Reduced Calorie Dressing
2 cups (6 ounces) corkscrew
    noodles, cooked, drained
1 cup broccoli florettes, partially
    cooked
½ cup chopped green bell pepper
½ cup chopped tomato
¼ cup green onion slices

Mix dressings in large bowl until well
blended. Add remaining ingredients; mix
lightly. Refrigerate. Serve with freshly
ground black pepper, if desired.

Makes 4 servings

Nutrients per serving:

Calories	260	Cholesterol	0 mg
Fat	9 g	Sodium	450 mg

THOUSAND ISLAND DRESSING

⅔ cup PET® Light Evaporated
    Skimmed Milk
⅔ cup bottled chili sauce
⅔ cup safflower oil
¼ cup sweet pickle relish
1 tablespoon lemon juice
1 tablespoon sugar
1 teaspoon salt
⅛ teaspoon ground black pepper

Using a wire whisk, combine all
ingredients in a small bowl. Refrigerate
until well chilled. Serve over tossed
green salad. *Makes about 2 cups*

Nutrients per serving (1 tablespoon):

Calories	54	Cholesterol	0 mg
Fat	5 g	Sodium	129 mg

Curried Fruit and Rice Salad

CURRIED FRUIT AND RICE SALAD

2 cups cooked rice, chilled
1 DOLE® Orange, sliced and
    quartered
1 cup halved seedless red
    DOLE® Grapes
⅓ cup mayonnaise
⅓ cup vanilla yogurt
½ teaspoon curry powder, or to
    taste
Zest and juice from 1 lime
1 DOLE® Banana, peeled, sliced

Combine rice, orange and grapes in
large bowl. Combine mayonnaise,
yogurt, curry, lime zest and juice; stir
dressing into rice mixture. Fold in
banana just before serving.

Makes 6 servings

Nutrients per serving:

Calories	189	Cholesterol	9 mg
Fat	10 g	Sodium	76 mg

Zesty Pasta Salad

ZESTY PASTA SALAD

2 cups (8 ounces) ARMOUR®
   Lower Salt Ham cut into
   julienne strips
2 cups pasta bow ties or shells,
   cooked according to
   package directions omitting
   salt and drained
8 ounces California-blend frozen
   vegetables, thawed
5 cherry tomatoes, cut in half
¾ cup bottled low-sodium,
   reduced-calorie zesty Italian
   salad dressing
4 cups mixed greens, washed and
   drained

Combine ham, pasta, vegetables,
tomatoes and salad dressing in large
bowl; toss to coat well. Cover; refrigerate
at least 1 hour before serving to blend
flavors. To serve, arrange pasta mixture
in lettuce-lined bowl or on platter.

Makes 6 servings

Nutrients per serving:

Calories	233	Cholesterol	19 mg
Fat	3 g	Sodium	344 mg

TACO SALAD

2 packages (4-serving size) or
   1 package (8-serving size)
   JELL-O® Brand Lemon
   Flavor Sugar Free Gelatin
2 cups boiling water
1 cup frozen corn
1 cup canned kidney beans,
   drained
½ cup medium salsa
¼ cup (1 ounce) grated Cheddar
   cheese
2 tablespoons vinegar
½ teaspoon chili powder

Completely dissolve gelatin in boiling
water. Chill until slightly thickened. Stir
in remaining ingredients. Spoon into
4 individual plastic containers or dishes.
Chill until firm, about 2 hours.

Makes 4 servings

Nutrients per serving:

Calories	140	Cholesterol	10 mg
Fat	4 g	Sodium	560 mg

FIESTA CORN SALAD

1 can (14½ to 15½ ounces) dark
   red kidney beans or black
   beans, drained, rinsed
1 package (10 ounces) frozen
   whole kernel corn, thawed
   (about 2 cups)
1 medium tomato, peeled,
   seeded, chopped
¼ cup sliced green onions
1 jalapeño pepper, minced
¼ cup HEINZ® Chili Sauce
3 tablespoons vegetable oil
2 tablespoons HEINZ® Apple
   Cider Vinegar
1 teaspoon chili powder
½ teaspoon cumin
¼ teaspoon salt
⅛ teaspoon black pepper
   Lettuce leaves

In large bowl, combine beans, corn,
tomato, green onions and jalapeño
pepper. In small bowl, combine chili
sauce and remaining ingredients except
lettuce leaves; pour over bean mixture
and stir to coat. Chill. Serve on lettuce
leaves. *Makes 4 to 6 servings*

Nutrients per serving:

Calories	190	Cholesterol	0 mg
Fat	8 g	Sodium	511 mg

CONFETTI RICE SALAD

2 chicken-flavored bouillon
  cubes
1 cup long grain white rice,
  uncooked
1 can (16 ounces) California
  cling peach slices in juice or
  extra light syrup
3 tablespoons tarragon-flavored
  white wine vinegar
1 tablespoon Dijon-style mustard
1 tablespoon olive oil
¼ teaspoon dried tarragon
1 cup chopped red bell peppers
½ cup frozen peas, thawed
⅓ cup raisins
¼ cup sliced green onions

In medium saucepan, combine bouillon cubes and 2 cups water; bring mixture to a boil. Stir in rice. Cover and simmer 20 minutes, until liquid is absorbed and rice is tender. Remove from heat; cool 5 minutes. Drain peaches, reserving ¼ cup liquid. Save remainder for other uses. Cut peach slices in half and set aside. Mix reserved peach liquid with vinegar, mustard, olive oil and tarragon. Stir into cooled rice; add remaining ingredients *except* reserved peaches. Cool completely, tossing occasionally. Stir in reserved peaches and chill before serving. *Makes 6 servings*

Nutrients per serving:

Calories	210	Cholesterol	trace
Fat	3 g	Sodium	317 mg

Favorite recipe from **California Cling Peach Advisory Board**

CHINESE CHICKEN SALAD

3 cups cooked rice, cooled
1 cup cooked chicken breast
  cubes
1 cup sliced celery
1 can (8 ounces) sliced water
  chestnuts, drained
1 cup fresh bean sprouts*
½ cup (about 2 ounces) sliced
  fresh mushrooms
¼ cup sliced green onions
¼ cup diced red bell pepper
3 tablespoons lemon juice
2 tablespoons reduced-sodium
  soy sauce
2 tablespoons sesame oil
2 teaspoons grated fresh ginger
  root
¼ to ½ teaspoon ground white
  pepper
Lettuce leaves

Combine rice, chicken, celery, water chestnuts, bean sprouts, mushrooms, onions, and red pepper in large bowl. Combine lemon juice, soy sauce, oil, ginger root, and white pepper in small jar with lid. Pour over rice mixture; toss lightly. Serve on lettuce leaves.

Makes 6 servings

*Substitute canned bean sprouts, rinsed and drained, for fresh bean sprouts, if desired.

Nutrients per serving:

Calories	248	Cholesterol	20 mg
Fat	6 g	Sodium	593 mg

Favorite recipe from **USA Rice Council**

ZESTY BEAN SALAD

1 medium onion, chopped
¼ cup freshly squeezed lemon
 juice
¼ cup vegetable oil
3 tablespoons chopped fresh
 mint
1 medium clove garlic, minced
 Grated peel of ½ SUNKIST®
 Lemon
2 teaspoons sugar
1 teaspoon Dijon-style mustard
¼ teaspoon white pepper
1 cup dry white beans or dry
 garbanzo beans (chick peas),
 cooked, drained*
½ cup chopped red bell pepper
 or tomato
⅓ cup chopped parsley

Combine onion, lemon juice, oil, mint,
garlic, lemon peel, sugar, mustard and
white pepper in large bowl. Stir in
cooked beans; chill well. To serve, stir in
remaining ingredients.

Makes 8 servings

*Bring 1 cup dry beans to a boil in 6 to
8 cups water. Boil 2 minutes. Cover;
remove from heat and let stand 1 hour.
Drain beans and replace water. Bring to
boil; cover and cook over low heat 1½ to
2 hours or until beans are tender. One
cup dry beans yields about 2¾ cups
cooked beans.

Nutrients per serving (½ cup):

Calories	162	Cholesterol	0 mg
Fat	7 g	Sodium	24 mg

MOSTACCIOLI SALAD NIÇOISE

1 package (1 pound)
 CREAMETTE® Mostaccioli,
 uncooked
2 pounds fresh green beans,
 steamed until tender-crisp
2 medium green bell peppers,
 cut into chunks
2 cups cherry tomatoes,
 quartered
2 cups sliced celery
½ cup sliced green onions
10 pitted ripe olives, sliced
2 (7-ounce) cans water-pack
 white tuna, drained and
 flaked
½ cup olive or vegetable oil
¼ cup red wine vinegar
3 cloves garlic, minced
4 teaspoons Dijon-style mustard
1 teaspoon salt-free herb
 seasoning
1 teaspoon dried basil leaves
¼ teaspoon black pepper

Prepare Creamette® Mostaccioli
according to package directions; drain.
In large bowl, combine mostaccioli,
vegetables, olives and tuna. In small
bowl, blend olive oil, vinegar, garlic,
mustard, herb seasoning, basil and
pepper; toss with salad mixture. Cover;
chill thoroughly. Stir before serving.
Refrigerate leftovers.

Makes 16 servings

Nutrients per serving:

Calories	236	Cholesterol	9 mg
Fat	9 g	Sodium	185 mg

Summer Fruit Salad

LANAI PASTA SALAD

1 can (20 ounces) DOLE®
    Pineapple Chunks
3 cups cooked spiral pasta
2 cups sugar peas or snow peas
1 cup sliced DOLE® Carrots
1 cup sliced cucumbers
½ cup bottled reduced-calorie
    Italian salad dressing
¼ cup chopped cilantro or
    parsley

Drain pineapple; reserve ¼ cup juice.

Combine pineapple and reserved juice
with remaining ingredients in large bowl;
toss to coat.   *Makes 6 to 8 servings*

Nutrients per serving:

Calories	181	Cholesterol	0 mg
Fat	trace	Sodium	219 mg

SUMMER FRUIT SALAD

1 DOLE® Fresh Pineapple
2 DOLE® Oranges, peeled, sliced
2 DOLE® Bananas, peeled, sliced
1 cup halved DOLE®
    Strawberries
1 cup seedless green DOLE®
    Grapes
    Strawberry-Banana Yogurt
    Dressing (recipe follows)
    Orange-Banana Yogurt
    Dressing (recipe follows)

Cut pineapple in half lengthwise through
crown. Remove fruit with curved knife,
leaving shells intact. Trim off core and
cut fruit into chunks. In large bowl,
combine pineapple, oranges, bananas,
strawberries and grapes. Spoon into
pineapple shells. Serve with your choice
of dressing.   *Makes 6 servings*

STRAWBERRY–BANANA YOGURT DRESSING

6 DOLE® Strawberries, halved
1 ripe DOLE® Banana, peeled
1 carton (8 ounces) vanilla
    yogurt
1 tablespoon brown sugar or
    honey

In blender or food processor, combine all
ingredients and blend until smooth.

ORANGE–BANANA YOGURT DRESSING

1 DOLE® Orange
1 ripe DOLE® Banana, peeled
1 carton (8 ounces) vanilla
    yogurt
1 tablespoon brown sugar or
    honey

Grate peel from ½ orange. Juice orange
(⅓ cup). In blender or food processor,
combine orange peel and juice with
remaining ingredients. Blend until
smooth.

*Nutrients per serving (with 1
tablespoon Strawberry-Banana Yogurt
Dressing):*

Calories	143	Cholesterol	4 mg
Fat	2 g	Sodium	15 mg

SUNSET YOGURT SALAD

**2 packages (4-serving size) or
1 package (8-serving size)
JELL-O® Brand Orange or
Lemon Flavor Sugar Free
Gelatin
2 cups boiling water
1 container (8 ounces) plain
low-fat yogurt
¼ cup cold water
1 can (8 ounces) crushed
pineapple in unsweetened
pineapple juice, undrained
1 cup coarsely grated carrots**

Completely dissolve gelatin in 2 cups
boiling water. Measure 1 cup and chill
until slightly thickened. Combine
thickened gelatin with yogurt and pour
into a 5-cup serving bowl. Chill until set
but not firm.

Add ¼ cup cold water to remaining
gelatin; then add pineapple with juice
and carrots. Chill until slightly
thickened. Spoon over gelatin-yogurt
mixture in bowl. Chill until firm, at least
4 hours. Garnish with carrot curls,
celery leaves and pineapple slices, if
desired.   *Makes 5 cups, 10 servings*

Nutrients per serving:

Calories	40	Cholesterol	0 mg
Fat	0 g	Sodium	65 mg

SWEET 'N' SOUR VINAIGRETTE

**1 cup white wine vinegar
¼ cup sugar
½ teaspoon dried parsley
¼ teaspoon dry mustard**

Combine all ingredients in jar with tight
fitting lid. Cover and shake vigorously.
Chill and shake again before serving.
Serve over green salad.

Makes 8 servings

Nutrients per serving (2 tablespoons):

Calories	28	Cholesterol	0 mg
Fat	0 g	Sodium	trace

Favorite recipe from **The Sugar
Association, Inc.**

Sunset Yogurt Salad

BLACK BEAN AND RICE SALAD

2 cups cooked rice, cooled to
    room temperature
1 cup cooked black beans*
1 medium tomato, seeded and
    chopped
½ cup (2 ounces) shredded
    Cheddar cheese (optional)
1 tablespoon snipped parsley
¼ cup prepared light Italian
    dressing
1 tablespoon lime juice
    Lettuce leaves

Combine rice, beans, tomato, cheese,
and parsley in large bowl. Pour dressing
and lime juice over rice mixture; toss
lightly. Serve on lettuce leaves.

Makes 4 servings

*Substitute canned black beans, drained,
for the cooked beans, if desired.

Nutrients per serving:			
Calories	210	Cholesterol	0 mg
Fat	1 g	Sodium	560 mg

Favorite recipe from **USA Rice Council**

REUNION FRUIT SLAW

1 can (20 ounces) pineapple
    tidbits in unsweetened
    pineapple juice, undrained
1 container (8 ounces)
    PHILADELPHIA BRAND®
    Soft Cream Cheese with
    Pineapple
½ teaspoon ground cinnamon
8 cups shredded cabbage
1 red apple, chopped
1 green apple, chopped
1 cup halved seedless red grapes

Drain pineapple; reserve 2 tablespoons
juice. Stir cream cheese, reserved juice
and cinnamon in large bowl until well
blended. Add remaining ingredients;
toss lightly. Cover. Refrigerate.

Makes 8 servings

Prep time: 20 minutes plus
refrigerating

Nutrients per serving:			
Calories	200	Cholesterol	25 mg
Fat	9 g	Sodium	100 mg

MEXICAN SURIMI SALAD

12 ounces crab-flavored SURIMI
    Seafood flakes, chunks or
    salad style, well flaked
1 large tomato, halved, seeded
    and diced
¼ cup sliced green onion
¼ cup sliced black olives
1 tablespoon chopped cilantro
    or parsley
¼ cup salsa (purchased or
    homemade)
3 cups salad greens, washed,
    drained, torn into bite-size
    pieces

Combine Surimi Seafood, tomato, green
onion, olives and cilantro in medium
bowl. Add salsa; toss gently to combine.
Arrange salad greens on 4 plates and
divide seafood mixture over greens.

Makes 4 servings

Nutrients per serving:			
Calories	122	Cholesterol	17 mg
Fat	3 g	Sodium	794 mg

Favorite recipe from **Surimi Seafood Education Center**

Black Bean and Rice Salad

PASTA PRIMAVERA SALAD

1 package (8 ounces or 2 cups)
    elbow macaroni, cooked,
    drained
2 cups DOLE® Broccoli florettes
2 cups sliced DOLE® Celery
1 cup sliced DOLE® Carrots
½ cup sliced green onions
½ cup diced green bell pepper
1 cup light sour cream
½ cup reduced-calorie
    mayonnaise
1 teaspoon dried dill weed
1 teaspoon garlic salt

Pasta Primavera Salad

Combine cooked macaroni, broccoli,
celery, carrots, onions and green pepper
in large bowl. For dressing, combine
remaining ingredients in small bowl.
Pour over pasta mixture; toss to coat
well. Refrigerate.   *Makes 6 servings*

Prep time: 20 minutes
Cook time: 10 minutes

Nutrients per serving:

Calories	240	Cholesterol	24 mg
Fat	7 g	Sodium	346 mg

GREEN BEAN, NEW POTATO AND HAM SALAD

3 pounds new potatoes,
    quartered
⅔ cup cold water
1 pound green beans, halved
¾ cup MIRACLE WHIP® FREE®
    Nonfat Dressing
⅓ cup stone-ground mustard
2 tablespoons red wine vinegar
2 cups OSCAR MAYER® Ham
    cubes
½ cup chopped green onions

Place potatoes and water in 3-quart
casserole; cover. Microwave on HIGH
(100%) 13 minutes. Stir in beans.
Microwave on HIGH 7 to 13 minutes or
until tender; drain. Mix dressing,
mustard and vinegar in large bowl until
well blended. Add potatoes, beans and
remaining ingredients; mix lightly.
Refrigerate.   *Makes 12 cups*

Prep time: 15 minutes plus
refrigerating
Microwave cook time: 26 minutes

Nutrients per serving (¾ cup):

Calories	100	Cholesterol	5 mg
Fat	1 g	Sodium	428 mg

CUCUMBER AND ONION SALAD

½ cup MIRACLE WHIP® FREE®
   Nonfat Dressing
4 cucumbers, peeled, halved
   lengthwise, seeded, sliced
2 onions, sliced, halved
½ cup thin red bell pepper strips

Mix together dressing, cucumbers and onions in large bowl. Top with peppers; refrigerate.

Makes 12 servings, 6 cups

Prep time: 10 minutes plus refrigerating

Nutrients per serving (½ cup):

Calories	30	Cholesterol	0 mg
Fat	trace	Sodium	143 mg

CANTALOUPE DRESSING

1 cup cantaloupe cubes
½ cup low-fat vanilla yogurt
4 teaspoons sugar

Place all ingredients in blender container or food processor; process until blended. Chill or serve immediately over fruit salad.   *Makes 6 servings*

For a tangier dressing: Substitute ½ cup kiwifruit for cantaloupe. Blend all ingredients as above.

For a thicker dressing: Substitute 1 cup pear cubes for cantaloupe. Blend all ingredients as above.

Nutrients per serving (2 tablespoons):

Calories	36	Cholesterol	1 mg
Fat	trace	Sodium	15 mg

Favorite recipe from **The Sugar Association, Inc.**

Cucumber and Onion Salad

RICE SALAD MILANO

3 cups hot cooked rice
2 tablespoons vegetable oil
2 tablespoons lemon juice
1 clove garlic, minced
½ teaspoon salt (optional)
½ teaspoon dried rosemary leaves
½ teaspoon dried oregano leaves
½ teaspoon ground black pepper
1 small zucchini, julienned*
1 medium tomato, seeded and
   chopped
2 tablespoons grated Parmesan
   cheese

Place rice in large bowl. Combine oil, lemon juice, garlic, salt, rosemary, oregano, and pepper in small jar with lid. Pour over rice; toss lightly. Cover; let cool. Add remaining ingredients. Serve at room temperature or chilled.

Makes 6 servings

*To julienne, slice zucchini diagonally. Cut slices into matchstick-size strips.

Nutrients per serving:

Calories	189	Cholesterol	1 mg
Fat	5 g	Sodium	620 mg

Favorite recipe from **USA Rice Council**

Ziti Salmon Salad

oven; roast for 20 to 25 minutes, or until tender. Cut pepper in half; remove seeds. Pat dry with paper towel. Place bell pepper and remaining ingredients in blender container or food processor; process until well blended. Chill or serve immediately over green salad.

Makes 6 servings

Nutrients per serving (2 tablespoons):

Calories	21	Cholesterol	1 mg
Fat	trace	Sodium	67 mg

Favorite recipe from **The Sugar Association, Inc.**

MICROWAVE OR ROASTED BELL PEPPER DRESSING

1 green or red bell pepper
½ cup buttermilk
2 teaspoons sugar
1 teaspoon parsley sprigs (optional)
¾ teaspoon lemon juice
¼ teaspoon paprika
⅛ teaspoon onion powder
⅛ teaspoon salt
⅛ teaspoon black pepper

Place bell pepper in microwave; heat on High power (100%) 5 minutes or until tender. *Or,* place bell pepper in 375°F

ZITI SALMON SALAD

½ of a (1 pound) package CREAMETTE® Ziti, uncooked
1 (16-ounce) can salmon, drained, skin and bones removed
1 (6-ounce) package frozen snow peas, thawed
1 medium red bell pepper, chopped
1 medium yellow bell pepper, chopped
½ cup sliced green onions
½ cup bottled Italian salad dressing
½ teaspoon salt-free herb seasoning

Prepare Creamette® Ziti according to package directions; drain. In large bowl, combine ziti and remaining ingredients; mix well. Cover; chill thoroughly. Toss gently before serving. Refrigerate leftovers. *Makes 6 to 8 servings*

Nutrients per serving:

Calories	173	Cholesterol	19 mg
Fat	4 g	Sodium	332 mg

SALAD VERONIQUE

1 package (4-serving size)
    JELL-O® Brand Lemon
    Flavor Sugar Free Gelatin
¼ teaspoon salt
1 cup boiling water
¼ teaspoon dried tarragon leaves
¾ cup cold water
1 tablespoon lemon juice
1 cup diced cooked turkey breast
    (white meat)
½ cup green or red seedless
    grapes, halved
½ cup diced celery

Completely dissolve gelatin and salt in
boiling water; add tarragon. Stir in cold
water and lemon juice. Chill until slightly
thickened. Stir in remaining ingredients.
Spoon into 3 individual plastic containers
or dishes. Chill until firm, about 2 hours.
Garnish with grapes and celery leaf, if
desired.   *Makes 3 servings*

Nutrients per serving:

Calories	100	Cholesterol	35 mg
Fat	2 g	Sodium	310 mg

Salad Veronique

GAZPACHO SALAD

1 cup diced tomato
½ cup diced peeled cucumber
¼ cup diced green bell pepper
2 tablespoons diced red bell
    pepper
2 tablespoons thinly sliced
    scallions
2 tablespoons vinegar
¼ teaspoon black pepper
⅛ teaspoon garlic powder
1½ cups tomato juice
1 package (4-serving size)
    JELL-O® Brand Lemon
    Flavor Sugar Free Gelatin
Salad greens

Combine vegetables, vinegar, black
pepper and garlic powder in medium
bowl; mix well and set aside. Bring
tomato juice to a boil in small saucepan.
Pour boiling tomato juice over gelatin in
large bowl; stir until completely
dissolved. Chill until slightly thickened.

Stir vegetable mixture into gelatin
mixture. Pour into 7 individual dishes or
4-cup bowl. Chill until firm, about 3
hours. Serve with salad greens.
          Makes 7 servings

Nutrients per serving:

Calories	25	Cholesterol	0 mg
Fat	0 g	Sodium	220 mg

Tuna and Fresh Fruit Salad

TUNA AND FRESH FRUIT SALAD

Lettuce leaves (optional)
1 can (12½ ounces) STARKIST® Tuna, drained and broken into chunks
4 cups slices or wedges fresh fruit*
¼ cup slivered almonds (optional)

Fruit Dressing
1 container (8 ounces) lemon, mandarin orange or vanilla low-fat yogurt
2 tablespoons orange juice
¼ teaspoon ground cinnamon

Line a large platter or 4 individual plates with lettuce leaves, if desired. Arrange tuna and desired fruit in a decorative design over lettuce. Sprinkle almonds over salad if desired.

For Fruit Dressing: In a small bowl stir together yogurt, orange juice and cinnamon until well blended. Serve dressing with salad.

Makes 4 servings

*Suggested fresh fruit: apples, bananas, berries, citrus fruit, kiwifruit, melon, papaya, peaches or pears.

Nutrients per serving:			
Calories	233	Cholesterol	39 mg
Fat	1 g	Sodium	434 mg

SOUTHWEST SALSA DRESSING

⅔ cup mild salsa*
2 tablespoons nonfat plain yogurt
4 teaspoons sugar
2 teaspoons chopped cilantro (optional)

In small bowl, stir together all ingredients. Or, for a less chunky dressing, blend together in food processor. Refrigerate or serve immediately over green salad, chicken or turkey salad, taco salad or seafood salad. *Makes about 5 servings*

*For a hotter and spicier dressing, use medium or hot salsa.

Nutrients per serving (2 tablespoons):			
Calories	30	Cholesterol	trace
Fat	trace	Sodium	226 mg

Favorite recipe from **The Sugar Association, Inc.**

WILD RICE AND PEPPER SALAD

1 package (6 ounces) MINUTE® Long Grain & Wild Rice
½ cup MIRACLE WHIP® FREE® Nonfat Dressing
2 tablespoons olive oil
½ teaspoon black pepper
¼ teaspoon grated lemon peel
1 cup chopped red bell pepper
1 cup chopped yellow bell pepper
¼ cup ½-inch green onion pieces

Prepare rice as directed on package. Cool.

Mix dressing, oil, black pepper and peel until well blended.

Add rice and remaining ingredients; mix lightly. Serve at room temperature or refrigerate. *Makes 6 servings*

Prep time: 30 minutes

Nutrients per serving (½ cup):			
Calories	140	Cholesterol	0 mg
Fat	5 g	Sodium	284 mg

Black and White Bean Salad

LEMONY APPLE–BRAN SALAD

- ½ cup plain low-fat yogurt
- 1 tablespoon chopped parsley
- 1 teaspoon sugar
- 1 teaspoon lemon juice
- ½ teaspoon salt
- 2 cups chopped, cored red apples
- ½ cup thinly sliced celery
- ½ cup halved green grapes *or*
  - ¼ cup raisins
- ½ cup KELLOGG'S®
  ALL-BRAN® Cereal

In medium bowl, combine yogurt, parsley, sugar, lemon juice and salt. Stir in apples, celery and grapes or raisins. Cover and refrigerate until ready to serve. Just before serving, stir in KELLOGG'S ALL-BRAN cereal. Serve on lettuce, if desired.

Makes 6 servings

Nutrients per serving:

Calories	60	Cholesterol	1 mg
Fat	1 g	Sodium	260 mg

BLACK AND WHITE BEAN SALAD

- ½ cup MIRACLE WHIP® FREE®
  Nonfat Dressing
- 1 can (15 ounces) *each* navy
  beans and black beans,
  drained and rinsed
- ½ cup *each* green bell pepper
  strips and red onion slices
- 1 cucumber, chopped
- 3 tablespoons chopped parsley
  Dash pepper

Mix together ingredients until well blended; refrigerate.   *Makes 4 cups*

Prep time: 10 minutes

Nutrients per serving (½ cup):

Calories	200	Cholesterol	0 mg
Fat	1 g	Sodium	214 mg

MOCK BLUE CHEESE DRESSING

- ¾ cup buttermilk
- ¼ cup low-fat cottage cheese
- 2 tablespoons blue cheese,
  crumbled
- 2 teaspoons sugar
- 1 teaspoon lemon juice
- ¼ teaspoon celery seed
- ⅛ teaspoon black pepper
- ⅛ teaspoon salt
- 4 drops hot pepper sauce

In blender, process all ingredients. Refrigerate. Serve over green salad.
Makes 6 servings, ¾ cup

Nutrients per serving (2 tablespoons):

Calories	33	Cholesterol	3 mg
Fat	1 g	Sodium	148 mg

Favorite recipe from **The Sugar Association, Inc.**

POPPY SEED FRUIT SAUCE

½ cup **MIRACLE WHIP® FREE®
Nonfat Dressing**
1 container (8 ounces)
lemon-flavored low-fat
yogurt
2 tablespoons skim milk
1 tablespoon firmly packed
brown sugar
1 tablespoon poppy seeds

Mix together ingredients until well
blended; refrigerate. Serve over fresh
fruit. *Makes 1⅔ cups*

Prep time: 5 minutes

Nutrients per serving (3 tablespoons):

Calories	70	Cholesterol	trace
Fat	1 g	Sodium	263 mg

PARMESAN CURRY DRESSING

½ cup nonfat yogurt
½ cup buttermilk
1 tablespoon **Parmesan** cheese
1½ teaspoons sugar
1 teaspoon capers
¼ teaspoon black pepper
⅛ teaspoon onion powder
⅛ teaspoon curry powder

Place all ingredients in blender container
or food processor; process until blended.
Makes 6 servings

Nutrients per serving (2 tablespoons):

Calories	27	Cholesterol	2 mg
Fat	1 g	Sodium	52 mg

Favorite recipe from **The Sugar
Association, Inc.**

Poppy Seed Fruit Sauce

TUNA CRACKED WHEAT SALAD

2½ cups water
1 package (8 ounces) wheat pilaf mix
¼ cup lemon juice
¼ cup vegetable oil
2 cans (6½ or 7 ounces each) tuna packed in water
1 cucumber, pared, seeded and diced
½ cup diced carrot
⅓ cup sliced scallions
¼ pound mushrooms, sliced
1 tomato, chopped
½ cup sliced pitted ripe olives
½ cup chopped parsley
½ teaspoon salt
½ teaspoon TABASCO® Pepper Sauce
    Salad greens
    Yogurt Dressing (recipe follows)

In large saucepan, bring water to a boil. Add pilaf mix and reduce heat to low; cover and simmer 15 minutes. Remove from heat; stir in lemon juice and oil. Let stand at room temperature until cool. Stir in remaining ingredients except salad greens and Yogurt Dressing. Cover and chill several hours. Turn into large bowl lined with salad greens. Serve with Yogurt Dressing.

Makes 6 to 8 servings

YOGURT DRESSING

2 cups plain low-fat yogurt
4 teaspoons chopped fresh mint *or* ¼ teaspoon dried dill weed
⅛ teaspoon TABASCO® Pepper Sauce

In small bowl combine yogurt, mint and TABASCO® sauce; mix well. Cover; refrigerate.   *Makes 2 cups*

Nutrients per serving (salad plus two tablespoons dressing):			
Calories	267	Cholesterol	7 mg
Fat	8 g	Sodium	385 mg

SHELLS AND SHRIMP SALAD ALFRESCO

½ of (1-pound) package CREAMETTE® Medium Shells, uncooked
2 cups cooked medium shrimp, shelled, deveined
2 medium fresh tomatoes, peeled, seeded and chopped
2 cups torn fresh spinach
1 cup sliced fresh cauliflowerets
½ cup sliced radishes
¼ cup sliced green onions
2 tablespoons vegetable oil
2 tablespoons lemon juice
1 tablespoon Dijon-style mustard
¼ teaspoon thyme leaves, crushed
¼ teaspoon lemon pepper seasoning

Prepare Creamette® Medium Shells according to package directions; drain. In large bowl, combine shells, shrimp, tomatoes, spinach, cauliflowerets, radishes and green onions. In small bowl, blend oil, lemon juice, mustard, thyme and seasoning; add to salad and toss to coat. Cover; chill thoroughly. Toss gently before serving. Refrigerate leftovers.   *Makes 10 servings*

Nutrients per serving:			
Calories	176	Cholesterol	68 mg
Fat	4 g	Sodium	89 mg

MARINATED VEGETABLE SPINACH SALAD

Mustard-Tarragon Marinade (recipe follows)
8 ounces fresh mushrooms, quartered
2 slices purple onion, separated into rings
16 cherry tomatoes, halved
4 cups fresh spinach leaves, washed and stems removed
3 slices (3 ounces) SARGENTO® Preferred Light Sliced Mozzarella Cheese, cut into julienne strips
Freshly ground black pepper

Prepare Mustard-Tarragon Marinade. Place mushrooms, onion and tomatoes in bowl. Toss with marinade and let stand 15 minutes. Arrange spinach on 4 individual plates. Divide marinated vegetables among plates and top each salad with one fourth of cheese. Serve with freshly ground black pepper, if desired. *Makes 4 servings*

MUSTARD-TARRAGON MARINADE

3 tablespoons red wine vinegar
1 tablespoon Dijon-style mustard
½ tablespoon dried tarragon
2 tablespoons olive oil

Combine first three ingredients in small bowl. Slowly whisk oil into mixture until slightly thickened.

Nutrients per serving:

Calories	186	Cholesterol	11 mg
Fat	10 g	Sodium	334 mg

SPROUT–GREEN BEAN SALAD

3 packages (9 ounces each) frozen French-cut green beans
½ cup CRISCO® PURITAN® Oil
¼ cup white vinegar
2 teaspoons sugar
½ teaspoon salt
¼ teaspoon black pepper
1 can (16 ounces) bean sprouts, rinsed and drained
1 cup thinly sliced celery
¾ cup chopped green onions
1 jar (2 ounces) diced pimento, drained
Cherry tomatoes (optional)

Cook beans in 3-quart saucepan according to package directions. Drain and cool. Blend Crisco® Puritan® Oil, vinegar, sugar, salt and pepper in small mixing bowl. Set aside.

Mix green beans, bean sprouts, celery, onion and pimento in large serving bowl. Stir dressing. Pour over bean mixture. Toss to coat. Cover and refrigerate at least 3 hours. Stir before serving. Garnish with cherry tomatoes, if desired. *Makes 12 servings*

Nutrients per serving:

Calories	112	Cholesterol	0 mg
Fat	9 g	Sodium	160 mg

Vegetables and Side Dishes

Left: Pasta Delight
Right: Tomatoes with Basil Cream
(page 154)

PASTA DELIGHT

1 medium zucchini, sliced
1 tablespoon olive oil
2 tablespoons chopped shallots
2 cloves garlic, chopped
1 medium tomato, diced
2 tablespoons chopped fresh
    basil *or* ½ teaspoon dried
    basil, crushed
2 tablespoons grated Parmesan
    cheese
12 ounces uncooked penne pasta,
    hot cooked and drained

Cook and stir zucchini in hot oil in large skillet over medium-high heat. Reduce heat to medium. Add shallots and garlic; cook 1 minute. Add tomato; cook and stir 45 seconds. Add basil and cheese. Pour vegetable mixture over penne in large bowl; toss gently to mix.

Makes 4 to 6 servings

Nutrients per serving:			
Calories	237	Cholesterol	51 mg
Fat	5 g	Sodium	51 mg

Favorite recipe from **National Pasta Association**

TOMATOES WITH BASIL CREAM

1 clove garlic
1 container (8 ounces) Light PHILADELPHIA BRAND® Pasteurized Process Cream Cheese Product
2 tablespoons white wine vinegar
2 tablespoons chopped fresh basil
2 tablespoons chopped fresh parsley, divided
½ teaspoon salt
¼ teaspoon black pepper
2 red tomatoes, thinly sliced
2 yellow tomatoes, thinly sliced

Place garlic in blender or food processor container; cover. Process until finely chopped.

Add cream cheese product, vinegar, basil, 1 tablespoon parsley, salt and pepper; blend until smooth.

Eggplant Italiano

Arrange tomatoes on serving platter. Spoon cream cheese mixture over tomatoes. Sprinkle with remaining 1 tablespoon parsley. Garnish with fresh basil leaves, if desired.

Makes 10 servings

Prep time: 15 minutes

Nutrients per serving:			
Calories	60	Cholesterol	15 mg
Fat	trace	Sodium	240 mg

EGGPLANT ITALIANO

1 eggplant (1 pound), peeled if desired
1 can (6 ounces) low-sodium cocktail vegetable juice (¾ cup)
½ cup QUAKER® Oat Bran hot cereal, uncooked
2 garlic cloves, minced
1 teaspoon dried basil leaves, crushed
½ teaspoon dried oregano leaves, crushed
2 medium tomatoes, chopped
1¼ cups (5 ounces) shredded part-skim mozzarella cheese

Heat oven to 350°F. Line cookie sheet or 15×10-inch baking pan with foil. Lightly spray with nonstick cooking spray, or oil lightly. Cut eggplant into ½-inch-thick slices; place in single layer on prepared pan. Combine vegetable juice, oat bran, garlic, basil and oregano. Spread evenly over eggplant; top with tomatoes. Sprinkle with mozzarella cheese. Bake 35 to 40 minutes or until eggplant is tender and cheese is melted. Sprinkle with additional basil or oregano, if desired. *Makes 4 servings*

Nutrients per serving:			
Calories	190	Cholesterol	20 mg
Fat	7 g	Sodium	190 mg

Risotto with Peas and Mushrooms

RISOTTO WITH PEAS AND MUSHROOMS

½ cup chopped onion
2 teaspoons margarine
1 cup uncooked rice
⅓ cup dry white wine
1 cup chicken broth
4 cups water
1 cup frozen peas, thawed
1 jar (2½ ounces) sliced
    mushrooms, drained
¼ cup grated Parmesan cheese
¼ teaspoon ground white pepper
⅓ cup 2% low-fat milk

Cook onion in margarine in skillet over medium-high heat until soft. Add rice, stirring constantly 2 to 3 minutes. Add wine; stir until absorbed. Stir in broth. Cook, uncovered, stirring constantly, until broth is absorbed. Continue stirring and adding water, one cup at a time, allowing each cup to be absorbed before adding another, until rice is tender and has a creamy consistency, 20 to 25 minutes. Stir in remaining ingredients. Stir until creamy, 1 to 2 minutes. Serve immediately.   *Makes 6 servings*

Tip: Medium grain rice will yield the best consistency for risottos, but long grain rice can be used.

Nutrients per serving:			
Calories	205	Cholesterol	4 mg
Fat	6 g	Sodium	316 mg

Favorite recipe from **USA Rice Council**

Dilled New Potatoes and Peas

DILLED NEW POTATOES AND PEAS

1 pound (6 to 8) small new potatoes, quartered
2 cups frozen peas
1 jar (12 ounces) HEINZ® HomeStyle Turkey Gravy
½ cup light dairy sour cream
1 teaspoon dried dill weed

Cook potatoes in 2-quart saucepan in lightly salted boiling water 10 to 15 minutes or until tender. Add peas; cook 1 minute. Drain well. Combine gravy, sour cream and dill; stir into vegetable mixture. Heat (*do not boil*), stirring occasionally.

Makes 8 servings, about 4 cups

To Microwave: Place potatoes and 2 tablespoons water in 2-quart casserole. Cover with lid or vented plastic wrap. Microwave at HIGH (100%) 6 to 7 minutes or until potatoes are just tender, stirring once. Stir in peas. Cover and microwave at HIGH 1 minute. Combine gravy, sour cream and dill; stir in vegetable mixture. Cover and microwave at HIGH 7 to 8 minutes or until heated through, stirring once.

Nutrients per serving (about ½ cup):

Calories	126	Cholesterol	6 mg
Fat	1 g	Sodium	332 mg

CHEESE–CRUMB BAKED TOMATOES

¾ cup (3 ounces) finely shredded Wisconsin Part-Skim Mozzarella Cheese, divided
⅓ cup fine, dry, unseasoned bread crumbs
1 to 1½ tablespoons fresh chopped herbs (oregano, parsley, rosemary) *or* 1 to 1½ teaspoons dried herbs
1 large clove garlic, minced
4 tomatoes (about 2½ inches in diameter), cored and cut into 3 slices *each*

In small bowl mix *half* the cheese, bread crumbs, herbs and garlic until thoroughly blended. Arrange tomato slices on oiled baking sheet. Top each with some of the crumb mixture, then with remaining cheese, dividing equally. Bake in 475°F oven 10 to 12 minutes until crumbs are lightly browned.

Makes 4 servings

Nutrients per serving:

Calories	112	Cholesterol	13 mg
Fat	4 g	Sodium	171 mg

Favorite recipe from **Wisconsin Milk Marketing Board** © 1992

LIGHT ITALIAN SPAGHETTI PRIMAVERA

½ of (1-pound) package CREAMETTE® Thin Spaghetti, uncooked
½ cup bottled reduced-calorie Italian salad dressing
1 medium green bell pepper, chopped
1 medium red bell pepper, chopped
1 medium yellow squash, cut into strips
1 cup sliced fresh mushrooms
¼ cup chopped onion
3 tablespoons sliced pitted ripe olives
¼ cup shredded part-skim mozzarella cheese
3 tablespoons chopped fresh parsley

Prepare Creamette® Thin Spaghetti according to package directions; drain. In large skillet, combine Italian dressing, vegetables and olives; simmer just until vegetables are tender-crisp. Serve over hot cooked spaghetti; sprinkle with cheese and parsley. Refrigerate leftovers.

Makes 6 servings

Nutrients per serving:

Calories	205	Cholesterol	8 mg
Fat	5 g	Sodium	218 mg

GUILT–FREE TURKEY GRAVY

4 tablespoons cornstarch
4 tablespoons water
4 cups Turkey Broth and defatted pan juices
Salt and pepper

Light Italian Spaghetti Primavera

In small bowl combine cornstarch and water. In large saucepan over medium heat, bring turkey broth and pan juices to a boil. Stir in cornstarch mixture and continue heating until gravy is thickened. Season to taste with salt and pepper.

Makes 4 cups

To make turkey broth: In large pan over high heat, bring 4 cups water, Turkey Giblets, 1 sliced celery stalk, 1 sliced carrot, 1 sliced onion, 1 bay leaf, 3 parsley sprigs and 4 peppercorns to a boil. Reduce heat to low; simmer for about 1 hour. Strain broth and use to make gravy.

Nutrients per serving (3 tablespoons gravy):

Calories	85	Cholesterol	41 mg
Fat	7 g	Sodium	22 mg

Favorite recipe from **National Turkey Federation**

157

SPINACH FETA RICE

1 cup uncooked long-grain white
  rice
1 cup chicken broth
1 cup water
1 medium onion, chopped
1 cup (about 4 ounces) sliced
  fresh mushrooms
2 cloves garlic, minced
  Nonstick cooking spray
1 tablespoon lemon juice
½ teaspoon dried oregano leaves
6 cups shredded fresh spinach
  leaves (about ¼ pound)
4 ounces feta cheese, crumbled
  Freshly ground black pepper
  Chopped pimiento for garnish
  (optional)

Combine rice, broth, and water in
medium saucepan. Bring to a boil; stir
once or twice. Reduce heat; cover and
simmer 15 minutes or until rice is tender
and liquid is absorbed. Cook onion,
mushrooms, and garlic in large skillet
coated with nonstick cooking spray until
onion is tender. Add mushroom mixture,
lemon juice, oregano, spinach, cheese,
and black pepper to hot cooked rice;
toss lightly until spinach is wilted.
Garnish with pimiento.

Makes 6 servings

To Microwave: Combine rice, broth,
and water in deep 2- to 3-quart
microproof baking dish. Cover and cook
on HIGH (100% power) 5 minutes.
Reduce setting to MEDIUM (50%
power) and cook 15 minutes or until rice
is tender and liquid is absorbed.
Combine onion, mushrooms, and garlic
in 1-quart microproof baking dish coated
with nonstick cooking spray. Cook on
HIGH 2 to 3 minutes. Add mushroom

mixture, lemon juice, oregano, spinach,
cheese, and black pepper to hot cooked
rice. Cook on HIGH 1 to 2 minutes or
until spinach is wilted. Garnish with
pimiento.

Nutrients per serving:

Calories	195	Cholesterol	17 mg
Fat	5 g	Sodium	387 mg

Favorite recipe from **USA Rice Council**

SAUCY SKILLET POTATOES

1 tablespoon MAZOLA®
  margarine
1 cup chopped onions
½ cup HELLMANN'S® or
  BEST FOODS® Light
  Reduced Calorie Mayonnaise
⅓ cup cider vinegar
1 tablespoon sugar
1 teaspoon salt
¼ teaspoon freshly ground black
  pepper
4 medium potatoes, cooked,
  peeled and sliced
1 tablespoon chopped parsley
1 tablespoon crumbled cooked
  bacon or real bacon bits

In large skillet, melt margarine over
medium heat. Add onions; cook 2 to
3 minutes or until tender-crisp. Stir in
mayonnaise, vinegar, sugar, salt and
pepper. Add potatoes; cook, stirring
constantly, 2 minutes or until hot (*do not
boil*). Sprinkle with parsley and bacon.

Makes 6 to 8 servings

Nutrients per serving:

Calories	128	Cholesterol	5 mg
Fat	6 g	Sodium	308 mg

Spinach Feta Rice

ANTIPASTO RICE

1½ cups water
½ cup tomato juice
1 cup uncooked rice*
1 teaspoon dried basil leaves
1 teaspoon dried oregano leaves
½ teaspoon salt (optional)
1 can (14 ounces) artichoke
    hearts, drained and
    quartered
1 jar (7 ounces) roasted red
    peppers, drained and
    chopped
1 can (2¼ ounces) sliced ripe
    olives, drained
2 tablespoons snipped parsley
2 tablespoons lemon juice
½ teaspoon ground black pepper
2 tablespoons grated Parmesan
    cheese

Combine water, tomato juice, rice, basil, oregano, and salt in 2- to 3-quart saucepan. Bring to a boil; stir once or twice. Reduce heat; cover and simmer 15 minutes or until rice is tender and liquid is absorbed. Stir in artichokes, red peppers, olives, parsley, lemon juice, and black pepper. Cook 5 minutes longer or until thoroughly heated. Sprinkle with cheese.

Makes 8 servings

To Microwave: Combine water, tomato juice, rice, basil, oregano, and salt in deep 2- to 3-quart microproof baking dish. Cover and cook on HIGH (100% power) 5 minutes. Reduce setting to MEDIUM (50% power) and cook 15 minutes or until rice is tender and liquid is absorbed. Add artichokes, red peppers, olives, parsley, lemon juice, and black pepper. Cook on HIGH 2 to 3 minutes or until mixture is thoroughly heated. Sprinkle with cheese.

*Recipe based on regular-milled long grain white rice. For medium grain rice, use 1¼ cups water and cook for 15 minutes. For parboiled rice, use 1¾ cups water and cook for 20 to 25 minutes. For brown rice, use 1¾ cups water and cook for 45 to 50 minutes.

Nutrients per serving:

Calories	131	Cholesterol	1 mg
Fat	2 g	Sodium	522 mg

Favorite recipe from **USA Rice Council**

Antipasto Rice

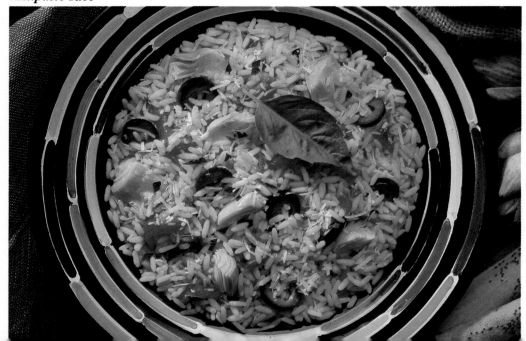

CORN OLÉ

2 tablespoons butter or
    margarine
3 cups chopped fresh tomatoes
2 cups fresh corn, cut off the cob
    (about 4 ears)
2 cups (about ¾ pound) summer
    squash slices, halved
⅓ cup chopped onion
¼ teaspoon black pepper

Melt butter in large skillet. Add
remaining ingredients; cover. Cook 10 to
15 minutes or until squash is tender,
stirring occasionally.

Makes 6 servings

Nutrients per serving:

Calories	111	Cholesterol	0 mg
Fat	5 g	Sodium	59 mg

Corn Olé

ITALIAN CAPELLINI AND FRESH TOMATO

½ of (1-pound) package
    CREAMETTE® Capellini,
    uncooked
2 cups peeled, seeded, finely
    chopped fresh tomatoes
    (about 3 medium)
2 tablespoons olive oil
1 teaspoon basil leaves
½ teaspoon salt
½ teaspoon coarse ground black
    pepper

Prepare Creamette® Capellini according
to package directions; drain. Quickly
toss hot cooked capellini with remaining
ingredients. Serve immediately.
Refrigerate leftovers.

Makes 6 servings

Nutrients per serving:

Calories	196	Cholesterol	0 mg
Fat	5 g	Sodium	170 mg

SUN VALLEY POTATO FRIES

2 large baking potatoes
¼ cup HELLMANN'S® or
    BEST FOODS® Light
    Reduced Calorie Mayonnaise

Preheat oven to 400°F. Cut potatoes into
¼-inch sticks. Spoon mayonnaise into
large plastic food bag. Add potatoes;
shake to coat well. Arrange in single
layer in jelly-roll pan so potatoes do not
touch. If desired, sprinkle with salt to
taste. Bake 20 minutes or until golden
brown and crisp, turning once with
spatula. *Makes 6 servings*

Nutrients per serving:

Calories	75	Cholesterol	3 mg
Fat	3 g	Sodium	3 mg

Alternately thread mushrooms and zucchini on four skewers. Grill kabobs over medium coals about 10 minutes, turning and brushing frequently with dressing mixture. Remove from heat. Thread cherry tomatoes onto ends of skewers. Continue grilling 5 minutes, turning and brushing with remaining dressing mixture. Garnish as desired.

Makes 4 servings

Nutrients per serving:			
Calories	44	Cholesterol	1 mg
Fat	2 g	Sodium	141 mg

CREOLE STUFFED PEPPERS

  6 **large green peppers**
    Boiling water
½ **cup chopped onion**
  1 **tablespoon butter or margarine**
  2 **cups chopped fresh tomatoes**
  2 **cups fresh okra slices**
  2 **cups fresh corn, cut off the cob**
    (about 4 ears)
⅛ **teaspoon black pepper**

Preheat oven to 350°F. Cut off tops of green peppers; remove seeds and membranes. Add green peppers to boiling water in large saucepan; cover. Boil 5 minutes; drain. Cool. Sauté onion in butter. Add tomatoes, okra, corn and black pepper; cook until mixture is thoroughly heated and slightly thickened. Fill green peppers with corn mixture; place in greased shallow baking dish. Bake 30 minutes or until green peppers are tender. *Makes 6 servings*

Nutrients per serving:			
Calories	119	Cholesterol	0 mg
Fat	3 g	Sodium	39 mg

Creole Stuffed Peppers

GRILLED VEGETABLE KABOBS

12 **large fresh mushrooms**
    Boiling water
¼ **cup Italian dressing**
  2 **tablespoons fresh lemon or**
    lime juice
1½ **teaspoons Worcestershire**
    sauce
  2 **medium zucchini, cut into**
    1-inch diagonal slices
  4 **cherry tomatoes**

Place mushrooms in medium bowl; cover with boiling water. Let stand 1 minute; drain. Combine dressing, lemon juice and Worcestershire sauce in small bowl.

PENNE WITH ARTICHOKES

    1 package (10 ounces) frozen
      artichokes
1¼ cups water
    2 tablespoons lemon juice
    5 cloves garlic, minced
    2 tablespoons olive oil, divided
    2 ounces sun-dried tomatoes in
      oil, drained
    2 small dried hot red peppers,
      crushed
    2 tablespoons chopped parsley
  ¼ teaspoon salt
  ¼ teaspoon black pepper
  ¾ cup fresh bread crumbs
    1 tablespoon chopped garlic
  12 ounces uncooked penne, hot
      cooked and drained
    1 tablespoon grated Romano
      cheese

Cook artichokes in water and lemon juice in medium saucepan over medium heat until tender. Cool artichokes, then cut into quarters. Reserve artichoke liquid. Cook and stir the 5 cloves minced garlic in 1½ tablespoons oil in large skillet over medium-high heat until golden. Reduce heat to low. Add artichokes and tomatoes; simmer 1 minute. Stir in artichoke liquid, red peppers, parsley, salt and pepper. Simmer 5 minutes.

Meanwhile, in small skillet, cook and stir bread crumbs and 1 tablespoon chopped garlic in remaining ½ tablespoon oil. In large bowl, pour artichoke sauce over penne; toss gently to coat. Sprinkle with bread crumb mixture and cheese.

Makes 4 to 6 servings

Nutrients per serving:			
Calories	287	Cholesterol	220 mg
Fat	7 g	Sodium	50 mg

Favorite recipe from **National Pasta Association**

Penne with Artichokes

Vegetables Italiano

ASPARAGUS DIJON

1 container (8 ounces) Light
   PHILADELPHIA BRAND®
   Pasteurized Process Cream
   Cheese Product
2 tablespoons lemon juice
2 tablespoons skim milk
1 tablespoon Dijon-style mustard
1½ pounds asparagus spears,
   cooked, chilled

Place all ingredients except asparagus in blender or food processor container; cover. Blend until smooth. Cover; refrigerate. Arrange asparagus on individual salad plates; pour dressing over asparagus. Garnish with lemon peel, if desired.   *Makes 6 servings*

Prep time: 15 minutes plus refrigerating

Nutrients per serving:

Calories	120	Cholesterol	20 mg
Fat	7 g	Sodium	300 mg

VEGETABLES ITALIANO

1 cup Italian seasoned bread
   crumbs
⅓ cup grated Parmesan cheese
⅔ cup HELLMANN'S® or
   BEST FOODS® Light
   Reduced Calorie Mayonnaise
6 cups assorted vegetables:
   broccoli florets, carrot
   slices, cauliflower florets,
   small mushrooms, green
   and/or red bell pepper
   strips, yellow squash slices
   and/or zucchini strips

In large plastic food bag combine crumbs and Parmesan; shake to blend well. In another large plastic food bag combine mayonnaise and vegetables; shake to coat well. Add mayonnaise-coated vegetables, half at a time, to crumb mixture; shake to coat well. Arrange in single layer on ungreased cookie sheet so that pieces do not touch. Bake in 425°F oven 10 minutes or until golden.   *Makes 8 servings*

Nutrients per serving:

Calories	119	Cholesterol	6 mg
Fat	5 g	Sodium	258 mg

SWEET AND SOUR RED CABBAGE

1 small head red cabbage
   (1 pound), shredded
1 medium apple, unpeeled,
   cored, shredded
1 small potato, peeled, shredded
1 small onion, chopped
   Grated peel of ½ SUNKIST®
   Lemon
   Juice of 1 SUNKIST® Lemon
3 tablespoons firmly packed
   brown sugar
1 tablespoon red wine vinegar

In large covered nonstick skillet, cook cabbage, apple, potato and onion in 1 cup water over low heat for 15 minutes; stir occasionally. Add remaining ingredients. Cover; cook over low heat an additional 10 minutes, stirring often, until vegetables are tender and mixture thickens slightly.   *Makes 6 servings*

Nutrients per serving (¾ cup):

Calories	74	Cholesterol	0 mg
Fat	0 g	Sodium	11 mg

165

Bacon Pilaf

To Microwave: Place margarine, tomatoes and green onions in large microwave-safe casserole dish. Cook, covered, on HIGH power (100%) for 5 minutes. Add 2 cups water and remaining ingredients; cover. Cook on HIGH power for 5 minutes. Reduce power to MEDIUM-HIGH (70%); cook about 10 to 12 minutes, or until liquid is absorbed. Let stand, covered, 5 minutes. Fluff rice with fork before serving. Garnish as above.

Nutrients per serving:

Calories	197	Cholesterol	8 mg
Fat	8 g	Sodium	175 mg

BACON PILAF

2 tablespoons unsalted margarine or butter
2 medium tomatoes, coarsely chopped
¼ cup sliced green onions
8 slices ARMOUR® Lower Salt Bacon, cooked crisp and crumbled
1 cup uncooked rice
1 teaspoon no-salt-added chicken flavor instant-bouillon

Melt margarine in large skillet or saucepan over medium heat. Add tomatoes and green onions; sauté for 2 minutes. Stir in 2 cups water and remaining ingredients. Heat to boiling; reduce heat and cover. Simmer 20 to 25 minutes, or until liquid is absorbed. Fluff rice with fork. Garnish with parsley, if desired. *Makes 4 to 6 servings*

LEMON HERB BROCCOLI

1 bunch DOLE® Broccoli, cut into florettes
2 tablespoons margarine
3 to 4 tablespoons lemon juice
1 tablespoon Dijon-style mustard
½ teaspoon dried marjoram, crumbled

Steam broccoli over boiling water in saucepan 3 to 4 minutes until tender-crisp.

Melt margarine in another saucepan over medium heat. Blend in lemon juice, mustard and marjoram. Spoon over broccoli. Serve with grilled chicken breasts or broiled fish steaks.
Makes 2 to 3 servings

Prep time: 5 minutes
Cook time: 10 minutes

Nutrients per serving:

Calories	118	Cholesterol	0 mg
Fat	8 g	Sodium	192 mg

GLAZED STIR–FRY HOLIDAY VEGETABLES

2 tablespoons sugar
½ teaspoon grated lemon peel
3 tablespoons fresh lemon juice (1 lemon)
1 tablespoon low-sodium soy sauce
2 teaspoons cornstarch
½ cup water
4 teaspoons vegetable oil
3 cups fresh broccoli florets
1 medium red bell pepper, cut into 1-inch pieces
1 cup peeled, julienne-cut jicama
Lemon zest (slivers of lemon peel)

In small bowl combine sugar, lemon peel, lemon juice, soy sauce and cornstarch. Stir in water; set aside.

Heat oil in large nonstick skillet. Add broccoli and pepper and stir-fry over high heat 2 minutes. Add jicama and cook 1 to 2 more minutes or until vegetables are crisp-tender, adding additional oil, if necessary. Pour lemon mixture over vegetables and continue cooking just until glaze thickens. Toss vegetables to coat thoroughly with glaze. Garnish with lemon zest.

Makes 6 servings, 3 cups

Nutrients per serving (½ cup):			
Calories	95	Cholesterol	0 mg
Fat	3 g	Sodium	72 mg

Favorite recipe from **The Sugar Association, Inc.**

GREEN BEANS WITH PINE NUTS

1 pound green beans, ends removed
2 tablespoons margarine or butter
2 tablespoons pine nuts
Salt
Pepper

Cook beans in 1 inch water in covered 3-quart saucepan 4 to 8 minutes or until crisp-tender; drain. Melt margarine in large skillet over medium heat. Add pine nuts; cook, stirring frequently, until golden. Add beans; stir gently to coat beans with margarine. Season with salt and pepper to taste.

Makes 4 servings

Nutrients per serving:			
Calories	127	Cholesterol	0 mg
Fat	10 g	Sodium	1 mg

Green Beans with Pine Nuts

Shrimp Stuffing

SHRIMP STUFFING

1 pound raw shrimp, cleaned,
    quartered
2 tablespoons margarine
1 package (6 oz.) KELLOGG'S®
    CROUTETTES®
    Stuffing Mix
½ cup chopped celery
½ cup sliced green onions
¼ cup chopped green pepper
1 can (10¾ ounces) condensed
    cream of mushroom soup
¾ cup water
1 teaspoon dry mustard
1 teaspoon lemon juice
½ teaspoon Cajun seasoning
¼ teaspoon salt (optional)
½ cup (2 ounces) shredded
    part-skim mozzarella cheese

In 12-inch skillet, cook shrimp in margarine over medium heat just until shrimp start to change color.

Stir in remaining ingredients *except* cheese, tossing gently to moisten. Reduce heat to low. Cover and cook 5 minutes. Remove from heat and stir in cheese.   *Makes 8 servings*

To Microwave: In 4-quart microwave-safe mixing bowl, melt margarine at HIGH (100%) 1 minute. Stir in remaining ingredients *except* cheese. Cover with plastic wrap, leaving a corner open as a vent. Microwave at HIGH 9 minutes or until stuffing is hot and shrimp are cooked, stirring every 3 minutes. (When stirring stuffing, carefully remove plastic from bowl to allow steam to escape.) Stir in cheese.

Nutrients per serving:

Calories	220	Cholesterol	95 mg
Fat	7 g	Sodium	827 mg

DELICIOUS SLICED APPLES

½ cup firmly packed brown sugar
2 tablespoons all-purpose flour
   Dash ground cloves
2½ pounds apples, pared, cored
   and sliced (about 8 cups)
¼ cup CRISCO® Shortening
¼ cup water

Combine brown sugar, flour and cloves in large bowl. Stir in apple slices and toss lightly. Melt Crisco® in large skillet. Stir in apple mixture and cook over high heat for 5 minutes, stirring occasionally. Stir in water. Bring mixture to boiling; cover and reduce heat. Simmer for 10 minutes or until apples are tender, stirring occasionally. Serve with roast beef or turkey, if desired.

Makes 6 to 8 servings

Nutrients per serving:

Calories	195	Cholesterol	0 mg
Fat	6 g	Sodium	7 mg

TANGY ASPARAGUS LINGUINI

¼ cup finely chopped onion
3 cloves garlic, minced
8 ounces fresh asparagus, peeled
   and sliced diagonally into
   ½-inch pieces
5 ounces linguini, uncooked
2 tablespoons light margarine
2 tablespoons dry white wine
2 tablespoons fresh lemon juice
   Freshly ground black pepper
¼ cup (1 ounce) SARGENTO®
   Grated Parmesan cheese
¾ cup (3 ounces) SARGENTO®
   Preferred Light Fancy
   Shredded Mozzarella Cheese

Chop and measure all vegetables. Bring water to a boil and cook linguini to al dente stage (firm to the bite). Drain. Meanwhile, melt margarine over medium heat in large skillet. Sauté onion and garlic until onions are soft. Add asparagus; sauté for an additional 2 minutes. Add wine and lemon juice; cook an additional minute. Season with pepper to taste. Remove from heat. In large bowl, toss hot pasta, Parmesan cheese and asparagus mixture. Remove to serving platter; sprinkle with mozzarella cheese. Garnish with strips of lemon zest, if desired. Serve immediately.

Makes 4 servings

Nutrients per serving:

Calories	254	Cholesterol	13 mg
Fat	8 g	Sodium	317 mg

WILD RICE SAUTÉ

½ cup sliced fresh mushrooms
¼ cup chopped green onions
1 clove garlic, minced
2 tablespoons HOLLYWOOD®
   Safflower Oil
3 cups cooked wild rice
¼ teaspoon salt
¼ teaspoon ground black pepper
¼ teaspoon dried rosemary
   sprigs
2 tablespoons peach schnapps
   liqueur

In a large skillet, sauté mushrooms, onions and garlic in hot oil for 1½ minutes. Add rice, seasonings and peach schnapps; cook 1½ minutes longer, stirring frequently.

Makes 6 servings

Nutrients per serving:

Calories	143	Cholesterol	0 mg
Fat	5 g	Sodium	97 mg

MICROWAVE MARINARA SAUCE

2 tablespoons olive oil
½ cup chopped onion
2 cloves garlic, minced
1¾ cups (14½-ounce can)
    CONTADINA® Whole Peeled
    Tomatoes, cut up, with juice
1 cup (8-ounce can)
    CONTADINA® Tomato Sauce
½ teaspoon salt
½ teaspoon dried basil leaves,
    crushed
½ teaspoon dried oregano leaves,
    crushed
    Pasta (tortellini, ravioli,
    spaghetti, fusilli, linguine,
    twists, fettucini, gnocchi or
    small shells), cooked and
    drained

In medium saucepan, heat oil. Sauté onion and garlic over medium-high heat until onion is translucent. Stir in tomatoes and juice, tomato sauce, salt, basil and oregano. Bring to a boil; reduce heat. Cook for 15 minutes, stirring occasionally. Toss with hot pasta before serving.   *Makes about 2 cups*

To Microwave: In 2-quart microwave-safe dish, microwave onion and garlic in oil on HIGH power (100%) for 3 minutes, or until onion is translucent. Stir in tomatoes and juice, tomato sauce, salt, basil and oregano. Microwave on HIGH power for additional 7 to 8 minutes. Toss with hot pasta before serving.

Nutrients per serving (½ cup sauce):

Calories	103	Cholesterol	0 mg
Fat	7 g	Sodium	705 mg

ALMOND BROWN RICE STUFFING

⅓ cup slivered almonds
2 teaspoons margarine
2 medium tart apples, cored and
    diced
½ cup chopped onion
½ cup chopped celery
½ teaspoon poultry seasoning
¼ teaspoon dried thyme leaves
¼ teaspoon ground white pepper
3 cups cooked brown rice
    (cooked in chicken broth)

Cook almonds in margarine in large skillet over medium-high heat until brown. Add apples, onion, celery, poultry seasoning, thyme, and pepper; cook until vegetables are tender-crisp. Stir in rice; cook until thoroughly heated. Serve or use as stuffing for poultry or pork roast. Stuffing may be baked in covered baking dish at 375°F for 15 to 20 minutes.   *Makes 6 servings*

To Microwave: Combine almonds and margarine in 2- to 3-quart microproof baking dish. Cook on HIGH (100% power) 2 to 3 minutes or until browned. Add apples, onion, celery, poultry seasoning, thyme, and pepper. Cover with waxed paper and cook on HIGH 2 minutes. Stir in rice; cook on HIGH 2 to 3 minutes, stirring after 1½ minutes, or until thoroughly heated. Serve as above.

Variations: For Mushroom Stuffing, add 2 cups (about 8 ounces) sliced mushrooms; cook with apples, onion, celery, and seasonings. For Raisin Stuffing, add ½ cup raisins; cook with apples, onion, celery, and seasonings.

Nutrients per serving:

Calories	198	Cholesterol	0 mg
Fat	6 g	Sodium	30 mg

Favorite recipe from **USA Rice Council**

Almond Brown Rice Stuffing

COLORFUL CAULIFLOWER BAKE

1 cup KELLOGG'S®
    ALL-BRAN® Cereal
2 tablespoons margarine, melted
¼ teaspoon garlic salt
¼ cup flour
½ teaspoon salt
⅛ teaspoon white pepper
1⅓ cups skim milk
1 chicken bouillon cube
1 package (16 ounces) frozen,
    cut cauliflower, thawed, well
    drained
½ cup sliced green onions
2 tablespoons drained chopped
    pimento

Combine KELLOGG'S ALL-BRAN cereal, margarine and garlic salt; set aside. In 3-quart saucepan, combine flour, salt and pepper. Gradually add milk, mixing until smooth, using a wire whip if necessary. Add bouillon cube. Cook, stirring constantly, over medium heat until bubbly and thickened. Remove from heat. Add cauliflower, onions and pimento, mixing until combined. Spread evenly in 1½-quart baking dish. Sprinkle with cereal mixture. Bake at 350°F about 20 minutes or until thoroughly heated and sauce is bubbly.

Makes 6 servings

Note: 3½ cups fresh cauliflower flowerets, cooked crisp-tender, may be substituted for frozen cauliflower.

Nutrients per serving:

Calories	120	Cholesterol	1 mg
Fat	4 g	Sodium	508 mg

STUFFED TOMATOES

6 to 8 medium tomatoes
2 tablespoons CRISCO®
    PURITAN® Oil
⅓ cup chopped celery
2 tablespoons chopped onion
2 cups cooked brown rice
¼ cup grated Parmesan cheese
1 tablespoon snipped fresh
    parsley
1 teaspoon dried basil leaves
⅛ teaspoon black pepper
⅛ teaspoon garlic powder

Cut thin slice from top of each tomato. Set aside. Scoop out centers of tomatoes; chop pulp and set aside. Place shells, upside-down, on paper towels to drain.

Preheat oven to 350°F. Heat Crisco® Puritan® Oil in medium saucepan. Add celery and onion. Sauté over moderate heat until celery is tender. Remove from heat. Add reserved tomato pulp, rice, Parmesan cheese, parsley, basil, pepper and garlic powder. Mix well. Fill each tomato shell with rice mixture. Replace tomato tops, if desired.

Lightly oil 9-inch pie plate or round baking dish with Crisco® Puritan® Oil. Place tomatoes in dish. Cover with aluminum foil.

Bake at 350°F for 30 to 45 minutes, or until tomatoes are tender.

Makes 6 to 8 servings

Note: Use 1 lightly oiled custard cup for each tomato instead of pie plate or baking dish, if desired.

Nutrients per serving:

Calories	125	Cholesterol	2 mg
Fat	5 g	Sodium	65 mg

ZUCCHINI AND CARROTS AU GRATIN

¼ cup HELLMANN'S® or
    BEST FOODS® Light
    Reduced Calorie Mayonnaise
¼ cup minced onion
2 tablespoons flour
1 tablespoon chopped parsley
¾ teaspoon salt
¼ teaspoon dried Italian
    seasoning
    Dash freshly ground black
    pepper
1 cup milk
3 medium carrots, sliced,
    cooked and drained
2 medium zucchini, sliced,
    cooked and drained
½ cup fresh bread crumbs
¼ cup grated Parmesan cheese
1 tablespoon MAZOLA®
    Margarine, melted

In 1-quart saucepan combine mayonnaise, onion, flour, parsley, salt, Italian seasoning and pepper. Cook over medium heat 1 minute, stirring constantly. Gradually stir in milk until smooth; cook until thick, stirring constantly (*do not boil*). In medium bowl combine carrots and zucchini. Add sauce; toss to coat well. Spoon into shallow 1-quart broilerproof casserole dish. In small bowl combine bread crumbs, Parmesan and margarine; sprinkle over vegetables. Broil 6 inches from heat source for 3 minutes or until golden. *Makes 4 to 6 servings*

Nutrients per serving:

Calories	134	Cholesterol	12 mg
Fat	7 g	Sodium	420 mg

RISOTTO MILANESE

1 small onion, thinly sliced
1 tablespoon margarine
1 cup uncooked Arborio or
    other short-grain rice
    Pinch saffron
½ cup dry white wine
¼ teaspoon TABASCO® Pepper
    Sauce
2 cups low-sodium chicken
    broth, divided
    Hot water
¼ cup grated Parmesan cheese
    Salt and freshly ground white
    pepper (optional)

In large skillet, sauté onion in margarine over medium-high heat until soft. Add rice and saffron; stir constantly 2 to 3 minutes. Add wine and TABASCO® sauce; stir until absorbed. Stir in one cup of broth. Cook, uncovered, stirring frequently until broth is absorbed. Add remaining broth and hot water, ½ cup at a time, stirring constantly from bottom and sides of pan. (Wait until rice just begins to dry out before adding more liquid.) Continue stirring and adding water until rice is tender but firm to the bite and has the consistency of creamy rice pudding. (The total amount of liquid used will vary. Watch rice carefully to ensure proper consistency.) Stir in cheese and salt and pepper, if desired.

Makes 6 servings

Nutrients per serving:

Calories	178	Cholesterol	3 mg
Fat	4 g	Sodium	94 mg

Cakes and Cheesecakes

Left: Mini-Almond Cheesecakes
Right: Orange Poppy Seed Cake
(page 176)

MINI–ALMOND CHEESECAKES

    ¾ cup ground almonds
     1 tablespoon PARKAY®
        Margarine, melted
     1 envelope unflavored gelatin
    ¼ cup cold water
     1 container (12 ounces) Light
        PHILADELPHIA BRAND®
        Pasteurized Process Cream
        Cheese Product, softened
    ¾ cup skim milk
    ½ cup sugar *or* 12 packets sugar
        substitute
    ¼ teaspoon almond extract
     3 cups peeled peach slices

Stir together almonds and margarine in small bowl. Press mixture evenly onto bottoms of 12 (2½-inch) paper-lined baking cups.

Soften gelatin in water in small saucepan; stir over low heat until dissolved.

Beat cream cheese product, milk, sugar and almond extract in large mixing bowl at medium speed with electric mixer until well blended. Stir in gelatin mixture. Pour into baking cups; freeze until firm.

Place peaches in food processor or blender container; process until smooth. Spoon peach purée onto individual plates.

Remove cheesecakes from freezer 10 minutes before serving. Peel off paper. Invert cheesecakes onto plates. Garnish with additional peach slices, raspberries and fresh mint leaves, if desired.   *Makes 12 servings*

Note: For a sweeter peach purée, add sugar to taste.

Nutrients per serving:

Calories	175	Cholesterol	11 mg
Fat	10 g	Sodium	180 mg

ORANGE POPPY SEED CAKE

1 (8 ounce) container Light PHILADELPHIA BRAND® Pasteurized Process Cream Cheese Product
⅓ cup PARKAY® Margarine, softened
1 cup sugar
3 eggs, separated
2 cups flour
1 teaspoon CALUMET® Baking Powder
1 teaspoon baking soda
1 cup BREAKSTONE'S® LIGHT CHOICE® Sour Half and Half
2 tablespoons poppy seed
1 tablespoon grated orange peel
½ cup sugar *or* 12 packets sugar substitute
½ cup orange juice
3 tablespoons powdered sugar

Preheat oven to 350°F.

Beat cream cheese product, margarine and 1 cup sugar in large mixing bowl at medium speed with electric mixer until well blended. Add egg yolks, one at a time, mixing well after each addition.

Mix together flour, baking powder and baking soda; add to cream cheese mixture alternately with sour half and half. Stir in poppy seed and peel.

Beat egg whites in small mixing bowl at high speed with electric mixer until stiff peaks form; fold into cream cheese mixture. Pour into greased 10-inch fluted tube pan. Bake 50 minutes.

Stir together ½ cup sugar and orange juice in small saucepan over low heat until sugar dissolves. Prick hot cake several times with fork. Pour syrup over cake; cool 10 minutes. Invert onto serving plate. Cool completely. Sprinkle with powdered sugar. Garnish with quartered orange slices, if desired.

Makes 16 servings

Nutrients per serving:			
Calories	228	Cholesterol	48 mg
Fat	9 g	Sodium	157 mg

CHOCOLATE CUPCAKES

6 tablespoons light corn oil spread
1 cup sugar
1¼ cups all-purpose flour
⅓ cup HERSHEY'S® Cocoa
1 teaspoon baking soda
Dash salt
1 cup nonfat buttermilk
½ teaspoon vanilla extract
Powdered sugar

Heat oven to 350°F. Line muffin pans with paper bake cups (2½ inches in diameter). In large saucepan, melt corn oil spread. Remove from heat; stir in sugar. In small bowl, stir together flour, cocoa, baking soda and salt; add alternately with buttermilk and vanilla to mixture in saucepan. Beat with whisk until well blended. Spoon into bake cups.

Bake 18 to 20 minutes or until wooden toothpick inserted in center comes out clean. Remove from pans to wire rack; cool completely. Sift powdered sugar over tops.

Makes 18 cupcakes

Nutrients per serving (1 cupcake):			
Calories	110	Cholesterol	0 mg
Fat	3 g	Sodium	95 mg

CHERRY ANGEL ROLLS

- **1 package DUNCAN HINES® Angel Food Cake Mix**
- **1 cup chopped maraschino cherries**
- **½ cup flaked coconut**
- **1 teaspoon maraschino cherry juice**
- **1 container (8 ounces) frozen whipped topping, thawed Confectioners sugar**

1. Preheat oven to 350°F. Line two 15½×10½×1-inch jelly-roll pans with aluminum foil.

2. Prepare cake mix following package directions. Divide batter into lined pans. Spread evenly. Cut through batter with knife or spatula to remove large air bubbles. Bake at 350°F for 15 minutes or until set. Immediately invert cakes onto towels covered with confectioners sugar. Remove foil carefully. Immediately roll up each cake with towel jelly-roll fashion. Cool completely.

3. Drain cherries, reserving 1 teaspoon juice. Fold cherries, coconut and cherry juice into whipped topping. Unroll cakes. Spread half of filling over each cake to edges. Reroll and place, seam-side-down, on serving plate. Dust with confectioners sugar. Refrigerate until ready to serve.

Makes 2 cakes, 16 servings

Tip: Use clean, lint-free dishtowels to roll up cakes.

Nutrients per serving:

Calories	211	Cholesterol	0 mg
Fat	6 g	Sodium	113 mg

Cherry Angel Rolls

Fudge Marble Pound Cake

CREAMY CITRUS CHEESECAKE

¾ cup crushed graham crackers
2 tablespoons margarine, melted
3 eggs
½ cup sugar
1 teaspoon finely shredded
    orange peel
¼ cup orange juice
3 teaspoons vanilla, divided
2 (8-ounce) packages light cream
    cheese
1 cup DANNON® Plain, Lemon
    or Vanilla Lowfat Yogurt,
    divided
2 tablespoons powdered sugar

In small bowl combine graham crackers and margarine. Press onto bottom of 7- or 8-inch springform pan. Bake at 325°F for 6 minutes; let cool.

In blender container, combine eggs, sugar, orange peel, orange juice and 2 teaspoons of the vanilla. Cut cream cheese into chunks; add to mixture and blend until smooth. Stir in ½ cup of the yogurt. Pour into crust. Bake at 325°F for 50 to 60 minutes or until nearly set.

Combine remaining ½ cup yogurt, powdered sugar and remaining 1 teaspoon vanilla. Spread over hot cheesecake. Loosen sides of pan. Cool on wire rack. Chill before serving. Garnish with orange peel, if desired.

Makes 8 servings

Nutrients per serving:

Calories	186	Cholesterol	88 mg
Fat	8 g	Sodium	286 mg

FUDGE MARBLE POUND CAKE

1 package DUNCAN HINES®
    Fudge Marble Cake Mix
1 package (4-serving size) vanilla
    instant pudding and pie
    filling mix
4 eggs
1 cup water
⅓ cup CRISCO® PURITAN® Oil

1. Preheat oven to 350°F. Grease and flour two 9×5×3-inch loaf pans.

2. Set aside cocoa packet. Combine cake mix, pudding mix, eggs, water and Crisco® Puritan® Oil in large bowl. Beat at medium speed with electric mixer for 2 minutes. Measure 1 cup batter; place in small bowl. Stir in cocoa packet.

3. Spoon half the yellow batter in each loaf pan. Spoon half the chocolate batter on top of each yellow batter. Run knife through batters to marble. Bake at 350°F for 45 to 50 minutes or until wooden toothpick inserted in center comes out clean. Cool in pans 5 minutes. Loosen cakes from pans. Invert onto cooling racks. Cool completely. Cut loaves in ½-inch-thick slices.

Makes 2 loaves, 18 slices each

Nutrients per serving (1 slice):

Calories	86	Cholesterol	24 mg
Fat	4 g	Sodium	108 mg

ROYAL BANANA FRUIT SHORTCAKE

2 extra-ripe, medium DOLE® Bananas, peeled
1 package (18 ounces) yellow cake mix
  Ingredients for cake mix
½ cup DOLE® Sliced Almonds
¾ cup DOLE® Pine-Orange-Guava Juice, divided
1 firm, medium DOLE® Banana, peeled
2 cups assorted sliced DOLE® fresh fruit
¼ cup semisweet chocolate chips
½ teaspoon margarine

Place 2 extra-ripe bananas in blender. Process until puréed. Prepare cake according to package directions, using puréed bananas as part of the liquid measured with water.

Spread batter in 2 greased 9-inch round cake pans. Sprinkle tops with almonds.

Bake and cool as directed. Use one layer for recipe; freeze second layer for future use.

Pour 3 tablespoons fruit juice onto large cake plate. Place cake on top to absorb juice. Pour another 3 tablespoons juice over top of cake.

Slice firm banana and combine with other fruits in small bowl. Reserve 1 tablespoon fruit juice for chocolate sauce; pour remaining juice over fruit. Arrange fruit and juice mixture over cake.

Combine chocolate chips, 1 tablespoon reserved fruit juice and margarine in small microwave-safe bowl. Microwave on HIGH (100%) 10 to 30 seconds or until soft. Stir until smooth. Drizzle over fruit and cake. Refrigerate 30 minutes.

Makes 8 servings

Prep time: 15 minutes
Bake time: 30 minutes

Nutrients per serving:

Calories	208	Cholesterol	81 mg
Fat	7 g	Sodium	60 mg

Royal Banana Fruit Shortcake

CHOCOLATE RASPBERRY CHEESECAKE

1 cup 1% low-fat cottage cheese
¾ cup cold skim milk
⅓ cup seedless raspberry fruit
    spread
1 package (4-serving size)
    JELL-O® Chocolate Flavor
    Sugar Free Instant Pudding
    and Pie Filling
2 cups thawed COOL WHIP®
    LITE® Whipped Topping
1 square BAKER'S® Semi-Sweet
    Chocolate, grated
½ cup raspberries

Process cottage cheese, milk and fruit spread in blender container until smooth. Add pudding mix; blend until smooth.

Pour into large bowl; gently stir in whipped topping. Pour into 8-inch pie plate. Freeze until firm, 6 hours or overnight. Garnish with chocolate and raspberries.   *Makes 8 servings*

Nutrients per serving:

Calories	120	Cholesterol	0 mg
Fat	4 g	Sodium	310 mg

SPICE CAKE WITH FRESH PEACH SAUCE

1 package DUNCAN HINES®
    Moist Deluxe Spice Cake Mix
Sauce
6 cups fresh sliced peaches
1 cup water
⅓ cup sugar
⅛ teaspoon ground cinnamon

Preheat oven to 350°F. Grease and flour 10-inch Bundt® or tube pan. Prepare,

Spice Cake with Fresh Peach Sauce

bake and cool cake following package directions for No-Cholesterol recipe. Dust with confectioners sugar, if desired.

For Sauce, combine peaches and water in large saucepan. Cook over medium heat 5 minutes. Reduce heat. Cover and simmer 10 minutes. Cool. Reserve ½ cup peach slices. Combine remaining peaches with any cooking liquid, sugar and cinnamon in blender or food processor. Process until smooth. Stir in reserved peach slices. To serve, spoon peach sauce over cake slices.

Makes 12 to 16 servings

Tip: Fresh peach sauce can be served either warm or chilled.

Nutrients per serving:

Calories	299	Cholesterol	0 mg
Fat	10 g	Sodium	294 mg

181

LOVELY LEMON CHEESECAKE

1 whole graham cracker, crushed
1 package (4-serving size) JELL-O® Brand Sugar Free Lemon Flavor Gelatin
⅔ cup boiling water
1 cup 1% low-fat cottage cheese
1 container (8 ounces) light pasteurized process cream cheese product, softened
2 cups thawed COOL WHIP® LITE® Whipped Topping
1 cup reduced-calorie cherry pie filling

Spray 8- or 9-inch springform pan or 9-inch pie plate with nonstick cooking spray. Sprinkle sides with half of the graham cracker crumbs. (If desired, omit graham cracker crumb garnish; sprinkle bottom of pan with remaining graham cracker crumbs.)

Completely dissolve gelatin in boiling water in small bowl. Pour into blender container. Add cheeses; blend at medium speed, scraping down sides occasionally, about 2 minutes or until mixture is completely smooth. Pour into large bowl. Gently stir in whipped topping. Pour into prepared pan; smooth top. Sprinkle remaining crumbs around outside edge, leaving center plain. Chill until set, about 4 hours.

Just before serving, decorate top of cheesecake with pie filling. Remove sides of pan and cut.

Makes 8 servings

Nutrients per serving:

Calories	160	Cholesterol	15 mg
Fat	7 g	Sodium	330 mg

BANANA UPSIDE–DOWN CAKE

3 tablespoons margarine
½ cup firmly packed brown sugar
4 firm, medium DOLE® Bananas, peeled, divided
1 egg
½ cup granulated sugar
3 tablespoons vegetable oil
2 tablespoons milk
1 teaspoon vanilla extract
½ teaspoon grated DOLE® Orange peel
1 cup all-purpose flour
1 teaspoon baking powder
½ teaspoon ground cinnamon
¼ teaspoon baking soda
⅛ teaspoon salt

Melt margarine in 9-inch square cake pan 2 to 3 minutes as oven preheats to 350°F. Remove pan from oven; stir in brown sugar. Slice 3 bananas; arrange in single layer in brown sugar mixture. Cut remaining banana into chunks. Place banana chunks, egg, granulated sugar, oil, milk, vanilla and orange peel in food processor or blender. Process until smooth.

In large bowl, combine flour, baking powder, cinnamon, baking soda and salt. Add banana mixture to flour mixture. Stir until blended. Pour batter over bananas in cake pan.

Bake in 350°F oven 30 minutes or until cake tester inserted in center comes out clean. Cool in pan on wire rack 5 minutes. Invert onto serving plate. Serve warm or cool. *Makes 9 servings*

Prep time: 15 minutes
Bake time: 30 minutes

Nutrients per serving:

Calories	271	Cholesterol	31 mg
Fat	9 g	Sodium	137 mg

Lovely Lemon Cheesecake

Danish Orange Loaves

DANISH ORANGE LOAVES

Cake
- 1 package DUNCAN HINES® Moist Deluxe Orange Supreme Cake Mix
- 1 package (4-serving size) vanilla instant pudding and pie filling mix
- 4 eggs
- 1 cup dairy sour cream
- ⅓ cup CRISCO® PURITAN® Oil

Frosting
- 2¼ cups confectioners sugar
- 3 tablespoons butter or margarine, melted
- 2 to 3 tablespoons CITRUS HILL® Orange Juice
- 1 tablespoon grated orange peel

1. Preheat oven to 350°F. Grease and flour two 9×5×3-inch loaf pans.

2. *For Cake,* combine cake mix, pudding mix, eggs, sour cream and Crisco® Puritan® Oil in large bowl. Beat at medium speed with electric mixer for 3 minutes. Pour batter into pans. Bake at 350°F for 50 to 60 minutes or until wooden toothpick inserted in center comes out clean. Cool in pans 15 minutes. Loosen loaves from pans. Invert onto cooling racks. Turn right side up. Cool completely.

3. *For Frosting,* combine confectioners sugar, melted butter and 1 tablespoon orange juice in small bowl. Beat at low speed with electric mixer until blended. Add remaining juice, 1 teaspoon at a time, until frosting is of spreading consistency. Fold in orange peel. Spread frosting over cooled loaves.

Makes 2 loaves, 12 slices each

Tip: This recipe may also be baked in a 10-inch Bundt® pan or tube pan for 50 to 60 minutes or until wooden toothpick inserted in center of cake comes out clean.

Nutrients per serving (1 slice):

Calories	212	Cholesterol	44 mg
Fat	9 g	Sodium	184 mg

CHOCOLATE CAKE FINGERS

1 cup granulated sugar
1 cup all-purpose flour
⅓ cup HERSHEY'S® Cocoa
¾ teaspoon baking powder
¾ teaspoon baking soda
½ cup skim milk
¼ cup frozen egg substitute, thawed
¼ cup canola oil or vegetable oil
1 teaspoon vanilla extract
½ cup boiling water
  Powdered sugar
1 teaspoon freshly grated orange peel
1½ cups frozen nondairy whipped topping, thawed
30 fresh strawberries or raspberries (optional)

Heat oven to 350°F. Line bottom of 13×9-inch baking pan with waxed paper. In large mixer bowl, stir together granulated sugar, flour, cocoa, baking powder and baking soda. Add milk, egg substitute, oil and vanilla; beat on medium speed of electric mixer 2 minutes. Add water, stirring with spoon until well blended. Pour batter into pan.

Bake 16 to 18 minutes or until wooden toothpick inserted in center comes out clean. Place towel on wire rack; sprinkle with powdered sugar. Invert cake on towel; peel off waxed paper. Turn cake right side up. Cool completely. Cut cake into small rectangles (about 2¼×1¼ inches). Stir orange peel into whipped topping; spoon dollop on each piece of cake. Garnish with strawberry or raspberry, if desired.

Makes about 30 servings

Nutrients per serving:

Calories	80	Cholesterol	0 mg
Fat	3 g	Sodium	35 mg

MAPLE WALNUT CREAM DELIGHT

Cake
1 package DUNCAN HINES® DeLights Yellow Cake Mix
1⅓ cups water
2 eggs
½ cup finely chopped walnuts
Filling
1 package (4-serving size) sugar-free vanilla flavor pudding and pie filling mix
2 cups skim milk
½ teaspoon maple flavoring
1 cup frozen nondairy whipped topping, thawed and divided
1 tablespoon chopped walnuts

1. Preheat oven to 350°F. Grease and flour two 8- or 9-inch round cake pans.

2. *For Cake,* empty mix into large bowl. Add water, eggs and nuts. Prepare, bake and cool cake following package directions.

3. *For Filling,* cook pudding as directed on package, using skim milk. Stir in maple flavor. Place plastic wrap on surface of pudding. Refrigerate until cool. Fold in ½ cup whipped topping.

4. *To assemble,* place one cake layer on serving plate. Spread with half of maple filling. Top with other cake layer. Spread remaining filling on top. Garnish top with remaining ½ cup whipped topping and nuts. Refrigerate.

Makes 12 servings

Nutrients per serving:

Calories	251	Cholesterol	71 mg
Fat	10 g	Sodium	318 mg

Desserts

Left: Blueberry Crisp
Right: Orange Terrine with
Strawberry Sauce (page 188)

BLUEBERRY CRISP

   3 **cups cooked brown rice**
   3 **cups fresh blueberries***
   ¼ **cup plus 3 tablespoons firmly**
       packed brown sugar, divided
      Nonstick cooking spray
   ⅓ **cup rice bran**
   ¼ **cup whole-wheat flour**
   ¼ **cup chopped walnuts**
   1 **teaspoon ground cinnamon**
   3 **tablespoons margarine**

Combine rice, blueberries, and 3
tablespoons sugar. Coat 8 individual
custard cups or 2-quart baking dish with
nonstick cooking spray. Place rice
mixture in cups or baking dish; set
aside. Combine bran, flour, walnuts,
remaining ¼ cup sugar, and cinnamon
in bowl. Cut in margarine with pastry
blender until mixture resembles coarse
meal. Sprinkle over rice mixture. Bake at
375°F for 15 to 20 minutes or until
thoroughly heated. Serve warm.

Makes 8 servings

To Microwave: Prepare as directed
using 2-quart microproof baking dish.
Cook, uncovered, on HIGH (100%
power) 4 to 5 minutes, rotating dish once
during cooking time. Let stand 5
minutes. Serve warm.

*Substitute frozen unsweetened
blueberries for the fresh blueberries, if
desired. Thaw and drain before using.
Or, substitute your choice of fresh fruit
or combinations of fruit for the
blueberries, if desired.

Nutrients per serving:

Calories	243	Cholesterol	0 mg
Fat	8 g	Sodium	61 mg

Favorite recipe from **USA Rice Council**

ORANGE TERRINE WITH STRAWBERRY SAUCE

1 package (3 ounces)
    ladyfingers, split
2 packages (4-serving size) *or*
    1 package (8-serving size)
    JELL-O® Brand Orange
    Flavor Sugar Free Gelatin
1½ cups boiling water
1 cup orange juice
    Ice cubes
1 tablespoon orange liqueur
    (optional)
2 teaspoons grated orange peel
3¼ cups (8 ounces) COOL WHIP®
    LITE® Whipped Topping,
    thawed, divided
1 package (10 ounces)
    BIRDS EYE® Strawberries
    in Syrup, thawed, puréed
    and strained

Line bottom and sides of 9×5-inch loaf pan with plastic wrap. Vertically line long sides of pan with ladyfingers, split sides facing in.

Completely dissolve gelatin in boiling water. Combine orange juice and ice cubes to make 1¾ cups. Add to gelatin, stirring until slightly thickened. Remove any unmelted ice. Stir in liqueur and orange peel.

Gently stir in 2½ cups whipped topping. Spoon into prepared pan, trimming ladyfingers even with filling, if necessary. Arrange remaining ladyfingers on top of creamy mixture. Chill until firm, at least 3 hours.

Unmold onto serving plate; remove plastic wrap. Cut into slices and serve on strawberry purée; garnish with remaining ¾ cup whipped topping.

Makes 12 servings

Nutrients per serving:

Calories	100	Cholesterol	25 mg
Fat	3 g	Sodium	60 mg

SILKY COCOA CREME

1 envelope unflavored gelatin
¼ cup cold water
½ cup sugar
⅓ cup HERSHEY'S® Cocoa
¾ cup skim milk
½ cup low-fat part-skim ricotta
    cheese
1 teaspoon vanilla extract
½ cup frozen non-dairy whipped
    topping, thawed
    Fresh strawberries (optional)

In small bowl, sprinkle gelatin over water; allow to stand 2 minutes to soften. In medium saucepan, stir together sugar and cocoa; stir in milk. Cook over medium heat, stirring constantly, until mixture is very hot. Add gelatin mixture, stirring until gelatin is dissolved; pour into medium bowl. Refrigerate until mixture is slightly cold (do not allow to gel). In blender container or food processor blend ricotta cheese and vanilla until smooth; transfer to small bowl. Add whipped topping; stir until combined. Gradually fold ricotta mixture into cocoa mixture; pour into 2-cup mold. Refrigerate until set, about 4 hours. Unmold; serve with strawberries.

Makes 8 servings

Nutrients per serving:

Calories	110	Cholesterol	5 mg
Fat	3 g	Sodium	35 mg

RASPBERRY RICE AUX AMANDES

3 cups cooked rice
2 cups skim milk
⅛ teaspoon salt
    Low-calorie sugar substitute to
        equal 2 tablespoons sugar
1 teaspoon vanilla extract
¾ cup frozen light whipped
        topping, thawed
3 tablespoons sliced almonds,
        toasted
1 package (16 ounces) frozen
        unsweetened raspberries,
        thawed*

Combine rice, milk, and salt in 2-quart saucepan. Cook over medium heat until thick and creamy, 5 to 8 minutes, stirring frequently. Remove from heat. Cool. Add sugar substitute and vanilla. Fold in whipped topping and almonds. Alternate rice mixture and raspberries in parfait glasses or dessert dishes.

Makes 8 servings

To Microwave: Combine rice, milk, and salt in 1½-quart microproof baking dish. Cover and cook on HIGH (100% power) 3 minutes. Reduce setting to MEDIUM (50% power) and cook 7 minutes, stirring after 3 and 5 minutes. Stir in sugar substitute and vanilla; cool. Fold in whipped topping and almonds. Alternate rice mixture and raspberries in parfait glasses or dessert dishes.

*Substitute frozen unsweetened strawberries or other fruit for the raspberries, if desired.

Nutrients per serving:

| Calories | 180 | Cholesterol | 2 mg |
| Fat | 3 g | Sodium | 369 mg |

Favorite recipe from **USA Rice Council**

FROZEN ORANGE CREAM

1 package (4-serving size)
        JELL-O® Brand Orange
        Flavor Sugar Free Gelatin
¾ cup boiling water
2 cups skim milk
1 can (6 ounces) frozen apple
        juice concentrate, thawed
1 cup thawed COOL WHIP®
        LITE® Whipped Topping
1 can (11 ounces) mandarin
        orange segments, well
        drained
    Mint leaves (optional)

Completely dissolve gelatin in boiling water. Stir in milk and apple juice concentrate. (Mixture will appear curdled but will be smooth when frozen.) Pour into 13×9-inch metal pan. Freeze until about 1 inch of icy crystals forms around edges, about 1 hour. Spoon mixture into chilled bowl; beat with electric mixer until smooth. Gently stir in whipped topping. Spoon a scant ⅔ cup mixture into each of 8 custard cups. Freeze about 6 hours or overnight.

To serve, reserve 8 orange segments for garnish. Process remaining oranges in blender until smooth. Remove custard cups from freezer; let stand 15 minutes. Run knife around edges of cups; invert onto dessert plates and unmold. Garnish each dessert with about 1 tablespoon puréed oranges, 1 reserved orange segment and mint leaf, if desired. Store leftover desserts in freezer.

Makes 8 servings

Nutrients per serving:

| Calories | 100 | Cholesterol | 0 mg |
| Fat | 1 g | Sodium | 75 mg |

BAVARIAN RICE CLOUD WITH BITTERSWEET CHOCOLATE SAUCE

   1 **envelope unflavored gelatin**
1½ **cups skim milk**
   3 **tablespoons sugar**
   2 **cups cooked rice**
   2 **cups frozen light whipped topping, thawed**
   1 **tablespoon almond-flavored liqueur**
   ½ **teaspoon vanilla extract**
     Nonstick cooking spray
     Bittersweet Chocolate Sauce (recipe follows)
   2 **tablespoons sliced almonds, toasted**

Sprinkle gelatin over milk in small saucepan; let stand 1 minute or until gelatin is softened. Cook over low heat, stirring constantly, until gelatin dissolves. Add sugar and stir until dissolved. Add rice; stir until well blended. Cover and chill until the consistency of unbeaten egg whites. Fold in whipped topping, liqueur, and vanilla. Spoon into 4-cup mold coated with nonstick cooking spray. Cover and chill until firm. To serve, unmold onto serving platter. Spoon Bittersweet Chocolate Sauce over rice dessert. Sprinkle with toasted almonds.

Makes 10 servings

BITTERSWEET CHOCOLATE SAUCE

   3 **tablespoons cocoa**
   3 **tablespoons sugar**
   ½ **cup low-fat buttermilk**
   1 **tablespoon almond-flavored liqueur**

Combine cocoa and sugar in small saucepan. Add buttermilk, mixing well.

Place over medium heat, and cook until sugar dissolves. Stir in liqueur; remove from heat.

Tip: Unmold gelatin desserts onto slightly dampened plate. This will allow you to move the mold and position it where you want it on the plate.

Nutrients per serving:

Calories	146	Cholesterol	1 mg
Fat	3 g	Sodium	211 mg

Favorite recipe from **USA Rice Council**

BLACK FOREST PARFAITS

   2 **cups cold 2% low-fat milk, divided**
   4 **ounces Neufchâtel Cheese**
   1 **package (4-serving size) JELL-O® Chocolate Flavor Sugar Free Instant Pudding and Pie Filling**
   1 **package (15 ounces) ENTENMANN'S® Fat Free Chocolate Loaf, cubed**
   1 **can (20 ounces) reduced-calorie cherry pie filling**
   1 **square BAKER'S® Semi-Sweet Chocolate, grated**

In blender container, process ½ cup of the milk and cheese until smooth. Add remaining 1½ cups milk and pudding mix; blend until smooth. Divide cake cubes evenly among 12 dessert dishes. Spoon cherry pie filling over cake cubes, reserving a few cherries for garnish. Top with pudding mixture. Refrigerate until ready to serve. Garnish with reserved cherries and chocolate.

Makes 12 servings

Nutrients per serving:

Calories	190	Cholesterol	10 mg
Fat	4 g	Sodium	340 mg

Bavarian Rice Cloud with Bittersweet Chocolate Sauce

191

Berry Good Sundaes

BERRY GOOD SUNDAES

**4 flour tortillas (6 inches
    diameter)
1½ cups diced peeled peaches
1½ cups diced raspberries
2 tablespoons sugar
1 tablespoon finely chopped
    crystallized ginger
½ teaspoon grated lemon peel
4 scoops (3 ounces each) vanilla
    ice milk
Sprigs of fresh mint**

Preheat oven to 350°F. Soften tortillas
according to package directions. Press
each tortilla down into ungreased

10-ounce custard cup. Bake 10 to
15 minutes or until crisp. Set aside
to cool.

Combine peaches, raspberries, sugar,
ginger and lemon peel in large bowl; mix
gently until well blended. To assemble,
remove tortillas from custard cups. Place
each tortilla shell on dessert plate and
fill with scoop of ice milk. Spoon equal
portions of fruit salsa over tops. Garnish
with mint sprigs.   *Makes 4 servings*

Nutrients per serving:			
Calories	278	Cholesterol	6 mg
Fat	4 g	Sodium	80 mg

CITRUS BERRY SHERBET

**1 envelope unflavored gelatin
    Juice of 3 SUNKIST® Oranges
    (1 cup)
    Grated peel and juice of
    1 SUNKIST® Lemon
¼ cup sugar
1½ cups mashed fresh or
    frozen strawberries or
    boysenberries, thawed (no
    sugar added)
½ cup applesauce**

In large saucepan, sprinkle gelatin over
orange and lemon juice; allow to stand 2
minutes to soften. Add sugar and lemon
peel. Stir over low heat until gelatin and
sugar are dissolved. Cool. Stir in
strawberries and applesauce. Pour into
shallow pan. Freeze until firm, about
4 hours.   *Makes 6 servings*

Nutrients per serving (½ cup):			
Calories	77	Cholesterol	0 mg
Fat	0 g	Sodium	3 mg

AMBROSIA FRUIT CUSTARD

1 package (4-serving size) sugar-free instant vanilla pudding
Ingredients for pudding
1 teaspoon grated DOLE® Lemon peel
1 tablespoon DOLE® Lemon juice
½ teaspoon coconut or almond extract
1 can (8 ounces) DOLE® Pineapple Tidbits, drained
1 cup assorted sliced DOLE® fresh fruit
¼ cup mini marshmallows *or* flaked coconut

Make pudding according to package directions in bowl. Stir in lemon peel, lemon juice and extract. Reserve ¼ cup pudding for topping. Spoon remaining pudding equally into 4 dessert bowls. Combine remaining ingredients in bowl. Spoon on top of pudding. Drizzle with reserved pudding.   *Makes 4 servings*

Nutrients per serving:

Calories	139	Cholesterol	0 mg
Fat	2 g	Sodium	203 mg

MELON BUBBLES

1 package (4-serving size) JELL-O® Brand Sugar Free Gelatin, any flavor
¾ cup boiling water
½ cup cold water
Ice cubes
1 cup melon balls (cantaloupe, honeydew or watermelon)
Mint leaves (optional)

Melon Bubbles

Completely dissolve gelatin in boiling water. Combine cold water and ice cubes to make 1¼ cups. Add to gelatin, stirring until slightly thickened. Remove any unmelted ice. In medium bowl, combine 1⅓ cups gelatin and melon balls. Pour into 7 individual dessert dishes or serving bowl.

Whip remaining gelatin at high speed of electric mixer until fluffy, thick and about doubled in volume. Spoon over gelatin in dishes or bowl. Chill until set, about 2 hours. Garnish with additional melon balls and mint leaves, if desired.
      Makes 7 (½-cup) servings

Nutrients per serving:

Calories	14	Cholesterol	0 mg
Fat	0 g	Sodium	50 mg

CRANBERRY APPLE ICE

1 can (12 ounces) frozen
   apple-cranberry juice
   concentrate, thawed
1½ cups MOTT'S® Chunky Apple
   Sauce
1 bottle (32 ounces) sugar-free
   lemon-lime flavored
   carbonated beverage
   (4 cups)

In 2-quart nonmetal bowl, combine all ingredients; mix well. Cover; freeze until firm. Scoop frozen mixture into 5-ounce drinking cups or spoon into dessert dishes. *Makes 14 servings, 7 cups*

Nutrients per serving (½ cup):

Calories	33	Cholesterol	0 mg
Fat	0 g	Sodium	14 mg

PINWHEEL CAKE AND CREAM

2 cups cold skim milk
1 package (4-serving size)
   JELL-O® Vanilla Flavor
   Sugar Free Instant Pudding
   and Pie Filling
1 cup thawed COOL WHIP®
   LITE® Whipped Topping
1 small peach, cut into bite-size
   pieces
1 teaspoon grated orange peel
1 package (10 ounces)
   ENTENMANN'S® Fat Free
   Golden Loaf Cake, cut into
   slices
2 cups summer fruits (peaches,
   nectarines, berries, seedless
   grapes)

Pour milk into small mixing bowl. Add pudding mix. Beat with wire whisk until well blended, 1 to 2 minutes. Gently stir in whipped topping, peach and peel. Arrange pound cake slices on serving plate. Spoon pudding mixture evenly over cake. Top with fruits. Serve immediately or cover and refrigerate until serving time.

Makes 12 servings

Nutrients per serving:

Calories	120	Cholesterol	0 mg
Fat	1 g	Sodium	230 mg

APPLE CINNAMON DESSERT

1 cup pared diced apple
2 teaspoons REALEMON®
   Lemon Juice from
   Concentrate
1½ tablespoons sugar
⅛ teaspoon ground cinnamon
2 slices BORDEN® Lite-line®
   American Flavor Process
   Cheese Product, cut into
   small pieces*
½ tablespoon low-calorie
   margarine
2 plain melba rounds, crushed

Preheat oven to 350°F. In small bowl, combine apples, ReaLemon® brand, sugar and cinnamon; mix well. Stir in cheese product. Divide mixture between 2 small baking dishes. Top with margarine; sprinkle with melba crumbs. Bake 12 to 15 minutes or until apples are tender. Refrigerate leftovers.

Makes 2 servings

*"½ the calories" 8% milkfat version

Nutrients per serving:

Calories	123	Cholesterol	5 mg
Fat	4 g	Sodium	315 mg

Pinwheel Cake and Cream

Frozen Banana Dessert Cups

FROZEN BANANA DESSERT CUPS

  2 extra-ripe, medium DOLE®
       Bananas, peeled
  1 cup DOLE® Fresh or frozen
       Strawberries
  1 can (8 ounces) DOLE®
       Crushed Pineapple in Juice,
       drained
  2 tablespoons honey
       Dash ground nutmeg
  1 cup frozen whipped topping,
       thawed
  ¼ cup DOLE® Chopped Almonds
  1 cup DOLE® Pure & Light
       Mountain Cherry Juice
  1 tablespoon cornstarch
  1 tablespoon sugar
       Sliced DOLE® fresh fruit for
       garnish

Place bananas, strawberries, pineapple, honey and nutmeg in blender container. Process until smooth. Fold in whipped topping and almonds. Line 12 (2½-inch) muffin cups with foil liners. Fill with banana mixture. Cover and freeze until firm. Blend cherry juice, cornstarch and sugar in small saucepan. Cook, stirring, until sauce boils and thickens. Cool.

To serve, spoon cherry sauce onto each serving plate. Remove foil liners from dessert. Invert on top of sauce. Arrange fresh fruit around mold.

Makes 8 to 12 servings

Nutrients per serving:			
Calories	99	Cholesterol	0 mg
Fat	3 g	Sodium	3 mg

196

CHOCOLATE PEANUT BUTTER PARFAITS

- 2 tablespoons skim milk
- 2 tablespoons chunky peanut butter
- 1 cup thawed COOL WHIP® LITE® Whipped Topping
- 2 cups cold skim milk
- 1 package (4-serving size) JELL-O® Chocolate Flavor Sugar Free Instant Pudding and Pie Filling

In small bowl, stir 2 tablespoons milk into peanut butter, mixing until smooth. Gently stir in whipped topping. Pour 2 cups milk into medium mixing bowl. Add pudding mix. Beat with wire whisk until well blended, 1 to 2 minutes. Alternately spoon whipped topping mixture and pudding into parfait glasses. Refrigerate.

Makes 3 cups, 6 servings

Nutrients per serving:

Calories	110	Cholesterol	0 mg
Fat	5 g	Sodium	290 mg

CHERRY ALMOND SUPREME

- 1 can (8 ounces) pitted dark sweet cherries in light syrup
- 1 package (4-serving size) JELL-O® Brand Cherry Flavor Sugar Free Gelatin
- ¾ cup boiling water
  Ice cubes
- 2 tablespoons chopped toasted almonds
- 1 cup thawed COOL WHIP® LITE® Whipped Topping

Drain cherries, reserving syrup. Add enough water to syrup to measure ½ cup. Quarter the cherries. Completely dissolve gelatin in boiling water. Combine measured syrup and ice to make 1¼ cups. Add to gelatin, stirring until slightly thickened. Remove any unmelted ice. Let stand or chill until thickened. In medium bowl, combine 1¼ cups gelatin, half the cherries and half the nuts; set aside.

In large bowl, gently stir whipped topping into remaining gelatin; add remaining cherries and nuts. Spoon mixture into individual glasses or cups. Chill until set but not firm, about 15 minutes. Top with reserved gelatin mixture. Chill until set, about 1 hour.

Makes about 3 cups, 6 servings

Nutrients per serving:

Calories	70	Cholesterol	0 mg
Fat	3 g	Sodium	65 mg

Chocolate Peanut Butter Parfaits

Rice Pudding

RICE PUDDING

3 cups 2% low-fat milk
1 large stick cinnamon
1 cup uncooked long-grain rice
2 cups water
½ teaspoon salt
   Peel of an orange or lemon
¾ cup sugar
¼ cup raisins
2 tablespoons dark rum

Heat milk and cinnamon in small saucepan over medium heat until milk is infused with flavor of cinnamon, about 15 minutes. Combine rice, water, and salt in 2- to 3-quart saucepan. Bring to a boil; stir once or twice. Place orange peel on top of rice. Reduce heat; cover and simmer 15 minutes or until rice is tender and liquid is absorbed. Remove and discard orange peel. Strain milk and stir into cooked rice. Add sugar and simmer 20 minutes or until thickened, stirring often. Add raisins and rum; simmer 10 minutes. Serve hot. To reheat, add a little milk to restore creamy texture. *Makes 6 servings*

Nutrients per serving:

Calories	297	Cholesterol	10 mg
Fat	3 g	Sodium	259 mg

Favorite recipe from **USA Rice Council**

PEACH MELBA PARFAITS

1 (10-ounce) package frozen red raspberries in syrup, thawed
¼ cup red currant jelly
1 tablespoon cornstarch
½ of a (½ gallon) carton BORDEN® or MEADOW GOLD® Peach Frozen Yogurt
⅔ cup granola or natural cereal

Drain raspberries, reserving ⅔ cup syrup. In small saucepan, combine reserved syrup, jelly and cornstarch. Cook and stir until slightly thickened and glossy. Cool. Stir in raspberries. In 6 parfait or wine glasses, layer raspberry sauce, frozen yogurt, raspberry sauce, then granola; repeat. Freeze. Remove from freezer 5 to 10 minutes before serving. Garnish as desired. Freeze leftovers. *Makes 6 servings*

Nutrients per serving:

Calories	268	Cholesterol	9 mg
Fat	5 g	Sodium	75 mg

RHUBARB CRISP

6 cups chopped fresh rhubarb
½ cup firmly packed brown sugar
⅓ cup all-purpose flour
⅓ cup rolled oats, uncooked
½ teaspoon ground cinnamon
3 tablespoons butter or margarine
   Whipped topping or ice cream (optional)

Preheat oven to 350°F. Place rhubarb in 8-inch square baking dish. Combine brown sugar, flour, oats and cinnamon in medium bowl; cut in butter with pastry blender until mixture resembles coarse crumbs. Sprinkle crumb mixture over rhubarb. Bake 30 minutes, or until lightly browned. Serve hot or cold with whipped topping or ice cream, if desired. Garnish as desired.

Makes 4 to 6 servings

Nutrients per serving:

Calories	187	Cholesterol	0 mg
Fat	6 g	Sodium	77 mg

PEAR FANS WITH CREAMY CUSTARD SAUCE

8 canned pear halves in juice, drained
Creamy Custard Sauce (recipe follows)
8 raspberries (optional)
8 mint leaves (optional)

Cut pear halves into thin slices with sharp knife, cutting up to, but not through, stem ends. Holding stem end in place, gently fan out slices from stem. Place on dessert plates. Spoon about ⅓ cup Creamy Custard Sauce around pears. Place raspberry and mint leaf at stem end of each pear, if desired.

Makes 8 servings

CREAMY CUSTARD SAUCE

3 cups cold 2% lowfat milk
1 package (4-serving size) JELL-O® Vanilla Flavor Sugar Free Instant Pudding and Pie Filling
¼ teaspoon ground cinnamon (optional)

Pear Fans with Creamy Custard Sauce

Pour milk into large mixing bowl. Add pudding mix and cinnamon. Beat with wire whisk until well blended, 1 to 2 minutes. Cover; refrigerate until ready to use.

Nutrients per serving:

Calories	160	Cholesterol	20 mg
Fat	4 g	Sodium	420 mg

ORANGE AND RAISIN BREAD PUDDING

4 cups (about 6 slices) raisin bread, cut into ¾-inch cubes
1 whole egg plus 2 egg whites
1½ cups (12-ounce can) *undiluted* CARNATION® Lite Evaporated Skimmed Milk
2 tablespoons honey
1 tablespoon margarine, melted
1 tablespoon grated orange zest

Preheat oven to 375°F. Arrange bread cubes in single layer on baking sheet; toast 6 to 8 minutes or until lightly browned. In large bowl, beat egg and egg whites. Add evaporated skimmed milk, honey, margarine and orange zest; beat until blended. Stir in toasted bread cubes; let stand 10 minutes. Spray 1-quart casserole dish with nonstick cooking spray; pour in bread mixture. Set casserole dish in 9-inch square baking pan; fill baking pan with 1 inch hot water.

Bake in 375°F oven 45 to 55 minutes or until puffed and golden brown. Remove casserole from water; cool 5 to 10 minutes. Garnish with powdered sugar and orange zest if desired. Serve warm.

Makes 6 servings

Nutrients per serving:

Calories	172	Cholesterol	39 mg
Fat	4 g	Sodium	220 mg

ALL–AMERICAN PINEAPPLE & FRUIT TRIFLE

1 DOLE® Fresh Pineapple
1 cup frozen sliced peaches, thawed
1 cup frozen strawberries, thawed, sliced
1 cup frozen raspberries, thawed
1 angel food cake (10 inch)
1 package (4-serving size) instant sugar-free vanilla pudding mix
⅓ cup cream sherry
½ cup frozen whipped topping, thawed

Twist crown from pineapple. Cut pineapple in half lengthwise. Refrigerate half for another use, such as fruit salad. Cut fruit from shell. Cut fruit into thin wedges. Reserve 3 wedges for garnish; combine remaining pineapple wedges with peaches, strawberries and raspberries.

Cut cake in half. Freeze half for another use. Tear cake into chunks.

Prepare pudding according to package directions.

In 2-quart glass bowl, layer half of each: cake, sherry, fruit mixture and pudding. Repeat layer once. Cover; chill 1 hour or overnight.

Just before serving, garnish with whipped topping and reserved pineapple wedges.   *Makes 8 to 10 servings*

Prep time: 20 minutes
Chill time: 1 hour

Nutrients per serving:

Calories	173	Cholesterol	4 mg
Fat	2 g	Sodium	129 mg

All-American Pineapple & Fruit Trifle

STRAWBERRY ICE

1 cup sugar
½ cup water
3 tablespoons REALEMON® Lemon Juice from Concentrate
1 quart fresh strawberries, cleaned and hulled (about 1½ pounds)
Red food coloring (optional)

In blender container, combine sugar, water and Realemon® brand; mix well. Gradually add strawberries; blend until smooth, adding food coloring, if desired. Pour into 8-inch square pan; freeze about 1½ hours. In small mixer bowl, beat until slushy. Return to freezer. Place in refrigerator 1 hour before serving to soften. Freeze leftovers.

Makes 6 servings

Nutrients per serving:

Calories	162	Cholesterol	0 mg
Fat	0 g	Sodium	3 mg

Frozen Apple Sauce 'n' Fruit Cup

FROZEN APPLE SAUCE 'N' FRUIT CUP

    1 can (11 ounces) mandarin
        orange segments, drained
    1 package (10 ounces) frozen
        strawberries, thawed
    1 cup MOTT'S® Chunky or
        Regular Apple Sauce
    1 cup grapes, if desired
    2 tablespoons orange juice
        concentrate

In medium bowl, combine all
ingredients. Spoon fruit mixture into
individual dishes or paper cups. Freeze
until firm. Remove from freezer about
30 minutes before serving. Garnish if
desired.   *Makes 7 servings, 3½ cups*

Nutrients per serving (½ cup):			
Calories	107	Cholesterol	0 mg
Fat	0 g	Sodium	5 mg

VANILLA PUDDING GRAHAMWICHES

 1½ cups cold skim milk
    1 package (4-serving size)
        JELL-O® Vanilla Flavor
        Sugar Free Instant Pudding
        and Pie Filling
 3¼ cups (8-ounce container)
        COOL WHIP® LITE®
        Whipped Topping, thawed
    1 cup miniature marshmallows
   22 whole cinnamon graham
        crackers, broken into
        44 squares
    2 squares BAKER'S® Semi-Sweet
        Chocolate, shaved or grated

Pour milk into large mixing bowl. Add
pudding mix. Beat with wire whisk until
well blended, 1 to 2 minutes. Gently stir
in whipped topping and marshmallows.
Spread about 2 tablespoons mixture on
each graham cracker square. Form
sandwiches by lightly pressing 2 graham
crackers together. Press edges of each
sandwich into chocolate to coat. (If filling
mixture begins to soften, refrigerate for a
few minutes.) Freeze until firm, about
6 hours or overnight. Remove from
freezer. Let stand about 5 minutes before
serving to soften.

Makes 22 sandwich cookies

Note: Store any leftover sandwich
cookies in freezer in airtight bag or
container.

Nutrients per serving (1 sandwich cookie):			
Calories	110	Cholesterol	0 mg
Fat	4 g	Sodium	160 mg

MERINGUE FRUIT CUPS WITH CUSTARD SAUCE

4 large egg whites, at room temperature
½ teaspoon cream of tartar
Pinch salt
1 cup sugar
1 can (17 ounces) DEL MONTE® Fruit Cocktail, drained
Custard Sauce (recipe follows)

Line baking sheet with parchment or waxed paper. With bottom of glass, trace eight 3-inch circles about 2 inches apart on paper. Turn paper over on baking sheet. Beat egg whites until frothy; add cream of tartar and salt. Beat until soft peaks form. Add sugar, 1 tablespoon at a time, and beat until meringue is stiff and shiny, about 10 minutes. Transfer to pastry bag fitted with star tip. Use a little meringue to secure paper to baking sheet.

Pipe 2 tablespoons meringue in center of each circle; spread to edges. Pipe 2 rings, one on top of the other, around edges of circles. Bake in preheated 200°F oven about 1½ hours or until dry but still white. Cool completely. (Can be made several days ahead and stored in airtight container.)

Spoon fruit cocktail into meringue cups. Place on individual dessert dishes. Spoon approximately ¼ cup Custard Sauce over each. Garnish with mint, if desired. *Makes 8 servings*

CUSTARD SAUCE

4 egg yolks,* slightly beaten
¼ cup sugar
Pinch salt
2 cups milk, scalded
1 teaspoon vanilla extract

In top of double boiler, mix egg yolks, sugar and salt until well blended. Slowly add milk, stirring constantly. Cook over hot water, stirring constantly, until mixture begins to thicken. Remove from heat; stir in vanilla. Chill.
Makes about 2½ cups

*Use only clean, uncracked eggs.

Nutrients per serving:			
Calories	217	Cholesterol	115 mg
Fat	5 g	Sodium	63 mg

Meringue Fruit Cups with Custard Sauce

Cookies
and Pies

Left: Top to bottom: Cocoa Brownies,
(page 206) Chocolate Chip Cookies
Right: Picnic Fruit Tart (page 206)

CHOCOLATE CHIP
COOKIES

2 cups all-purpose flour
1 teaspoon baking soda
½ teaspoon salt
1 egg
3 tablespoons water
1 teaspoon vanilla extract
1 cup firmly packed brown sugar
¼ cup CRISCO® PURITAN® Oil
½ cup semi-sweet chocolate chips

Heat oven to 375°F. Oil cookie sheets
well. Combine flour, baking soda and
salt. Set aside. Combine egg, water and
vanilla. Set aside.

Blend brown sugar and Crisco® Puritan®
Oil in large bowl at low speed of electric
mixer. Add egg mixture. Beat until
smooth. Add flour mixture in three parts
at lowest speed. Scrape bowl well after
each addition. Stir in chocolate chips.

Drop dough by rounded teaspoonfuls
onto cookie sheets. Bake at 375°F for
7 to 8 minutes or until lightly browned.
Cool on cookie sheets 1 minute. Remove
to wire racks.   *Makes 3 dozen cookies*

Nutrients per serving (1 cookie):			
Calories	74	Cholesterol	6 mg
Fat	3 g	Sodium	57 mg

PICNIC FRUIT TART

Crust
- ¾ cup flour
- ¼ cup oat bran
- 2 tablespoons sugar
- ¼ cup (½ stick) PARKAY® Margarine
- 2 to 3 tablespoons cold water

Filling
- 1 envelope unflavored gelatin
- ½ cup cold water
- 1 container (8 ounces) Light PHILADELPHIA BRAND® Pasteurized Process Cream Cheese Product, softened
- ¼ cup sugar *or* 6 packets sugar substitute
- 1 teaspoon grated lemon peel
- ¼ cup skim milk
- ⅓ cup KRAFT® Apricot Preserves
- ¾ cup grape halves
- ¾ cup plum slices

Crust: Heat oven to 375°F.

Mix flour, oat bran and 2 tablespoons sugar in medium bowl; cut in margarine until mixture resembles coarse crumbs. Sprinkle with 2 to 3 tablespoons water, mixing lightly with fork just until moistened. Roll into ball. Cover; refrigerate.

On lightly floured surface, roll out dough to 11-inch circle. Place in 9-inch tart pan with removable bottom. Trim edges; prick bottom with fork.

Bake 16 to 18 minutes or until golden brown; cool.

Filling: Soften gelatin in ½ cup water in small saucepan; stir over low heat until dissolved. Cool.

Beat cream cheese product, ¼ cup sugar and peel in large mixing bowl at medium speed with electric mixer until

well blended. Gradually add gelatin mixture and milk, mixing until well blended.

Pour over crust. Refrigerate until firm.

Heat preserves in small saucepan over low heat until thinned. Spread evenly over tart. Arrange fruit over preserves. Carefully remove rim of pan.

Makes 14 servings

Prep time: 40 minutes plus refrigerating
Cook time: 18 minutes

Nutrients per serving:

Calories	150	Cholesterol	10 mg
Fat	6 g	Sodium	130 mg

COCOA BROWNIES

- 4 egg whites
- ½ cup CRISCO® PURITAN® Oil
- 1 teaspoon vanilla
- 1⅓ cups granulated sugar
- ½ cup cocoa
- 1¼ cups all-purpose flour
- ¼ teaspoon salt
- Confectioners sugar (optional)

Heat oven to 350°F. Oil bottom of 9×9-inch pan. Set aside.

Place egg whites in large bowl. Beat with spoon until slightly frothy. Add Crisco® Puritan® Oil and vanilla. Mix thoroughly. Stir in sugar and cocoa. Mix well. Stir in flour and salt until blended. Pour into pan.

Bake at 350°F for 26 to 28 minutes. *Do not overbake.* Cool completely on wire rack before cutting. Sprinkle with confectioners sugar, if desired.

Makes 1½ dozen brownies

Nutrients per serving (1 brownie):

Calories	150	Cholesterol	0 mg
Fat	7 g	Sodium	43 mg

EASY PINEAPPLE PIE

1 can (20 ounces) DOLE®
    Crushed Pineapple in Syrup*
1 package (4-serving size)
    instant lemon pudding and
    pie filling mix
1 cup milk
1 carton (4 ounces) frozen
    whipped topping, thawed
2 tablespoons DOLE® Lemon
    juice
1 teaspoon grated DOLE®
    Lemon peel
1 (8- or 9-inch) graham cracker
    pie crust

Drain pineapple well. Combine pudding mix and milk in medium bowl. Beat 2 to 3 minutes until very thick.

Fold in whipped topping, pineapple, lemon juice and lemon peel. Pour into crust. Cover and refrigerate 4 hours or overnight. Garnish as desired.

Makes 6 to 8 servings

Prep time: 5 minutes
Chill time: 4 hours or overnight

*Use pineapple packed in juice, if desired.

Nutrients per serving:

Calories	251	Cholesterol	2 mg
Fat	10 g	Sodium	321 mg

Easy Pineapple Pie

Apricot-Pecan Tassies

APRICOT–PECAN TASSIES

- **1 cup all-purpose flour**
- **½ cup butter, cut into pieces**
- **6 tablespoons light cream cheese**
- **¾ cup firmly packed light brown sugar**
- **1 egg, lightly beaten**
- **1 tablespoon butter, softened**
- **½ teaspoon vanilla extract**
- **¼ teaspoon salt**
- **⅔ cup Dried California Apricot Halves, diced (about 4 ounces)**
- **⅓ cup chopped pecans**

In food processor, combine flour, ½ cup butter and cream cheese; process until mixture forms a ball. Wrap dough in plastic wrap and chill 15 minutes.

Meanwhile, prepare filling by combining sugar, egg, 1 tablespoon butter, vanilla and salt in medium bowl; beat until smooth. Stir in apricots and nuts.

Preheat oven to 325°F. Shape dough into 24 (1-inch) balls and place in paper-lined or greased (1½-inch) miniature muffin cups or tart pans. Press dough on bottom and sides of each cup; fill with 1 teaspoon apricot-pecan filling. Bake 25 minutes or until golden and filling sets. Cool slightly and remove from cups. Cooled cookies can be wrapped tightly in plastic and frozen for up to 6 weeks.   *Makes 24 cookies*

Nutrients per serving (1 cookie):

Calories	110	Cholesterol	13 mg
Fat	7 g	Sodium	85 mg

Favorite recipe from California Apricot Advisory Board

APPLESAUCE COOKIES

1 cup all-purpose flour
1 teaspoon baking powder
1 teaspoon ground allspice
¼ teaspoon salt
½ cup margarine, softened
½ cup sugar
2 egg whites
2 cups rolled oats, uncooked
1 cup unsweetened applesauce
½ cup chopped raisins

Preheat oven to 375°F. Grease cookie sheet. Mix flour, baking powder, allspice and salt; set aside. In large bowl, beat margarine and sugar until creamy. Add egg whites; beat well. Add reserved flour mixture. Stir in oats, applesauce, and raisins, mixing well. Drop by level tablespoonfuls onto prepared cookie sheet. Bake 11 minutes or until edges are lightly browned. Cool on wire rack.

Makes about 5 dozen cookies

Nutrients per serving (1 cookie):

Calories	45	Cholesterol	0 mg
Fat	2 g	Sodium	34 mg

Favorite recipe from **Western New York Apple Growers Association**

CAPPUCCINO BON BONS

1 package DUNCAN HINES®
    Fudge Brownie Mix, Family
    Size
2 eggs
⅓ cup water
⅓ cup CRISCO® PURITAN® Oil
1½ tablespoons FOLGERS®
    Instant Coffee
1 teaspoon ground cinnamon
    Whipped topping
    Ground cinnamon or fresh
    fruit for garnish

Preheat oven to 350°F. Place 1½-inch foil cupcake liners on cookie sheet.

Combine brownie mix, eggs, water, oil, instant coffee and 1 teaspoon cinnamon. Stir with spoon until well blended, about 50 strokes. Fill each cupcake liner with 1 measuring tablespoon batter. Bake at 350°F for 12 to 15 minutes or until wooden toothpick inserted in centers comes out clean. Cool completely. Garnish each bon bon with whipped topping and a dash of cinnamon or piece of fruit. Refrigerate until ready to serve.

Makes 40 bon bons

Tip: To make larger bon bons, use 12 (2½-inch) foil cupcake liners and fill with ¼ cup batter. Bake for 28 to 30 minutes.

Nutrients per serving (1 bon bon):

Calories	87	Cholesterol	11 mg
Fat	4 g	Sodium	53 mg

Cappuccino Bon Bons

EASY DARK CHERRY TART

1¾ cups QUAKER® Oats (quick or old fashioned, uncooked)
½ cup all-purpose flour
⅓ cup firmly packed brown sugar
¼ teaspoon salt (optional)
⅓ cup (5⅓ tablespoons) margarine, melted
2 cans (16 ounces each) pitted dark sweet cherries, undrained
2 tablespoons granulated sugar
1 tablespoon cornstarch
½ teaspoon almond or vanilla extract

Heat oven to 350°F. Lightly oil 9-inch springform pan or pie plate. Combine oats, flour, brown sugar and salt. Add margarine; mix well. Reserve ⅓ cup for topping; press remaining mixture onto bottom and 1 inch up sides of prepared pan. Bake 15 minutes.

Drain cherries, reserving ⅓ cup liquid. In medium saucepan, combine granulated sugar and cornstarch. Gradually add reserved liquid, stirring until smooth. Add cherries and extract. Bring to a boil, stirring occasionally. Reduce heat; simmer about 1 minute or until thickened and clear, stirring constantly. Pour over baked crust. Sprinkle with reserved oat topping. Bake 15 to 18 minutes or until edges of crust are lightly browned. Store tightly covered in refrigerator. *Makes 10 servings*

Nutrients per serving:

Calories	235	Cholesterol	0 mg
Fat	7 g	Sodium	75 mg

COCOA BANANA BARS

Bars
⅔ cup QUAKER® Oat Bran hot cereal, uncooked
⅔ cup all-purpose flour
½ cup granulated sugar
⅓ cup unsweetened cocoa
½ cup mashed ripe banana (about 1 large)
¼ cup liquid vegetable oil margarine
3 tablespoons light corn syrup
2 egg whites, slightly beaten
1 teaspoon vanilla

Glaze
2 teaspoons unsweetened cocoa
2 teaspoons liquid vegetable oil margarine
¼ cup powdered sugar
2 to 2½ teaspoons warm water, divided
Strawberry halves (optional)

For Bars, heat oven to 350°F. Lightly spray 8-inch square baking pan with nonstick cooking spray, or oil lightly. In large bowl, combine oat bran, flour, granulated sugar and ⅓ cup cocoa. Add combined banana, ¼ cup margarine, corn syrup, egg whites and vanilla; mix well. Pour into prepared pan, spreading evenly. Bake 23 to 25 minutes or until center is set. Cool on wire rack. Drizzle glaze over brownies. Top with strawberry halves, if desired. Cut into bars. Store tightly covered.

For Glaze, in small bowl combine 2 teaspoons cocoa and 2 teaspoons margarine. Stir in powdered sugar and 1 teaspoon of the water. Gradually add remaining 1 to 1½ teaspoons water to make medium-thick glaze, mixing well. *Makes 9 bar cookies*

Nutrients per serving (1 bar):

Calories	210	Cholesterol	0 mg
Fat	7 g	Sodium	60 mg

Cocoa Banana Bars

Deep-Dish Peach Pie

DEEP–DISH PEACH PIE

Pastry for 1-crust pie
1 cup sugar
2 tablespoons cornstarch
3 pounds peaches, seeded, pared and sliced (about 6 cups)
2 tablespoons REALEMON® Lemon Juice from Concentrate
1 tablespoon margarine, melted
¼ teaspoon almond extract
2 tablespoons sliced almonds

Preheat oven to 375°F. Remove and reserve *1 tablespoon* sugar. In small bowl, combine remaining sugar and cornstarch. In large bowl, toss peaches with ReaLemon® brand; add sugar mixture, margarine and extract. Turn into 8-inch square baking dish. Roll pastry to 9-inch square; cut slits near center. Place pastry over filling; turn under edges, seal and flute. Sprinkle with reserved 1 tablespoon sugar and almonds. Bake 45 to 50 minutes or until golden brown. Cool on wire rack.

Makes 1 (8-inch) pie, 8 servings

Nutrients per serving:

Calories	292	Cholesterol	0 mg
Fat	10 g	Sodium	163 mg

CRANBERRY APPLE PIE WITH SOFT GINGERSNAP CRUST

20 gingersnap cookies
1½ tablespoons margarine
2 McIntosh apples, pared and cored
1 cup fresh cranberries
5 tablespoons firmly packed dark brown sugar
¼ teaspoon vanilla extract
¼ teaspoon ground cinnamon
1 teaspoon granulated sugar

Preheat oven to 375°F. Place gingersnaps and margarine in food processor; process until gingersnaps are finely ground. Press gingersnap mixture into 8-inch pie plate. Bake 5 to 8 minutes; cool. Chop apples in food processor. Add cranberries, brown sugar, vanilla and cinnamon; pulse just until mixed. Spoon apple-cranberry filling into another 8-inch pie plate or casserole dish. Sprinkle with granulated sugar. Bake 35 minutes or until tender. Spoon filling into gingersnap crust and serve immediately.

Makes 1 (8-inch) pie, 8 servings

Nutrients per serving:

Calories	124	Cholesterol	0 mg
Fat	3 g	Sodium	90 mg

Favorite recipe from **The Sugar Association, Inc.**

DOUBLE CHOCOLATE CLOUD COOKIES

   3 egg whites
   ⅛ teaspoon cream of tartar
   ¾ cup sugar
   1 teaspoon vanilla extract
   2 tablespoons HERSHEY'S®
       Cocoa or HERSHEY'S®
       Premium European Style
       Cocoa
   ¾ cup HERSHEY'S® Semi-Sweet
       Chocolate Chips
       Chocolate Drizzle Glaze
       (recipe follows)

Heat oven to 300°F. Place parchment paper on cookie sheet. In large mixer bowl, beat egg whites and cream of tartar until soft peaks form. Gradually add sugar and vanilla, beating until stiff peaks hold their shape, sugar is dissolved and mixture is glossy. Sift cocoa onto egg white mixture; gently fold just until combined. Fold in chocolate chips. Drop by heaping teaspoonfuls onto prepared cookie sheet. Bake 20 to 25 minutes or just until dry. Carefully peel cookies off paper; cool completely on wire rack. Prepare Chocolate Drizzle Glaze; drizzle glaze lightly over cookies. Store, covered, at room temperature.

Makes about 4 dozen cookies

Chocolate Drizzle Glaze: In top of double boiler over hot, not boiling, water, melt ⅓ cup HERSHEY'S® Semi-Sweet Chocolate Chips and ½ teaspoon shortening, stirring until smooth. Remove from heat; cool slightly, stirring frequently.

Nutrients per serving (3 cookies):			
Calories	100	Cholesterol	0 mg
Fat	4 g	Sodium	12 mg

Chocolate Chip Raspberry Jumbles

CHOCOLATE CHIP RASPBERRY JUMBLES

   1 package DUNCAN HINES®
       Chocolate Chip Cookie Mix
   ½ cup seedless red raspberry
       preserves

1. Preheat oven to 350°F.

2. Prepare chocolate chip cookie mix following package directions. Reserve ½ cup dough.

3. Spread remaining dough into ungreased 9-inch square pan. Spread preserves over base. Drop teaspoonfuls of reserved dough randomly over top. Bake at 350°F for 20 to 25 minutes or until golden brown. Cool; cut into bars.

Makes 16 bar cookies

Nutrients per serving (1 cookie):			
Calories	178	Cholesterol	13 mg
Fat	6 g	Sodium	95 mg

TROPICAL BAR COOKIES

½ cup DOLE® Sliced Almonds, divided
1 cup all-purpose flour
⅓ cup margarine, melted
½ cup sugar, divided
1 can (20 ounces) DOLE® Crushed Pineapple in Syrup, drained
1 package (8 ounces) light cream cheese, softened
1 egg
1 teaspoon vanilla extract
⅓ cup flaked coconut

Preheat oven to 350°F. Chop ¼ cup almonds for crust; mix with flour, margarine and ¼ cup sugar in medium bowl until crumbly. Press into bottom of 9-inch square pan. Bake 12 minutes.

Beat pineapple, cream cheese, egg, remaining ¼ cup sugar and vanilla in large bowl until blended. Pour over crust. Top with coconut and remaining ¼ cup sliced almonds.

Tropical Bar Cookies

Bake 35 to 40 minutes or until golden brown. Cool on wire rack. Refrigerate at least 2 hours before cutting into bars.
Makes 16 bars

Nutrients per serving (1 cookie):			
Calories	199	Cholesterol	28 mg
Fat	10 g	Sodium	111 mg

ICED COFFEE AND CHOCOLATE PIE

2 envelopes unflavored gelatin
¼ cup cold skim milk
1 cup skim milk, heated to boiling
2 cups vanilla ice milk
⅓ cup sugar
2 tablespoons instant coffee granules
1 teaspoon vanilla extract
1 (6-ounce) KEEBLER® READY-CRUST® Chocolate Flavored Pie Crust
Reduced-calorie whipped topping (optional)
Chocolate curls (optional)

In blender container, sprinkle gelatin over ¼ cup cold milk; mix on low. Let stand 3 to 4 minutes to soften. Add hot milk; cover and mix on low until gelatin dissolves, about 2 minutes. Add ice milk, sugar, coffee granules and vanilla. Cover and mix until smooth. Pour into KEEBLER® READY-CRUST®. Refrigerate at least 2 hours. Garnish with whipped topping and chocolate curls, if desired. *Makes 1 pie, 8 servings*

Nutrients per serving:			
Calories	220	Cholesterol	6 mg
Fat	6 g	Sodium	210 mg

PEANUT BUTTER BARS

1 package DUNCAN HINES®
    Peanut Butter Cookie Mix
2 egg whites
½ cup chopped peanuts
1 cup confectioners sugar
2 tablespoons water
½ teaspoon vanilla extract

1. Preheat oven to 350°F.

2. Combine cookie mix, peanut butter packet from mix and egg whites in large bowl. Stir until thoroughly blended. Press in ungreased 13×9×2-inch pan. Sprinkle peanuts over dough. Press lightly. Bake at 350°F for 16 to 18 minutes or until golden brown. Cool completely in pan on wire rack.

3. Combine confectioners sugar, water and vanilla extract in small bowl. Stir until blended. Drizzle glaze over top. Cut into bars.   *Makes 24 bar cookies*

Nutrients per serving (1 cookie):

Calories	65	Cholesterol	0 mg
Fat	7 g	Sodium	104 mg

Peanut Butter Bars

In medium bowl, with electric mixer at medium speed, beat ¾ cup sugar, margarine, orange peel and vanilla until creamy. Add Egg Beaters®; beat 1 minute. Gradually stir in flour mixture until blended. Chill dough 1 hour.

Shape dough into 42 (¾-inch) balls; roll in remaining ¼ cup sugar. Place 2 inches apart on lightly greased cookie sheets. Bake at 375°F for 8 to 10 minutes or until light golden brown. Remove from cookie sheets. Cool on wire racks.

Makes about 3½ dozen cookies

Nutrients per serving (1 cookie):

Calories	60	Cholesterol	0 mg
Fat	2 g	Sodium	49 mg

ORANGE SUGAR COOKIES

2 cups all-purpose flour
1½ teaspoons baking soda
1 cup sugar, divided
½ cup FLEISCHMANN'S®
    Margarine, softened
2 teaspoons grated orange peel
1 teaspoon vanilla extract
¼ cup EGG BEATERS®
    99% Real Egg Product

In small bowl, combine flour and baking soda; set aside.

Acknowledgments

*The publishers would like to thank the companies and organizations
listed below for the use of their recipes in this book.*

American Lamb Council
Armour Swift-Eckrich
Best Foods, a Division of CPC International Inc.
Black-Eyed Pea Jamboree—Athens, Texas
Borden Kitchens, Borden, Inc.
California Apricot Advisory Board
California Cling Peach Advisory Board
Carnation, Nestlé Food Company
Clear Springs Trout Company
Contadina Foods, Inc., Nestlé Food Company
The Creamette Company
The Dannon Company, Inc.
Del Monte Corporation
Dole Food Company, Inc.
Florida Tomato Committee
The Fresh Garlic Association
Heinz U.S.A.
Hershey Chocolate U.S.A.
Keebler Company
Kellogg Company
Kraft General Foods, Inc.
Thomas J. Lipton Co.
McIlhenny Company
Mott's U.S.A., A division of Cadbury
    Beverages Inc.

Nabisco Foods Company
National Broiler Council
National Live Stock & Meat Board
National Pasta Association
National Pork Producers Council
National Turkey Federation
Norseland Foods, Inc.
Oscar Mayer Foods Corporation
Pace Foods, Inc.
Perdue Farms
Pet Incorporated
Pollio Dairy Products Corporation
The Procter & Gamble Company, Inc.
The Quaker Oats Company
Sargento Cheese Company, Inc.
StarKist Seafood Company
The Sugar Association, Inc.
Sunkist Growers, Inc.
Surimi Seafood Education Center
The Times-Picayune
USA Rice Council
Western New York Apple Growers
    Association, Inc.
Wisconsin Milk Marketing Board

Photo Credits

*The publishers would like to thank the companies and organizations
listed below for the use of their photographs in this book.*

Armour Swift-Eckrich
Best Foods, a Division of CPC International Inc.
Borden Kitchens, Borden, Inc.
California Apricot Advisory Board
Carnation, Nestle Food Company
Contadina Foods, Inc., Nestlé Food Company
The Creamette Company
Del Monte Corporation
Dole Food Company, Inc.
Heinz U.S.A.
Kellogg Company
Kraft General Foods, Inc.
Thomas J. Lipton Co.
Mott's U.S.A., A division of Cadbury
    Beverages Inc.

Nabisco Foods Company
National Broiler Council
National Live Stock & Meat Board
National Pork Producers Council
National Turkey Federation
Oscar Mayer Foods Corporation
Pollio Dairy Products Corporation
The Procter & Gamble Company, Inc.
The Quaker Oats Company
Sargento Cheese Company, Inc.
StarKist Seafood Company
Surimi Seafood Education Center
USA Rice Council

Index

A

All-American Pineapple & Fruit Trifle, 201
Ambrosia Fruit Custard, 193
Antipasto Rice, 160
Appetizers (*see also* **Dips & Spreads**)
    Artichoke Puffs, 36
    Bruschetta, 8
    Cheddar-Rice Patties, 26
    Chili Tortilla Chips, 19
    Garden Vegetable Platter, 23
    Ginger Shrimp, 10
    Greek Isles Appetizers, 13
    Grilled Mushrooms with Lamb and Herbs, 16
    Ground Turkey Chinese Spring Rolls, 14
    Indonesian Satay, 7
    Italian Bread Pizza, 33
    Pan-Roasted Herbed Almonds, 36
    Party Ham Sandwiches, 28
    Peppered Pecans, 30
    Pickle Roll-em-Ups, 30
    Pineapple Shrimp Appetizers, 17
    Scandinavian Smörgåsbord, 20
    Shanghai Party Pleasers, 25
    Sherried Turkey Cocktail Meatballs, 36
    Spicy Zucchini and Bacon Canapés, 28
    Spinach Rice Balls, 17
    Steamed Mussels in White Wine, 30
    Toasted Sesame Seed Wafers, 35
    Tuna-Stuffed Artichokes, 13
    Tuna-Stuffed Endive, 17
    Twelve Carat Black-Eyed Pea Relish, 18
    Two-Tone Ricotta Loaf, 11
Apples
    Almond Brown Rice Stuffing, 170
    Apple Cinnamon Dessert, 194
    Apple Salad, 131
    Applesauce Cookies, 209
    Applesauce-Stuffed Tenderloin, 96
    Apple Streusel Coffee Cake, 55
    Cheese 'n' Apple Spread, 41
    Cranberry Apple Ice, 194
    Cranberry Apple Pie with Soft Gingersnap Crust, 212
    Delicious Sliced Apples, 169
    Frozen Apple Sauce 'n' Fruit Cup, 202
    Lemony Apple-Bran Salad, 148
    Microwave Lemon-Apple Fish Rolls, 105
    Sweet and Sour Red Cabbage, 165
Apricot Muffins, 52
Apricot-Pecan Tassies, 208
Artichoke Puffs, 36
Asparagus and Surimi Seafood Soup, 86
Asparagus Dijon, 165

B

Bacon Morning Muffins, 59
Bacon Pilaf, 166
Baja Fish and Rice Bake, 106
Baked Tomatoes Florentine, 96
Bananas
    Banana Bran Loaf, 59
    Banana-Cinnamon Rolls, 44
    Banana-Raspberry Smoothie, 27
    Banana Upside-Down Cake, 182
    Cocoa Banana Bars, 210
    Curried Fruit and Rice Salad, 133
    Frozen Banana Dessert Cups, 196
    Gone Bananas Shake, 37
    Northern California Banana Bread, 54
    Orange-Banana Yogurt Dressing, 138
    Royal Banana Fruit Shortcake, 180
    Strawberry-Banana Yogurt Dressing, 138
Barbecue Bacon Meatloaf, 99
Basil-Vegetable Soup, 72
Bavarian Rice Cloud with Bittersweet Chocolate Sauce, 190
Beans
    Green Bean, New Potato and Ham Salad, 142
    Green Beans with Pine Nuts, 167
    Mostaccioli Salad Niçoise, 137
    Salade Niçoise, 124
    Sprout-Green Bean Salad, 151
    Warm Turkey Salad, 132
Beef
    Beef Cubed Steaks Provençale, 114
    Butterflied Eye Round Roast, 108
    Creole-Flavored Beef Soup, 83
    Fast Beef Roast with Mushroom Sauce, 116
    Greek Isles Appetizers, 13
    Herb-Marinated Chuck Steak, 100
    Lasagna, 110
    Meatball & Vegetable Soup, 73
    Saucy Stuffed Peppers, 120
    Southwestern Beef Stew, 71
    Spaghetti Pizza Deluxe, 103
Belgian Waffle Dessert, 64
Berry Good Sundaes, 192
Beverages
    Banana-Raspberry Smoothie, 27
    Birthday Punch, 10
    Cherry Punch, 20
    Double Strawberry Coconut Punch, 28
    Frosty Fruit Shake, 33
    Gone Bananas Shake, 37

Beverages (*continued*)
    Grape ReaLemonade, 22
    Hawaiian Tea, 9
    Hot Orchard Peach Cup, 15
    Kokomo Quencher, 24
    Lemony Light Cooler, 8
    Low Calorie ReaLemonade, 22
    Minted ReaLemonade, 22
    Mulled Cider, 16
    Orange Milk Shake, 35
    Orange Tea Punch, 23
    Pink ReaLemonade, 22
    ReaLemonade, 22
    Skim Milk Hot Cocoa, 15
    Slushy ReaLemonade, 22
    Sparkling Raspberry Mint Cooler, 24
    Sparkling ReaLemonade, 22
    Strawberry ReaLemonade, 22
    Strawberry Watermelon Slush, 35
    Sunlight Sipper, 24
    White Sangria, 18
Bittersweet Chocolate Sauce, 190
Black Bean and Rice Salad, 140
Black Bean Dip, 8
Black Forest Parfaits, 190
Black Pepper Patties, 95
Blueberry Crisp, 187
Bran
    Banana Bran Loaf, 59
    Bran-Cherry Bread, 52
    Bran Pita Bread, 74
    Cranberry Oat Bran Muffins, 48
    Double Bran-Lemon Muffins, 51
    Double Oat Muffins, 42
    Eggplant Italiano, 154
    Lemony Apple-Bran Salad, 148
    Shanghai Party Pleasers, 25
    Touch of Honey Bread, 68
Breakfast Foods (*see also* **Beverages; Quick Breads; Yeast Breads**)
    Belgian Waffle Dessert, 64
    Breakfast Burrito, 49
    Breakfast in a Cup, 58
    Breakfast Sausage Bake, 56
    Brown Rice, Mushroom, and Ham Hash, 54
    Brunch Potato Cassoulet, 53
    Brunch Quesadillas with Fruit Salsa, 60
    Brunch Rice, 39
    Country Breakfast Cereal, 51
    Fruit & Ham Kabobs, 47
    Ham & Fruit Pancake Rolls, 48
    Ham Breakfast Sandwich, 51
    Mexican Egg Muffin, 61
    Praline Pancakes, 55
    Rainbow Trout Breakfast Fillets, 63
    Rice Bran Buttermilk Pancakes, 44
    Rice Bran Granola Cereal, 65
    Rice Crêpes, 56
    Tangy Fruit and Nut Muesli, 53
    Weekend Skillet Breakfast, 46